PSI National Real Estate License Exam Prep 2023-2024

Complete Review + 9 Tests and Answer Explanations for Brokers and Salespersons

3rd Edition – Aug 23, 2023

Table of Contents

A link to the downloadable materials is on the last page.

Chapter 1: Brokers and Salespersons

There are four major players in real estate transactions at any one time, namely the broker, the salesperson, the buyer and the seller. Both the broker and the salesperson are professionals in the field of real estate, and they are the ones that facilitate a smooth transactional process.

Although sometimes people use the term 'real estate agent' to refer to either the broker or the salesperson, technically the terms refer to different professionals. The general distinction between the two is that a salesperson is not qualified to do the work of a broker but a broker can perform the duties of a salesperson as well as those of a broker. In fact, one of the major requirements for a person to qualify to become a real estate broker is to have worked as a real estate salesperson for a period of time.

It's important to note that there are separate licenses for real estate salespeople and real estate brokers. Hence, if you aspire to become a broker you should work towards being licensed as a salesperson first and gain the necessary experience in that capacity. Then you can take the licensing exam to become a real estate broker. Essentially, a real estate salesperson's job is only one step away from becoming a real estate broker.

A broker works as an independent contractor while a salesperson works under the license of a broker. This means as a salesperson you have no right to contact clients directly. Only the broker can and then sends you as his/her agent to carry out the tasks required for the client.

Role of a Broker

The responsibility of a real estate broker is to carry out negotiations on behalf of the client, and to make arrangements for the necessary transactions regarding the real estate. The daily tasks that a licensed broker carries out include drafting of contracts and overseeing sales and purchase transactions involving residential and commercial property or land.

Since the broker's license is higher in level than that of a salesperson, the broker has the authority to hire real estate salespeople to work under his/her supervision, whether individually or as a team.

There are a few states where all professionals handling real estate transactions on behalf of clients are expected to acquire a broker's license. In such instances, the license the salesperson receives is also referred to as a broker's license. This gives the person the go-ahead to work as a real estate agent, but he/she can still not hire others.

In those states that do not distinguish between licenses for salespersons and brokers, such as Colorado and New Mexico, brokers who only have the basic license have to work towards acquiring a higher one in order to qualify to hire others to work as agents under their supervision.

It's very important that a broker only hire appropriately licensed salespersons because if they act against any regulations pertaining to real estate, the broker or brokerage firm under which the salesperson operates will be liable for anything, including breach of contract, errors, etc.

If a salesperson you have hired sets up a website, as many do, it's up to you as the broker to inspect the website every now and then to ensure the salesperson doesn't violate any regulations. Otherwise, again, you could be liable since the person is working under your agency.

Brokers are expected to list homes that clients have asked them to sell on their behalf, and even if salespeople receive the requests, they have to do it under the name of the broker. Salespeople earn their income from the broker who has contracted them.

One of the main takeaways here is that even if a salesperson in real estate needs to be licensed as much as a broker does, acquiring a salesperson's license is easier than getting one as a broker.

The buck stops with the broker under whose license both the salesperson and the broker transact. Property listings are all placed under the name of the licensed broker and never in the salesperson's name.

Broker's Relationship with Seller & Buyer

When a brokerage firm is trying to sell a particular piece of real estate property, the owner of the property—ideally the seller—is considered the principal in the transaction. In the same transaction, the broker is the agent who liaises between his/her principal and the property buyer. The role of the salesperson in this scenario is that of a subagent, who does the fieldwork for the principal on behalf of the broker who has hired him/her.

Likewise, when a brokerage firm is trying to buy a particular piece of real estate, the individual or entity interested in acquiring the property—ideally the buyer—is the principal. Brokers are the agents who liaise between the principal and the person willing to sell and salespeople are the subagents who handle the negotiations and transactions on behalf of the broker under whose license they operate.

Serving a Buyer vis-à-vis Serving a Seller

Brokers and salespersons serve both sellers and buyers of real estate property. Nevertheless, when you take up the responsibility of working for a buyer, you need to focus solely on the interests of the buyer, including doing your best to acquire the best property for the lowest possible price. The inverse is true, so when you are working for someone selling property, you should do your best to find a buyer who offers the highest price and meets the seller's requirements.

Tasks Brokers Do On Behalf Of Sellers

Brokers are expected to list homes that clients have asked them to sell on their behalf, be it in the local market or via the Multiple Listing Service (MLS). Brokers can also become part of the MLS by joining other members who are also brokers in their bid to find people to buy the properties they have listed. As a member of the MLS, you are able to see the properties that other brokers with the MLS have on offer.

As a broker you are expected to advise your principal, the seller, on how to prepare his/her home before listing it where anyone can see it. It is your responsibility to supervise how the property is listed and to keep the seller updated on the market response and also other feedback including the results of the listing.

It is incumbent upon you as the broker to present the seller with any offers you think are suitable, and to explain why you think the individual offers are worth considering. When acting on behalf of sellers, it's your responsibility to help them carry out any negotiations that may help in the execution of a contract of purchase between them and the buyer. This should be the culmination of the process you will have helped to coordinate all along.

During the transaction process, including the sale, you are expected to deliver the documents involved to the principal and to clearly explain them, along with making any necessary disclosures. It is your responsibility to ensure the closing of the sale and handing over of the property is carried out smoothly. If the subject of the transaction is a home, your job is also to ensure that it is vacated at the right time as per agreement.

Tasks Brokers Do On Behalf Of Buyers

When the principal the broker is working with wants to buy real estate property, it is the broker's responsibility to provide him/her with advice and the necessary services geared towards finding the preferred piece of property. It is the broker's responsibility to take the necessary steps in order for the transaction to be successfully completed.

Brokers are responsible for helping buyers identify properties in the location they prefer which are within their price range and meet the criteria specified by the buyers.

It is also the broker that coordinates any visits to the property and handles all the logistics to enable the buyer to view it. When it is time to initiate the purchase, the broker helps the buying principal to craft the starting offer and purchase agreement.

The buyer's broker seeks out the broker for the potential seller and negotiates with him/her on behalf of the buyer. After the purchase contract has been executed, the same broker coordinates the entire process on the side of the buyer until the transaction has been concluded.

During the process of acquiring the property and buying it, it is the broker's job to deliver all the documents to the buyer and to explain them. The broker also coordinates inspections of the property, compiles reports and streamlines negotiations. In short, it is the buyer's broker job to facilitate the entire process until the purchase deal has been closed and the buying principal has taken possession of the property.

Listing and Selling Real Estate Agents

When you see the term 'real estate agent' used, remember it could be in reference to either a broker or a salesperson. In some contexts, the difference may be ignored, particularly when the point being made pertains to the broker just as much as it does to the salesperson.

In this section we will explain the difference between the selling agent and the listing agent. A seller's agent is the broker or salesperson that has already been described earlier; the one who handles the property's selling process on behalf of the property owner. This one traces his/her counterpart on the side of potential buyers and engages them in negotiations in an attempt to sell the property the principal has authorized him/her to sell.

Listing agents sell through the MLS, where the property they handle on behalf of a principal is listed among others that belong to other selling agents within the MLS. In this latter scenario, all the agents can view what their counterparts have for sale and also what others are interested in buying. This essentially means that the seller's agent and the listing agent work on behalf of the property owner. In fact, a listing agent is sometimes referred to as the seller's agent.

'Selling agent' is a term that often poses a problem when trying to understand the titles given to different agents in the real estate market. This is because contrary to what the name 'selling' suggests, a selling agent does not deal actively with the selling of property. On the contrary, this is the agent you engage when you want to buy property. In short, a selling agent works on behalf of the buyer. While the listing agent helps you to market your property, the selling agent helps you acquire property.

The logic in using this rather confusing term, selling agent, seems to be that since this is the agent responsible for bringing the buyer to the negotiating table, he/she can also be credited with effecting the selling of the property. In practice, this individual is referred to as the buyer's agent during the period when he/she is searching for the appropriate piece of property to be bought, but once the purchase contract has been signed he/she assumes the title of selling agent.

Buyers and sellers are at an advantage when they can tell the difference between a selling and a listing agent because they are best able to identify a suitable agent to help them transact business in the real estate market.

It is important to understand that once you have entered into an agreement with a listing broker you effectively become his/her client. Consequently, he/she is your representative in all the ensuing transactions and is obliged to be loyal to you and to maintain confidentiality in your affairs. This broker is also accountable to you insofar as transactions pertaining to your property are concerned. When negotiations are being held regarding that particular property, the broker needs to keep your best interests uppermost in mind—negotiating for the highest price while looking out for the best terms of sale as well.

Note that a salesperson performs activities that are similar to those of a broker for the most part, with the exception that he/she cannot bring the negotiations to completion in terms of entering into a formal agreement. A salesperson also does not have the authority to control any funds or items in escrow—only the broker does. When something is held in escrow it means it is under the custody of a neutral person or entity. Once some set conditions are fulfilled, the item or funds will be released to the right person.

How Real Estate Agents are Compensated

There are some people who opt to sell their real estate property directly to a willing buyer, meaning they choose not to engage the services of a broker. These properties are commonly described as being FSBO—'For Sale By Owner.' The biggest advantage for property owners in such cases is that they save on commission because there is no broker to pay.

The downside is that you may end up getting a raw deal for your property as you may not be as conversant as the salespersons or brokers are with the real estate market.

Individuals looking to buy property without the assistance of a real estate agent risk not having a wide spread of appropriate properties to choose from. This is because some listing agents do not take offers placed by buyers directly, preferring to deal with professional agents representing the buyers.

Compensation of Real Estate Agents

Real estate agents are compensated differently. The way a listing agent is compensated is not necessarily the way another seller's agent is compensated. There are several transactions that are completed within a listing agreement where representation is exclusive. This means the owner of the property cannot enter into a transaction agreement involving the particular property with another agent.

Compensation of a Listing Agent

A listing agent is not prohibited from occasionally accepting a token fee for rendering clerical services for a home owner who wants property entered into the MLS. In these rare instances, the listing agent is not considered a representative of the property owner and owes the seller no obligation after the property has been listed. Alternatively, a property owner might consent to have the listing agent execute an open listing, so that the property owner still has leeway to list the same property with different other agents. This latter case is rare.

The most common arrangement is when the seller enters into a representation agreement with the listing agent and gives the seller the exclusive right to sell the property. Exclusive right to sell means the property owner owes the agent a commission once the property has been bought, and engaging another agent to sell the same property would be contravening the agreement. Nevertheless, you need to always keep in mind that a seller's agent transacts on behalf of a broker or brokerage firm, and so any commission paid will go to the brokerage and the agent will then be paid his/her share.

Exclusive listings are essentially bilateral agreements that exist between individual brokers and sellers, and although at face value they appear to be between individual sellers and salespersons, this is not the case unless the listing agent or salesperson is also the broker whose license is in use.

Compensation of a Selling Agent

Overall, a listing broker operates by liaising with a brokerage firm representing a buyer. In such instances, they handle the transaction together although back in the real estate market they are fundamentally competitors. The seller's agent, who is the listing broker, receives a commission from the principal. The seller's agent then pays a share of that commission to the buyer's agent or selling agent, to compensate him/her for having referred the buyer.

Such a commission, known as a co-op commission, is only paid if the buyer ends up committing to buying the property under the terms the seller agrees to and a deal is sealed.

Compensation for Listing cum Selling Agent

Although normally the listing and selling agents are on opposite sides of a real estate transaction, there are also opportunities for one agent to act as both the listing and selling agent. When that happens, the situation is described as one of 'dual agency.' Mostly dual agency exists in cases where the brokerage firm representing a seller is the same brokerage firm representing the buyer, so you have one salesperson from the brokerage trying to sell property for a property owner and another salesperson from the same brokerage looking for a property to buy on behalf of a willing buyer.

Sometimes salespersons may work for the same brokerage yet not know one another. It is important to point out that not all states allow dual representation of principals in real estate.

Chapter 2: Real & Personal Property & Conveyance

Everything that can be given ownership can be referred to as property. If it can be owned, it qualifies as property. Property can be further broken down into personal property and real property.

What is Real Property?

The term 'real property' is used in reference to land itself and the things that are attached directly to a piece of land, plus all the rights that are inherent to that particular land. When speaking of land, it is common to use the terms 'real estate' or just 'realty.'

In most cases, real property refers to immovable things like homes or buildings. When there are wooden or steel structures attached to a piece of land, these are also considered part of the real property, as are trees and plants. However, if the land has food crops like grains or vegetables, these are not included in the valuation of the real property for marketing purposes.

What is Personal Property?

Personal property comprises chattel and other intangible items. Clearly they cannot be part of real estate as they are not attached to land. As such, when real estate agents are said to deal in property, items like these are not included. The term 'chattel' refers to any moveable, tangible items.

However, there are some items that are considered chattel, like a furnace, that, because they are affixed to the owner's land, are considered part of the owner's real property. Any such chattel is technically referred to as a fixture. That is the reason valuation reports contain an item referred to as 'buildings and fixtures'; the chattel affixed to the owner's land is grouped together with the buildings.

What is Conveyance?

Conveyance is the transfer of ownership interest from an individual entity to another or from one person to another, where that interest is in reference to a given piece of property. The term 'conveyance' is also used in reference to the actual written instrument, such as a lease or deed that shows that legal right has been transferred from the person who has sold the property to the person who has bought it.

Conveyance is a common term in real estate, used in reference to the contract between the person selling a particular piece of property and the one interested in buying it. Such a written contract contains details that include the obligations each party has with regards to the ongoing transaction. Conveyance of ownership can also be referred to as 'conveyancing.' The person handling the legal angle of the transaction is called a conveyor.

You can describe a conveyance as a contract, which implies that the person interested in buying the property and the one interested in selling the property are legally bound to keep their side of the agreement.

Any of the two parties that fail to fulfill their obligations are considered to have defaulted and can be taken to court in order to demand that they fulfill their responsibilities. Alternatively, the court can award damages to the party that has been wronged by the breaking of the contract.

It is through conveyancing that a property buyer is furnished with information pertaining to the property, including all restrictions, if any, on the property such as mortgages or liens. In short, conveyancing enables a potential buyer to ascertain the cleanliness of the real estate property in advance. In some cases, property buyers also buy insurance for the title, so that in case fraud occurs during the process of transferring the title, they can be compensated.

In real estate, conveyance includes a review to check liens or other encumbrances, ensuring that all contract conditions have been fulfilled. It also ensures that any taxes are paid and that financing is properly in place as documents are prepared in order to finalize the contract. Formal documents required for conveyancing include those pertaining to mortgages, deeds, lien certificates, binders for title insurance and any other agreements made in the transaction process.

Conveyance on Mineral Rights

Conveyance is also applicable to mineral rights, where such rights are transacted without necessarily changing the title to the piece of land. Conveyance can be applied in establishing the correct way for a company to conduct its operations when using land that belongs to someone who is the landowner. The landowner in this case is compensated because of having transferred the mineral rights to the company.

Conveyance is also used in the oil and gas industry. In this case, and also where minerals are concerned, the land is real estate that has other rights attached to it, and it is those rights that exploration and mining companies pursue. They make use of the term 'conveyance' to indicate the contracts meant to transfer the rights to particular pieces of land to the company. Sometimes such companies, through conveyance, acquire rights of ownership of particular land parcels for their exploration.

Chapter 3: Encumbrances and Other Property Effects

Having title to your land means you are the only one entitled to use that land, and anyone else must seek your permission before using any part of it. Nevertheless, there are cases where you may not be able to use a part of your land because someone else has not made use of it. Such interference with your real estate property can be seen where there is encumbrance.

What Encumbrance Means

When dealing with real estate, the term 'encumbrance' is used to mean someone apart from the property owner believes he/she has a right to use that particular property. Encumbrance, therefore, is the right or interest which someone or an entity has in real estate property, although that property has a different owner.

The best way to understand encumbrance is to view it as a liability attached to a real estate property. Encumbrance limits the extent to which a property owner can use a particular property. Such a restriction has an impact on the property value, and the impact is normally negative.

Although encumbrance does not necessarily prevent real estate property from being sold and its ownership rights from being transferred, it is likely to continue putting restrictions upon the extent to which the property can be used. The new owner is therefore limited in how much he/she can enjoy the newly acquired property. Restrictions put on a piece of real estate can lower the value of property or hamper the owner's ability to find a willing buyer.

Types of Encumbrances

There are different types of encumbrances, but the major ones are liens, easements and encroachments, and deed restrictions.

Meaning of Property Easements

Property easements apply after you have requested that someone allow you to make use of their land. They are property rights of a non-possessory nature, where one can use land that belongs to another party for a particular purpose. Usually such a right involves the use of the airspace above the piece of land or the use of the space beneath the surface of the land.

If you permit such use and all parties agree on all terms, the easement is formalized and a legal deed is drawn up to make the agreement official.

Ordinarily the party you have allowed the use of your land will compensate you accordingly. However, it is important to note that if you end up selling the land, the new buyer and any others that buy it thereafter are not entitled to any compensation from the person with easement rights.

Easement in Gross

Property easements can be grouped into two, one being easement in gross and the other appurtenant easement. Easement in gross is linked to someone opposed to the particular property. This means the property owner has only extended the right to use the property to the individual that signed the deed and that individual does not have the right to transfer the right to anyone else by any means; whether through a will or a sale. In short, if the owner of the easement dies, the easement is terminated.

Appurtenant Easements

Appurtenance easements remain attached to the real estate property every time the property is sold to a new owner or transferred to someone else. Good examples are easements involving the establishment of public utilities or ditches for drainage.

Easements can also be exemplified by cases where one party gives another the right to use a part of his/her land to pass to another area, often for the sake of accessing a particular resource. Examples of these include a public beach or fishing pond that is owned by an individual. In the US, such easements are often equated to real covenants or equitable servitudes.

Some easements are acknowledged under common law even if deeds are not drawn. Nevertheless, in modern-day real estate transactions, easements are normally drawn to give right-of-way, access to light and air, construction, use of artificial waterways and so on.

Restrictions on Real Estate Deeds

Restrictions on deeds constitute encumbrance with regards to real estate. They are attached to the land and remain with it even when land ownership changes, very much like appurtenant easements. Restrictions on real estate deeds are referred to as 'Conditions, Covenants & Restrictions'—CC & Rs. These are agreements entered into privately regarding land use, but which are still entered into the public record.

A good example is where developers enter into an agreement with homeowners associations. The deeds they raise stipulate restrictions enacted to ensure there is uniformity in the way the neighborhood is developed. A good example of these restrictions is where the minimum size of a single housing unit is stipulated. Often a restriction of this nature is meant to ensure the neighborhood residents do not have RVs or boats on their property.

Homeowners Association

A homeowners association (HOA) is an association a property developer incorporates before selling the housing units that have been developed, and all the relevant CC & Rs are recorded at the same time within the public records at the local office. It is estimated that there approximately 63 million Americans that are members of HOAs, either knowingly or not.

Remember, CC & Rs regulate what homeowners can and cannot do where their own housing units are concerned, how a development's common areas are handled and other such matters that may affect the neighbors and the neighborhood. They contain detailed rules which any property buyer is required to abide by as a member of the development community. At times people simply refer to the CC & Rs as a "declaration."

CC & Rs are sometimes referred to as 'running with the land.' This essentially means that every homeowner in a particular housing development is a member of the HOA by default and cannot opt out as long as he/she owns a property there. That position preempts any necessities for drawing up a special agreement between the developer selling the property and the buyer.

Alongside the by-laws of the local area and laws of the state, the CC & Rs help to enhance management of the particular community. By the time a property buyer signs a purchase agreement, it is assumed he/she is aware of what the CC & Rs stipulate about the expectations of a member of the HOA.

How to Opt Out of an HOA

Since every property owner in the housing development with an HOA has to be a member, the only way you can cease to be a member is to sell your property or relinquish ownership in any other manner. In that case, the person who owns the property after you automatically becomes a member of the HOA.

Automatic membership within an HOA is one of those cases where ignorance is no defense, and so you cannot fail to pay any required fees or to conform to any of the regulations of the HOA and claim you were not aware of them.

Still, it should be understood that the rules of an HOA are not meant to be punitive on the members, but rather to help maintain and enhance the look of the properties and their value. Usually HOAs and condominiums have a board of directors that monitors adherence to the regulations on behalf of the property owners.

How HOAs are Formed

HOAs are first incorporated by the respective developers of housing projects. When a certain threshold of property sales is reached, the developer relinquishes management of the HOA to the property owners who now form the association's membership. On their inception, HOAs help in the marketing of housing units in a development or in the marketing and sale of lots after a residential property has been subdivided.

Forming an HOA involves filing specified documents of public record both at the state and county level. It is worth noting that the state government has typically not been involved much in the operation of HOAs, but that seems to be changing of late.

Governance by the Homeowners Association

A planned community normally has a homeowners association, and it is often established as a nonprofit corporation, meant to manage, oversee and regulate how the planned community exists and runs its affairs.

Once you buy a housing unit within a planned community you automatically become a member of the homeowners association and you are expected to pay any dues paid by other homeowners. Homeowners have a right to vote during meetings held by the association, when members participate in matters of governance. They also have a right to inspect the association's business records.

Dues by homeowners, which the US Census Bureau puts at around $400, are meant to be used on cost of property maintenance and on operations of the common areas belonging to the community, equipment and other shared amenities. Residents of the planned community normally elect directors who form the association's board, and this board is in charge of setting the annual fees to be paid by every member, depending on the projected cost of maintenance.

How CC & Rs are enforced

An HOA can enforce its regulations by issuing a threat, ultimatum or fines to offending members. The association can also seek to enforce any of its regulations through a court of law, where civil law would be applied. Whatever measure the association decides to take against its members, including levying of fines, is not inhibited by any government constraints that affect the public in general.

It is in the HOA's power to discipline any homeowner who fails to comply with any rules set by the community, and hearings on disciplinary matters are regulated by the laws of respective states. Taking the state of California as an example, disciplinary hearings are carried out as per Civil Code 5850, alongside Civil Code 5855A.

Whenever such a hearing is being planned, the errant property owner is given a minimum of 10 days' written notice preceding the hearing. He/she is informed of the time, venue and also date of that meeting, and also the violation he/she is being cited for. The property owner is informed that there will be an opportunity to speak directly to the board during the meeting.

After the disciplinary hearing has taken place, the HOA has 15 days within which to inform the property owner in writing of the disciplinary measures that are to be taken against him/her.

If a homeowner is not pleased by an action taken by the HOA, he/she is at liberty to seek recourse from a court of law, which will review the decision made by the association. Normally the court ends up upholding the HOA's decision unless it is clear its action was not taken in good faith. Any homeowner who takes a case to court has the duty to prove that the HOA was unreasonable or unfair.

Encroachments

Encroachments are buildings or sections of buildings that extend beyond the land owned by the building owner. These extensions are deemed to be encroachment because legally they intrude on land that is someone else's property.

Often encroachments are discovered when the property is being inspected before it's sold. Encroachments are often not deliberate and are easy to solve, such as when a hedge matures over time and ends up overgrowing onto a neighbor's property, or when habitual heavy rains end up altering a line of boundary due to soil erosion.

However, when neighboring parties are not friendly with each other, one can be found to be deliberately encroaching onto the other's property just to cause provocation. Although you may choose to ignore a neighbor's encroachment, you need to disclose it to a potential buyer at the time you sell the property.

It's preferable to solve any issues of encroachment early, as they can end up delaying your sales transaction even after you have found a willing buyer, given that people do not want to buy property that has signs of potential problems. Buyers who accept to buy your property despite the encroachment might end up bargaining for a price much lower than what they would have paid if the property had no encroachment. In short, encroachments, whether deliberate or not, can lower the value of your real estate property.

Liens

The term 'lien' is used to mean a claim made on a given property because of an unsettled debt. That property has been used in this case as collateral. If you fail to settle the debt, the person who holds the lien can rightfully have the property sold, after attaining a court order, to recoup his/her money.

Any time you take out a mortgage, you automatically raise a mortgage lien because your financier can sell the home to repay any debt if you default on payment.

Other liens include tax liens and taxes on real estate; taxes under the special assessment category; mechanic's liens and judgment liens. It is important to note that liens continue to remain in effect even when the real estate property changes ownership. For that reason, brokers need to determine whether a property they are trying to acquire on behalf of a principal has any liens placed upon it.

Brokers also need to advise their principals to settle any liens before they put a property on the market. Otherwise the lien might cause a significant drop in the value of the property.

Distinction between Easement & License

A license gives authority to the holder to use the piece of land, and such authority can be revoked at any moment. The interest in a piece of land afforded through an easement is for a specific period of time, although there are cases where such interest is meant to last indefinitely.

Having a license means you can use land that belongs to someone else just as it means when you have an easement, so in this aspect the two agreements are similar. In cases where the written agreements are not explicit on whether the authority to use the real estate property was meant to exist as a license or an easement, a court of law can help decide. Such a decision is normally arrived at when the owner of the property wants to revoke authority.

Evidence Used By Courts

Courts use certain types of evidence to help them make a decision on whether an existing agreement allows one of the parties to use the land belonging to the other on a perpetual basis, or for a limited time, in which case the license would be revocable.

For one, the court will look for any indication that permission granted before was meant to be permanent or to last for a particular time. If it is established that this is the case, such an encumbrance is understood to be an easement.

The court also seeks to establish the area designation meant for use by the grantee. A license can be revoked any time the property owner wills it, in which case the licensor may have refrained from specifying any particular area for the grantee to use. This differs in the case of an easement because since easement involves land interests, it is normal for the fraud statute to require that the piece of land that is the subject of easement be specified.

If nothing else, the easement grantor would have been specific regarding the rights extended to the grantee. This is particularly so because when parties enter into such an agreement, there is the clear notion that the agreement cannot be broken at the whim of the property owner. This helps to give the grantee confidence when investing to utilize the land allowed through the easement.

How to Check Property for Encumbrances

As a broker you need to do your due diligence before committing your principal to buying or selling any real estate property. Through a title search, you can establish who a property belongs to, and also determine whether the title has any defects. Defects can include liens or other encumbrances that are likely to reduce the property value.

It is always worth remembering that real property can still be sold or bought despite its liens and other encumbrances. The important thing is to include the relevant clause in the agreement: 'subject to all liens and encumbrances.'

In order to be protected from any encumbrances you may not have discovered at the time of buying the property, you should require a general warranty. A general warranty is a deed that has the clause, 'covenant against encumbrances,' and it provides a guarantee that the real estate property does not have any encumbrances other than any that have already been indicated in the particular deed. If things go wrong for some reason, there are real estate attorneys who deal specifically with disputes pertaining to property liens.

Chapter 4: Land Ownership in the US

In the US, land belongs either to the federal government or to private individuals, and each of these two types of land ownership is different. The size of the US is slightly less than $2^{1}/_{3}$ billion acres.

Land that the government owns is said to be federally owned and the federal government manages a third of it, much of which is within the western region of the country. The federal government owns over half the land in states like Nevada, Idaho, Alaska, Oregon and Utah. However, private citizens are still allowed to use this federally owned land within their respective states.

The main uses for federally owned land are national parks. The government protects this land from modern development and keeps the parks open all year round for visitors to explore. A good example of these parks is Yellowstone National Park, found within the western area of Wyoming, with some of its land extending up to Montana and even reaching Idaho.

The government has also set aside approximately 150 million acres of land and water for the conservation of various plants, fish and wildlife.

The government also uses its land for building federal prisons and military bases. In some cases, the land is leased to various companies. Such companies or corporations use the land for commercial purposes such as agriculture, forestry and mining. Federally owned land is regulated by the Department of Interior.

Tenancy in Common

The term 'tenancy-in-common' (TIC) is used in reference to the arrangement made between two or more parties to share the rights of the land or other property ownership. The use of this property could be residential or commercial, but its use notwithstanding, if a TIC dies, the ownership of the property goes straight to the estate of that tenant.

In TIC, the partner tenants do not have to own equal percentages of the property. Also, individual partners have a right to leave the share they hold in the property to their respective beneficiaries as part of their own estate. The terms of the contract in TIC can be found in the title or deed or any other legal document drafted to show the ownership of the property.

How to Dispose of Tenancy-in-Common

Co-tenants may choose to sell their ownership rights to the other partners. If one partner buys the rights of all the others, this means the TIC is dissolved. Also, there may be cases where tenants differ in the manner in which the property is being used, and in this case they must agree on how to proceed, one option being selling the property and sharing the proceeds. In cases where the partners cannot agree on the use of the property, a partition action can be taken either voluntarily or through a court order.

If the issue goes to court, normally there is a legal partition of the property, where the entire property is divided among the TIC so that every member can do as he/she wishes with his/her portion of the property. This action is referred to as 'partition in kind,' and it is often used when tenant partners become adversarial.

Taxes on Property under TIC

Tax liability with regards to property owned under a TIC agreement is distributed among the partners who own the property together. Since the property has not been legally divided, the co-owners receive a single bill of tax just like any individual who owns personal property, and they have to agree on how to share the liability.

Still, there are jurisdictions that insist on having agreements of TIC stipulate how liabilities will be apportioned. Such liability is referred to as 'joint & several liability.' The stipulation is that every co-owner in TIC is liable for any property tax due to the entire extent of the assessment. It is important to note that no property co-owner is exempt from such liability, irrespective of how small his/her ownership percentage is.

Be aware that although every tenant is liable for property tax, such an expense is deductible when it comes to filing income taxes. Some tax jurisdictions recognize joint & several liability while others do not, but in either case every individual co-owner is allowed to deduct the extent of the tax he/she contributed in settling the single property tax.

TIC versus Joint Tenancy

The two property ownership arrangements, TIC and joint tenancy, are often similar, but they are different in some aspects. In the case of joint tenancy, each of the property co-owners has an equal share of the common property and they all acquire ownership at the same moment. The main similarity between the two is that the deed is one and it covers all the partners as far as right of ownership is concerned.

There is a difference between the two arrangements when it comes to adding or removing a member or a property co-owner. In the TIC agreement, the agreement remains intact even after one member has left or has been replaced. On the contrary, an agreement under joint tenancy breaks the moment one of the property co-owners expresses an intention to sell his/her interest. Partners in a joint tenancy have two options, one of them being to agree to sell the co-owned property and then share the proceeds among themselves. The alternative is getting the property legally partitioned so that everyone gets an equal share, if division of that particular property is feasible.

What Happens If a Joint Tenant Dies

If a real estate co-owner dies in TIC, the part of the property that belonged to the deceased is passed to his/her estate while the part that belongs to the deceased in joint tenancy becomes the property of the surviving co-owner.

In short, the survivorship right that is automatic in joint tenancy does not exist in TIC. The only time the deceased partner's portion can pass to the surviving co-owners is if the partner has expressly said so in his/her will.

Ownership of Property in Marriage

In a number of states, real estate property is owned by married couples through automatic joint tenancy. In other states, the default form of ownership between married couples is TIC.

Tenancy by Entirety

There is a third model of real estate property ownership referred to as 'Tenancy By Entirety' (TbyE), which 25 states use. In this model, each spouse owns half of the property. If one of the partners wants to do something with his/her portion of the real estate property, the other partner must afford consent. Without both partners coming to an agreement, neither of them can make any adjustments to the property that they co-own under TbyE.

Also in TbyE, if one of the partners dies, the surviving spouse becomes the full owner of the property that was previously co-owned. No partner on his/her own can use a part of the property as collateral.

Common Interest Ownership

Common interest ownership of real estate property is the same as property held under 'community interest.' In real estate, this form of ownership is common where the property is in the form of condominiums, within associations of homeowners, planned communities or timeshares.

Categories of Common Interest Property

In the US, like many parts of the world, common interest properties (CIPs), are becoming more and more popular, as people opt to live in condominiums or make use of timeshares while on vacation. Different states have varying laws that regulate ownership and use of CIPs, but one law is the basis on which those other laws are developed across all the states.

That fundamental law is the Uniform Common Interest Ownership Act that was enacted in 1980 by the National Conference of Commissioners on Uniform State Laws. It addresses not only how communities with common interests are formed but also how they operate. It also provides guidance on how a common interest community can be dismantled or terminated.

According to this law, full disclosure of relevant facts must be made in advance to any person who expresses interest in buying property whose ownership is under CIP. Another stipulation is that the seller must inform interested buyers if a property is being resold and if so, must clearly state if there are warranties attached to the particular sale.

When buying property that is under CIP, any monies meant for the purchase should, according to the act, be put in an escrow account where they can be refunded to the prospective buyer if there is a disagreement. There are some circumstances that justify a person's rescinding a prior decision to enter into a purchase agreement, in which case said person is entitled to a full refund of his/her money.

Planned Communities

Planned communities are also referred to as 'Planned Unit Developments.' These are properties that have been developed in such a manner as to have some open common space, where every property owner can move around. Resources for common use are protected in such developments, and there are protocols unique to the property, required to be observed by everyone.

Many planned communities comprise homes of single families, which collectively sometimes cover a vast area in terms of acreage. In developing planned communities, there is a comprehensive plan in place with information and materials meant to guide developers. It's clear from the plan where a single home fits within the overall larger community that has been planned.

Although the plan has a framework to be used and shows policy context to guide decision-making as far as the envisioned development is concerned, the zoning set by the local board must be adhered to. As such, developers of properties for planned communities must first seek the approval of the relevant board.

CC & Rs are the constitution that guides the community, and are kept in the custody of the recording office of the county just like deeds; all are filed before any transaction involving housing units has taken place. This filing of documents at the county office is crucial because it shows the person who buys the property has been bound by the same restrictions that the rest of the community is required to adhere to.

Condominiums

If you want to own a condominium, you should understand that although you own the property you buy as an individual, the arrangement actually comprises a joint ownership. This is because your condominium is one of several in a big housing development, where all individual condominium owners have shared ownership of some areas that they use in common. Some of those areas that you co-share include stairways, roofs and areas of recreation. You are also expected to co-share the cost of maintenance of those areas and the building as a whole.

Before building condominiums, the developer is expected to file a contract, referred to as a condominium declaration and condominium plan, that indicates the exact location the private units and common areas are meant to be. This declaration is also termed the 'master deed' or 'master lease,' and is maintained in the public record to guide every condominium owner—current tenants and future ones—on how to handle the property and how to behave as a person who owns property in a real estate development that has co-owners.

Timeshares

The term 'timeshare' is used in reference to an arrangement where several people have rights of ownership to a given real estate property, using it as their holiday home within a scheme of time sharing.

This arrangement is often preferred by people who like making use of a particular piece of property for a short time every year, and so owning it on their own on a full-time basis would mean the property would be underutilized. Such people prefer to own the particular property with other people who also like to utilize the property for short periods of time, ensuring that when one party is at the property, the others are not.

Timeshares are popular with holiday resorts as well as various other vacation destinations. A timeshare gives a co-owner the right to occupy the property and use its facilities, or to have access to the recreation areas.

Timeshare ownership takes different legal forms, but in all cases the buyer is entitled to the use of the property for a limited amount of time. The two major forms timeshare interests take are fee simple ownership and a lease arrangement, also referred to as license arrangement.

Life Estate

The term 'life estate' is used in reference to interest in real estate that only lasts the life of the person with that interest. This means anyone with a life estate has no leeway to leave such interest to anyone else, including in a will. In other words, interest in a life estate never survives the interest holder. Such a person can transfer the interest they have to someone else as long as they are alive at the time they are making the transfer. What is prohibited is misusing the real estate so that the next interest holder takes over something in ruins.

Property Trusts

A trust is a document written for legal use, often written when the person creating it is still alive. This legal document continues to be in force even after the owner has died.

There are also times when a trust is created by a person's will, which means the trust is created after the death of the person who enacted it. After putting the person's assets into a trust, they become the property of the trust but not the appointed trustee. This means they are subject to the rules contained in the particular trust contract.

A trustee is the person or the organization charged with managing property on behalf of someone else while it is held in trust. Essentially, the trust holds the right to the property while in a fiduciary position in relation to the property beneficiary. Trusts can be either revocable or irrevocable, although there are also other categories of trusts.

Once you have bought a home or other real estate property, you have an option to put it in a trust, which holds it for your personal benefit and those to whom you want to leave the property when you die.

It is also legal for you to create a trust that has you as the trustee, and then after your death, the person you have chosen to succeed you becomes the new trustee. A trustee in real estate is the person in charge of the property or asset administration for as long as those assets are under the trust. If you personally create a trust, you automatically acquire particular powers such as designating the person who will inherit the property you put into the trust after your death. One reason it is beneficial to create a trust is that it legally protects the assets and property under the trust, and this can shield your personal estate from any future problems of an economic nature.

How to Buy Real Estate Property in Trust

If you want to buy a home or any other real estate property in trust, begin by establishing what is referred to as a 'living trust.' This form of trust is established when the person creating it is still alive. A living trust has a designated trustee who is expected to manage all the assets and properties for the beneficiary's benefit.

It is incumbent upon the property owner creating the trust to choose the kind of living trust he/she prefers since there are different types. The choice is based on the person the property chooses to take up the legal right of inheritance or to sell the property.

You can, for instance, decide to appoint your son to be your successor upon your death with regards to the trust ownership, but it is also important that you indicate if that son is to benefit from the properties held in the trust. If the home and other properties under the trust are to be sold, you need to elaborate on how you want the distribution of the proceeds to be carried out.

How to Acquire Property with a Revocable Trust

Buying a home or other real estate property under revocable trust means you will be bound by a trust agreement, which essentially provides an explanation of what the revocable trust entails. A trust declaration is contained therein. You can consider a revocable trust to be a contract that spells out who the heirs to the property are and the rights that they have with regard to your estate.

Under the revocable trust, you as the property owner are the 'grantor,' and so you have complete control of what goes on in the trust. You can make whatever changes you deem appropriate if and when you please. As the grantor you can also be the trust beneficiary, or you can appoint a beneficiary as you please. You are at liberty to make any changes to your choice of beneficiary or beneficiaries whenever you desire.

Example: How to Amend a Revocable Trust

You have chosen your son to be the trustee of your estate upon your death, but certain developments have now led you to change your mind and you would like instead to appoint your daughter to succeed you as trustee of your estate. Since what you have is a revocable trust, this change is legal and within your right as the trustee.

What you need to do is alter the parameters within the revocable trust so that you express your decision to appoint your daughter to replace your son. You have leeway to appoint more than one trustee for the revocable trust, just as it is within your right to appoint more than one beneficiary to the properties under the trust.

You can also create a document defining under what circumstances any changes can be made, and also specifying the trustee who has the capacity to make such changes. The term 'revocable' means 'being in a position to be canceled,' and so it follows that there are circumstances under which a revocable trust can be canceled.

Purchase of Property under a Revocable Trust

If you buy a home that is under revocable trust, you should be aware that the home still remains under the ownership of the trust. Nevertheless, if you are the person who created the trust, you are essentially the homeowner through your legal position. This means you have the capacity to appoint beneficiaries of the trust and also those who will inherit that property when you die. Although it is within your right to be the trustee in the revocable trust you have created, you can also appoint someone else to serve as the trustee especially for the purposes of managing the legal aspects of matters. One benefit of having a revocable trust is that such trusts do not undergo the lengthy probate legal process that seeks to review the actual beneficiaries of your estate.

By circumventing the probate, whoever you choose as your beneficiaries does not become a matter for public record the way it does when the beneficiaries are spelled out in a will. A will here refers to the document that legally indicates the individuals or institutions you have chosen to become heirs to the properties when you die.

The main characteristic of a revocable trust that makes it unique is the fact that you are wholly its controller, and you have the sole right to dissolve it at will.

Purchase of Property under an Irrevocable Trust

An irrevocable trust is the inverse of the revocable trust. For one, it has no room for either modification or termination unless the beneficiary affords his/her consent. This means the trustee only plays the role of fiduciary to the extent of managing the properties under the trust, which he/she does on the beneficiary's behalf.

To understand the difference between a revocable and irrevocable trust, consider that while all properties in a revocable trust remain in the estate of the beneficiary, all properties in an irrevocable trust immediately shift from the estate of the beneficiary to the trust. There are different reasons why a property owner might choose an irrevocable trust, one of them being tax avoidance.

When it comes to gifts, there is a limit on taxation when the property is under irrevocable trust, particularly with regards to real estate. When changes occur in the financial arena at a future date, the estate being run under irrevocable trust is also unlikely to be adversely affected.

If the trust is registered as a charitable irrevocable trust, then the property owner can claim a deductible tax on the transfer of the property to the trust. If he/she does not make the claim, the beneficiary can still claim it after the grantor's demise.

Example: Property Protection under an Irrevocable Trust

Suppose you put your properties under an irrevocable trust and name your son as the beneficiary. If your son falls into financial trouble sometime in the future, nobody can use the assets under the irrevocable trust as compensation for creditors. The reasoning is that those properties under the trust were put there before the beneficiary fell into debt.

In short, your son can continue enjoying the benefits you bestowed on him via the irrevocable trust, irrespective of what else transpires with his own estate. At the same time, if you eventually need long-term care at a nursing home, the institution cannot claim any of your properties under the irrevocable trust in order to pay your care costs.

Still, it is important for property owners to carefully consider the people they choose to be their beneficiaries in cases of an irrevocable trust. This is because there have been cases of grantors putting their estate under irrevocable trust and at an advanced age they are unable to revoke the trust even when their beneficiaries have failed them or have been unable to assist them.

Chapter 5: Land Characteristics & Ownership

There are three characteristics of a physical nature that land has, and all of them contribute to making it a very valuable resource.

Immobility of Land

Under no circumstances can you shift a piece of land from one location to another. When it is time for ownership of the land to change, the land remains in its location and only the title deed changes to reflect the name of the new land owner.

Indestructibility of Land

Not being destructible makes land durable and hence very valuable as property.

Non-homogeneity of Land

Different pieces of land can't be homogeneous because they can't be physically interchanged. Land is said to be non-fungible and there is no single piece of land that can be a perfect substitute for another. In short, different pieces of land can be comparable but are not replaceable.

Developments that are made on land can have similar layouts and designs, good examples being condominiums or houses that are built in clusters, but because each stands on a different piece of land, individual properties still retain their uniqueness.

How Land is Legally Described

Land is often described in the legal terms 'metes and bounds,' and to establish these measurements a surveying system is used in which the land involved is split into different sections, each one of them comprising 640 acres. When describing the exact place where the piece of land is located, the spot within the township is identified as well as the range, plus the section, and these specifications sometimes incorporate the distance and degrees.

A good example is when a township that is six square miles, meaning acreage of 23,040, is split into sections that total 36, and each one of them is a square mile. Each of these sections is 640 acres in size. Townships are known to run from north to south, and they also range from east to west, and they are essentially lines cutting each other at right angles. The US government land surveys adopted the township and range system in 1785.

The best way to understand this description of land is to visualize it as a massive grid comprising numerous squares, with every section being 640 acres in size. This means half of one section is 320 acres, a quarter is 160 acres, an eighth is 80 acres and one-sixteenth of a section is 40 acres.

When designating a specific piece of land that covers 20 acres, if the property is divided evenly, you can refer to it as 'S ½ of the SW ¼ of the SE ¼ of Section 32, T1N.' With such a description, it is quite easy to identify that piece of land on the relevant map.

Metes & Bound

Using metes and bounds to describe a location can be somewhat complex, and it is therefore important to ensure the starting point is well known. That starting point is known as the Point of Beginning (POB). If, for instance, you start considering a parcel of land from the SW corner of the SE ¼ of Section 32, T1N, then proceed some distance in terms of feet and at a given degree.

Describing a parcel of land in legal terms involves the use of varying degrees and angles, so that at the end you will have linked back to your POB. By this time you will have completed accurately drawing the boundaries of your property.

You can use a protractor when drawing your personal property description in legal terms, the way searchers of titles used to as they drew descriptions of metes and bounds obtained from the record entries the grantor and grantee kept at the courthouse.

Grantor

The term 'grantor' is used in the legal sense when dealing with real estate transactions, where it represents the party selling the property like a house. The 'grantor,' therefore, is the one expected to give the title he/she holds to the party buying the property, referred to as the 'grantee.'

The instrument used to effect the transfer of title from the grantor to the grantee is referred to as the 'deed.' It's usual to have the closing attorney in a real estate transaction ensure the title transfer is duly recorded, mostly at the courthouse at the local county. This deed is proof that the real estate property was legally transferred from the grantor to the grantee, particularly because it is certifiable.

Some deeds are not meant to last for perpetuity, with some allowing for the grantor or grantee to modify them. There can be room for either of them to have covenants or other limitations put in place to indicate the way the property ought to be used, sold or reclaimed.

Importance of Language

It is crucial that language is used effectively in the deed so that it clearly identifies who the grantor and grantee are, and also provides an appropriate description of the real estate property that is the subject of the transaction.

If a deed is not drawn up appropriately and in sufficient detail there is a risk of it being questioned, and the grantor and grantee can be exposed to the risk of a lawsuit. It is advisable for the parties involved to have a title insurance policy to cover any such eventuality.

Role of Grantor in Deeds

The role of the grantor in different deeds depends on the laws of respective states. Every state has its own stipulations in this regard, and you could, for example, have rules that regulate transactions in Iowa which are not acceptable in Illinois. It is advisable to have potential buyers and sellers discuss matters with their own attorneys prior to transacting, for the purposes of determining the appropriate deed type to convey or receive and the reasons for choosing it.

Title companies often do not advise the parties involved, one reason being that a deed is a legal document and the employees of title companies are not legal professionals. In fact, title offices and their counterparts, escrow officers, are not permitted to give any advice of a legal nature to real estate buyers and sellers.

General Warranty Deed

A general warranty deed is used by a grantor to provide confirmation that the particular title is both valid and marketable. This essentially means that the title has no liens attached to it that can prevent the title holder from putting the property up for sale.

A general warranty deed protects the grantee against any claim that may be deemed to exist against the title, which dates back to the origin of the property. This kind of warranty offers the property buyer the utmost protection in a real estate transaction. It is important to note that not all states make use of deeds like general warranties.

Special Warranty Deed

Under a special warranty deed, the buyer of the real estate property is protected in a limited way. For one, the grantor of such a warranty does not bear any responsibility for the defects on the title that existed prior to him/her owning the property. This means that such defects could potentially surface later on and become a problem for the new property owner.

Grant Deeds

A grant deed provides assurance that the property the grantor is offering for sale has not been concurrently offered for sale to another party. The grantor also gives assurance through the deed that the real estate property does not have undisclosed liens or encumbrances.

Quitclaim Deed

In a 'quitclaim deed,' the grantee does not receive any guarantee from the grantor. In fact the grantor transfers only the interest he/she has in the property to the grantee, which means if such interest is less than what is indicated on paper, then the grantee receives only the portion of interest that the seller really had, irrespective of the amount of money he/she may have paid for the property.

Essentially, therefore, a quitclaim deed does not guarantee any level of quality for the title. In fact a quitclaim deed explicitly states that there is no warranty that the grantor provides, either express or implied, regarding the title to the particular property in question. If the grantor does not have any interest at all in the property that is the subject of the deed, the grantee does not acquire anything at all going by the deed.

The takeaway here is that you should only agree to a quitclaim deed if you trust the party providing it. Owing to their lack of a guarantee, quitclaim deeds are often used when transactions bear minimal risk, such as when property is being transferred among family members. A good example of an appropriate time to use a quitclaim deed is when an individual is transferring property to an adult child or sibling. Another good example is when a newly wedded person wants to include his/her spouse on a property title.

There are also situations when a quitclaim deed can be legally of help, such as in a case where someone has received a warranty but the records on the documents for the real estate contain a misspelling. A quitclaim deed can be used to indicate the correct name, and the discrepancy will henceforth be ignored.

It is important to note that a quitclaim deed is not expected to make any alterations to an existing mortgage, but it may affect ownership of the relevant property.

Brokers and salespersons need to note the importance of having clear documents that indicate who the grantor and the grantee are, whether such documents are documents of a business partnership, a financing contract, a will, etc. Before the era of computers, people sought to establish the existence of quitclaim deeds that had the potential to alter the state of ownership of a given property.

Areas Livable & Rentable plus Usable

This part of the book explains how ground space of real estate property is measured using varying methods, especially when assessing the square area of apartments and other types of housing units. The three major methods of measurement are explained next.

Brokers and salespersons should be able to understand these methods so that they can explain them clearly to their clients. If you are thinking of buying an apartment and want to make sure the details provided by a realtor or landlord are accurate, you need to have a full understanding of the distinction between space that is described as 'livable,' 'rentable' and 'usable.' Worth noting is that it is possible to measure one particular area using the three varying methods as well as square footage.

Meaning & Calculation of Rentable Space

Rentable space is considered the most liberal when it comes to calculating property space, and it reports the biggest space. When you want to determine the size of an apartment in terms of rentable space, you are supposed to include the closets, hallways and stairs in addition to the living areas and part of what is considered a common area.

Example Rentable Space Calculation

An apartment space is 100,00 sq ft and one apartment within it that is yours measures 10,000 sq feet. The space you occupy as a percentage of the whole space is 10 percent. The common area measures 50,000 sq ft and 10 percent of that area is the portion added to your own rental area or space. Note that a common area constitutes the lobby, fitness space, place where meetings are held and any other such areas meant for use by all apartment owners. That, in its entirety, is your rentable space.

In the case just described, it would be correct to say you have rented 15,000 sq ft because that measure would be inclusive of the 10 percent of common space apportioned to you, which is 5,000 sq ft. It is good to always remember that your rentable space is not equivalent to the livable space. For purposes of marketing an apartment development, quoting the rentable space may be very impressive whereas individual housing units may not have such remarkable livable spaces.

Meaning & Calculation of Usable Space

The term 'usable space' is used to denote the space of the apartment that constitutes your home. Basically it is the space within the walls of your housing unit, inclusive of all spaces in the interior. Usable space is typically inclusive of patios or porches, particularly if they are included in the house air conditioning or heating setup.

To be sure you are calculating your usable space right, you need to keep in mind that all common spaces are excluded and all spaces on the inside of the apartment are included. This includes the storage area, laundry room, closets and other such spaces.

Chapter 6: Terms used in Land Measurement

Acre/Arpent/Aspect/Calc/Perch/Pole/Rod/Centimeter

The term 'acre' is used as a measure of an area of land, and it is given in square measures. It is the most common land measure in the US, and one unit of it is made up of 43,560 sq ft. It is also equivalent to 4,046.9 square meters (sq m). Another acre equivalent is 0.405 hectares (ha).

Other Units Equivalent to an Acre

If you know the units of one measure equivalent to another unit you can use those equivalents to carry out conversions.

An acre is equivalent to 10 square chains, 160 square rods, 160 square poles and 160 square perches. The same one unit of an acre is equivalent to 4,840 square yards (sq yd), 0.0016 sections, 0.004 square kilometers (sq km), and 0.000043 townships. One acre is also equivalent to 1.18368 arpents or 4.0 roods.

The Arpent Unit of Measure

An arpent gives area measurements and is often used on land, and it is equivalent to roughly 5/6th of one acre. In the US this unit is mostly made use of in Louisiana. An arpent is the equivalent of 0.845 acres or 36,800 sq ft.

Aspect

The term 'aspect' in real estate is used to indicate how a building is positioned, or how a structure on land other than a building is positioned towards a given direction. You can, for example, speak of 'a gazebo with a northern aspect.' Aspect is an indication of which direction a slope is facing, and when recorded it is given as a bearing or an azimuth.

Calc Acres

The term 'calc acres' is used in reference to the acreage calculated during a survey or from a given map, and sometimes the number of units found in terms of acres may differ from the ones indicated on the property deed.

Perch

The term 'perch' is used in reference to a unit that gives the measurement of length when land is being surveyed. Other terms used interchangeably with 'perch' are rod and pole, with 'rod' being the most commonly used among the three terms. A perch comprises 25 links, and it is equivalent to 16.5 ft. It is also equivalent to a quarter chain.

Pole

The term 'pole' is used in real estate as a unit indicating length measurements, and it can also mean a portion of land equivalent to a single linear rod or a single square rod. These are units which are made use of when land is being surveyed, and the three terms of rod, perch and pole are all equivalent and can be interchanged. Nevertheless, 'rod' is the most commonly used term.

Rod

The term 'rod' is used in real estate as a measurement during a land survey. It can be used interchangeably with 'perch' or 'pole,' but 'rod' is used most commonly. A single rod comprises 25 links and is equivalent to 16½ ft or a quarter chain.

Other Equivalents of the Rod

A rod is equivalent to 0.025 furlongs, 198 inches, 5.5 yd and 0.003 miles. It is also equivalent to 502.9 centimeters, 5.0292 meters and 0.00503 kilometers.

The Centimeter

The centimeter (cm) is a unit used to measure length, and it is equivalent to one hundredth of a meter or 0.01 meters (m). This unit is also equivalent to 0.394 inches (in). Other equivalents of a centimeter include 0.00001 km, 0.033 ft, 0.0497 links and 0.011 yards. One centimeter unit is also equivalent to 0.002 rods, poles or perches, and it is equivalent to 0.0005 chains. Other equivalents of a centimeter are 0.00005 furlongs and 0.000006 miles.

Engineer's Chain/Gunter's Chain/Density

The term 'engineer's chain' is used to refer to a metallic chain used in measuring length and distance. Sometimes the term is substituted with 'Ramsden's chain.' The use of this equipment is not as common as 'Gunter's chain' or 'surveyor's chain.'

The length of an engineer's chain is 100 ft and it has 100 links measuring a foot each. It is worth noting that an engineer's chain is used to indicate the equipment and is not to be mistaken as a measure of length.

Gunter's chain

The term 'Gunter's chain' (sometimes referred to simply as 'chain') is commonly used in forestry as well as in a land survey. When used as a measure, its equivalent is 66 linear feet.

A mile is equivalent to 80 chains and an area of land that is a square mile is equivalent to 640 acres in area. At the same time, this size of land has 80 chains on every one of its four sides.

Other Chain Equivalents

A chain is not only 66 ft but also 4 rods, poles or perches. It is also equivalent to 22 yards, 20.12 m, 0.0125 miles, 0.020 km, 0.1 furlongs, 792 in and 2011.68 cm.

Density

The term 'density' is used often where zoning is required, and that means there is a maximum set for the number of housing units that can be built within one acre of land. Sometimes zoning is done in terms of a maximum number of families per given piece of land measured in acres, square miles or other such units. Still, there are times when zoning is described in terms of the ratio of land that is developed to the entire area of the land in question.

Distinction between Square Units & Units Square

When using square units to measure an area of land, the term 'square units' is used in reference to the entire area. In the meantime, the term 'units square' is used in reference to the total unit number on each side of the square.

Example of Square Unit vs. Units Square

If you have a square of land that is 8 square miles and another one that is 8 miles square, the area of the first piece of land is 8 square miles, with every one of its sides being 2.8 miles long. To find the side lengths all you need to do is calculate the square root of the area already given. Hence, the square root of 8 square miles is 2.8 miles.

On the other hand, the area of the second piece of land is 64 square miles because 8 miles x 8 miles = 64 square miles.

Foot/Field Notes/Fractional Section/Furlong/Hectare/Inch

Foot

The term 'foot,' is used in real estate as a unit of measuring length, and it is equivalent to 12 in. The measure was originally derived from the measure of a person's foot on average. A human being's foot is considered on average to measure 0.31 m.

Foot Equivalent

A measure of a foot is equivalent to 12 in, and it is also equivalent to 0.305 m. Other foot equivalents include 30.5 cm, 0.0152 chains, 0.002 furlongs, 0.0003 km, 1.52 links and 0.0002 miles. It is also the equivalent of 0.0606 perches, rods or poles, and 0.3333 yards.

Field Notes

In real estate, when the term 'field notes' is used it means the official record that has been documented following a survey of a given piece of land.

Fractional Section

When you have a parcel of land whose completeness is impacted by something like a mass of water, that parcel is said to be a 'fractional section.' A fractional section is normally below 160 acres in size.

Furlong

The term 'furlong' is used in reference to a length measuring 220 yd, which is also the equivalent of 40 rods, perches, poles or 10 chains. This term was derived from 'furrow long,' which is a phrase meaning the distance which is considered sufficient for oxen to plow before being allowed a rest.

A furlong is equivalent to 600 ft, 201.17 m, 1,000 links and 40 perches, rods or poles. It is also equivalent to 10 chains, 0.125 miles, 0.2012 km and 220 yd. It is also equivalent to 7,920 in and 20,116.8 cm.

Hectare

The term 'hectare' is used in reference to a measure of an area of land that is equivalent to 10,000 sq m. The hectare is also equivalent to 0.01 sq km, and it is 2.47 in terms of acres.

Other Equivalents of a Hectare

A hectare given in terms of sq km is 0.01, while in terms of square miles it is 0.004. In terms of townships, a hectare is 0.0001. It is also equivalent to 107,639.1 sq ft and 11,959.9 sq yd.

At the same time, 395.367 square rods, which you can also term sq perches or sq poles, make 1 ha, which is also equivalent to 24.71 square chains. A hectare is also equivalent to 9.88 roods and 2.925 arpents.

Inch

An inch is a unit is used in the measurement of length, and its equivalent in terms of feet is 0.0833, which is essentially 1/12th of a foot. It is also equivalent to 2.54 cm.

Other Inch Equivalents

An inch is also equivalent to 0.1262 links, 0.0278 yd, 0.0051 perches, rods or poles, and 0.0013 chains. It is also equivalent to 0.00013 furlongs, 0.00002 miles and 0.0254 m. In terms of kilometers, one inch is equivalent to 0.00003.

Kilometer/Link/Littoral Rights/ Meander Line/Meter

Kilometer

The term 'kilometer' is used in real estate as a measurement unit of length, where it is the equivalent of a thousand meters.

Other Kilometer Equivalents

A kilometer is also equivalent to 0.6214 miles, 3280.8 ft and 39,370.08 in. It is equivalent to 100,000 cm. At the same time, 1,093.613 yd make one km and 4,970.96 links. A kilometer is also made up of 198.839 perches, rods or poles, 49.7 chains and 4.97 furlongs.

Link

The term 'link' is used in the survey of land, and it is associated with the chain links that surveyors previously used. A single chain comprises a hundred links, and every one of those links is equivalent to 0.66 ft and 0.201 m. It is also equivalent to 0.04 rods, perches or poles and 0.01 chains.

Other Equivalents of Link

Other link equivalents include 0.001 furlongs, 7.92 inches, 0.22 yards, 0.0001 miles and 0.0002 km. A single link comprises 20.1168 cm.

Littoral Rights

The term 'littoral rights' refers to the rights pertaining to real estate properties that abut the waters of a lake.

Meander Line

The term 'meander line' refers to a line artificially made for use by surveyors, who use it as they measure the lines that rivers have formed marking the property, or streams or other water routes that border the particular property.

Meter

The term 'meter,' is used as a unit of measuring length, where a single meter is equivalent to 1,650,763.7 radiation wavelengths emanating from one krypton isotope. A meter comprises 3.281 ft and is also equivalent to 1.094 yd.

Other Equivalents of Meter

A meter is equivalent to 100 cm and also 0.001 km. Other equivalents include 39.37 in, 0.00497 furlongs, 0.0497 chains and 4.971 links. A meter is also equivalent to 0.0006 miles and 0.199 perches, rods or poles.

Miles & Plat

Mile

Miles is the unit primarily used for length in the US, and formally it is referred to as a 'statute mile.' It is equivalent to 5,280 ft and 1.609 km.

Other mile equivalents include 80 chains, 8,000 links, 8 furlongs, 1,760 yd and 63,360 in. A mile is also equivalent to 320 perches, rods or poles, as well as 160,934 cm and 1,609.34 m, just as it is equivalent to 1.609 km.

Plat

The term 'plat' is used in reference to a map of a town or a section of it, or any other subdivision that has been surveyed so that it precisely indicates locations, street and easement boundaries and locations meant for recreation.

Normally plats are required in order to receive approval from the government during subdivision of land. Plats are treated as public documents.

The Term 'Plus or Minus'

The term 'plus or minus,' when used in advertisement or listings for real estate property, is meant to provide a disclaimer that the portion of land stated in square feet, square meters, acres and so on could be slightly smaller or bigger owing to errors of survey, numbers having been rounded up or other such discrepancies.

Often the 'plus or minus' expression is written as '+/-' or '±'.

Rancho/Range/Rood/Section

Rancho

'Rancho' is a term used in reference to a parcel of land beyond 1,000 acres in size. The term is also used to refer to a small-sized farm or building. It can also be used in reference to a cluster of small-sized buildings like huts or bunkhouses which workers at a ranch occupy. Other times people say 'rancho' when they just mean 'ranch.'

Range

The term 'range' is used in real estate in reference to a US measurement applicable in the United States Public Lands Survey System (PLSS). A range covers a six-mile wide land strip that runs north/south.

The term is also used to refer to a single row of townships that lie on the eastern or western side of the principal or main meridian and which are numbered in a successive order towards the east or west from that meridian. The numbering is in the form of R1E, meaning 'range 1East'; R2E, meaning 'range 2East' and so on, or R1W, meaning 'range 1West' etc.

Rood

The term 'rood' is used in real estate as a unit of measurement that defines an area measuring a quarter of an acre. It is equivalent to 40 square rods and 10,890 sq ft.

Other Equivalents of Rood

A rood is also equivalent to 2½ square chains, 1,210 sq yd and 0.296 arpents. It is equivalent to 0.0004 sections (square miles). Other equivalents of the rood include 0.00001 townships, 1,011.714 sq m, 0.001 sq km and 0.101 ha.

Section

In real estate, the term 'section' is used in reference to a land area in a township which is roughly a single mile square and comprises 640 acres. The PLSS uses sections in housing, and in comparison to an entire township every one of these sections is 0.0278 sq ft.

Owing to the curvature of the earth, irregularities are inevitable, but these are normally made up for within the western and northern tiers of the township sections. A single section is equivalent to a square mile, and also to 640 acres. It is also equivalent to 27,878.400 sq ft.

Other Equivalents of Section

Other equivalents of a section include 2.59 sq km, 3,097,600 sq yd and 102,399.6 square rods. Others are 6,399,974 square chains, 2,560 roods, 757.55 arpents and 1/36th of a township. A section is also equivalent to 2,589,988.11 sq m, as well as 258.999 ha.

Setback Lines/Square Chain/Square Foot

Setback Lines

'Setback lines' is a term used in reference to lines set at distances ideal for structures to be located when taking the property perimeter into account.

Square Chain

The term 'square chain' is used in real estate as a unit of measuring the area of a parcel of land; a square measure. Its length on every side is equivalent to that of the surveyor's chain. One acre contains 10 such square chains, with every one of them being equivalent to 4,356 sq f or 404.39 sq m.

Equivalents of the Square Chain

The equivalents of the square chain include 4,356 sq ft, 484 sq yd, 16 square rods, 0.4 roods, 0.118 arpents, 0.1 acres, 0.0405 ha, 0.0004 sq km, 0.0002 sq mi and 0.000004 townships.

Square Foot

The square foot is the unit measure of an area whose every side is a single foot in length. For example, within a parcel of land one acre in size there are 43,560 sq f, which are equivalent to 0.09 in sq m.

Equivalents of the Square Foot

A square foot has its equivalents in other units of measurement, and they include 0.004 square rods, 0.0002 square chains, 0.00002 acres, 0.00001 ha, 0.0001 roods and 0.00003 arpents.

Square Kilometer/Square Measure/Square Meter

Square Kilometer

A 'square kilometer' or 'sq km' is a unit of measurement used to state the area of a parcel of land whose length on every side is 1 km. One square kilometer is equivalent to 1,000,000 sq m, and it is also equivalent to 100 ha.

Other Equivalents of a Square Kilometer

Other equivalents of a square kilometer include 0.39 sq mi, 247.1 acres, 10,763,910.4 sq ft, 1,195,990.05 sq yd, 39,536.7 square rods, 2471.04 square chains, 988.4 roods and 292.5 arpents. In terms of townships, a square kilometer is 0.0107.

Square Measure

The term 'square measure' is used in real estate as a system of measurement for area. It is worth noting that a square foot, which is a square measure, is equivalent to 144 sq in, another square measure. A square meter is equivalent to 10,000 sq cm.

A square measure is also used as a land survey system that is employed in mapping. In using the square measure in measuring, mapping or surveying, the surveyor's chain serves as the base unit.

Square Meter

The term 'square meter' is used in real estate as a unit measure of area, meaning it is a square measure. It denotes an area whose every side is a meter in length. When land is being measured, it is considered that there are 10,000 sq m in a single hectare. Among the equivalents of a square meter are 1.12 sq yd and 10.76 sq ft.

Other Equivalents of a Square Meter

Other equivalents of a square meter include 0.04 squarc rods, 0.0025 square chains, 0.001 roods, 0.0003 arpents and 0.00025 acres. A square meter is also equivalent to 0.0001 ha and 0.000001 sq km. Note that a square kilometer is the equivalent of 1,000,000 sq m, and a square meter is the equivalent of 10,000 sq cm.

Square Mile/Square Perch/Square Pole/Square Yard

The term 'square mile' is used in real estate as a unit to measure the area, especially in the Government Rectangular Survey system. This unit is equivalent to a section of a township, which is essentially $1/36^{th}$ of it, which comprises 640 acres.

Equivalents of a Square Mile

Among the equivalents of a square mile are 27,878,400 sq ft, 2.6 sq km, 3,097,600 sq yd, 102399.6 square rods, 6399.97 square chains, 2,560 roods and 757.6 arpents. Other square mile equivalents are 0.028 or $1/36^{th}$ of a township, 2,589,988.11 sq m and 259 ha.

Square Perch

The term 'square perch' is used in real estate as a unit measure of area, where each side of the parcel of land under consideration is one perch in length. Some of the equivalents of a square perch include 272.3 sq ft, 0.063 square chains and 0.0063 acres. The measure of one square perch can also be referred to as one square rod or one square pole.

Square Pole

The term 'square pole' is used in real estate as a unit measure of area, where every one of the sides of the parcel of land under consideration is a single pole long. A square pole is equivalent to 0.063 square chains, 272.3 sq ft and 0.0063 acres.

Square Rod

The term 'square rod' is used in real estate as a unit measure of area, where every one of the sides of the parcel of land under consideration is a rod long. A square rod is equivalent to 0.063 square chains, 272.3 sq ft and 0.0063 acres.

Other Equivalents of Square Perch/Rod/Pole

Other equivalents of the square perch, square rod or square pole include 30.25 sq yd, 0.025 roods, 0.007 arpents, 25.3 sq m, 0.0025 ha and 0.000025 sq km. Another equivalent is 0.00001 sq mi.

Square Yard

A square yard is used in real estate as a unit for measuring the area, and each of a square yard's sides are a yard in length. Equivalents of a square yard include 0.84 sq m or 9 sq ft. Others include 0.033 square rods, 0.002 square chains, 0.0008 roods, 0.00024 arpents, 0.0002 acres and 0.00008 ha.

Statute Mile/Subdivider/Subdivision/Survey

The term 'statute mile' is used in real estate in reference to one mile, which is equivalent to 5,280 ft and also to 1.61 km.

Subdivider

In real estate, the term 'subdivider' means an individual who carries out the division, separation or apportioning of a parcel of land into smaller pieces.

Subdivision

Subdivision in real estate refers to the process where someone buys land that is yet to be developed, subdivides it into lots of smaller sizes and then sells those lots to other people who may include investors.

The term 'subdivision' is also used in reference to land already subdivided into lots that have then been organized into blocks.

The lots, streets, alleys, parks, schools, planned areas for commercial activity and for easement of public utilities all have their records put on the plat. Before a subdivision is started, both state and local regulations have to be fulfilled first. Often this process is long and you will be required to pay a fee for your application.

Survey

The term 'survey' is used in real estate to denote that process used to measure land boundaries and to determine not only the location of land parcels but also their forms. It is actually the measurement used on the site on lot lines and dimensions, as well as individual structure positions on the lot. It helps to determine when there is encroachment or easement.

Township/Yard

Township

In real estate, the term 'township' is used as a way by which land is measured within the PLSS. One township is six miles long on every one of its sides, and its entire area is 36 sq mi. That area that is the township comprises 36 sections, each 640 acres. This means the total amount of land comprising the township is 23,040 acres in size.

It is important to note that owing to the earth's curvature there is always a need to make an adjustment of 198 ft after every interval of 24 miles. For that reason, there are several townships whose size ends up being below 36 sq mi.

Equivalents of a Township

Other measurements in real estate that are equivalent to one township include 1,003,622,400 sq ft, 93,239,572 sq m, 111,514,046.52 sq yd and 3,686,400 square rods. A township is also equivalent to 230,400 square chains, 92,160.4 roods, 27,272 arpents, 9,324 ha and 93.2 sq km.

Yard

The term 'yard' is used in reference to a unit of measure used to determine the length of a given part, and it is equivalent to 3 ft and 36 in. It is also equivalent to 0.9 m, 0.0009 km and 91.4 cm.

Other yard equivalents include 4.55 links, 0.182 rods, 0.046 chains, 0.005 furlongs and 0.0006 miles.

Chapter 7: Rights to Minerals, Water & Air

If you own a parcel of land it is assumed that you also own everything else on it, including the trees and buildings unless you decide to sell them or rent them out. However, there is an exception to some natural resources such as minerals and water.

In the US, it is possible to sell or convey rights to minerals separately from the right to the land itself. For that reason, when you acquire a parcel of land you should not assume that the rights to any minerals under the surface belong to you. You will learn in this part of the book what it means to own rights to minerals and how you can convey those rights to another party.

Rights to Minerals

Mineral rights are rights a particular party has to exploit a particular area due to the minerals it has. These minerals include those beneath the ground like oil and natural gas as well as those that are said to be sedentary—on the surface of the earth.

The person who owns the minerals is the one with the right to extract and make use of them. To determine who the real owner of the minerals is and the specific minerals involved you have to look at the conveyance, which is the formal document indicating the sale or purchase of the mineral rights. You may find the conveyance has covered every kind of mineral found under the parcel of land, or that the ownership has been limited to several specified minerals.

Though minerals for extraction typically include coal, oil and natural gas, rights to minerals can also be extended to gold and silver and other precious metals. In some cases when someone transfers the rights to minerals they include the rights to the surface ground as well, so that the same party with rights of extracting minerals also has the right to dig out gravel and clay at will.

How to Separate Rights to Minerals from Rights to Land

When you buy a piece of land, it is assumed you also own the rights to any minerals beneath the ground and the conveyance confirms it, unless that ownership is separated in the process either by the owner or seller. There are different ways that you as a land owner can separate mineral rights from those of your piece of land.

Conveying Land Minus Minerals

It is possible to sell or transfer your piece of land, meaning to convey it, to another party but then retain the rights to the minerals the land holds. To accomplish this, the deed must contain a statement that clearly indicates that while the right to the parcel of land has been transferred to the buyer, the rights to all minerals on the land remain with the property seller.

Conveying Minerals Minus Land

It is also possible to sell or transfer the rights to minerals to another party as you retain the rights to the land you own. The way this is done is by issuing a deed to the buyer specifically for the mineral or minerals, showing you have conveyed only the rights to the minerals. This means you will retain your land deed even as the new mineral owner holds his/her mineral deed.

Conveying Land and Minerals to Different Parties

It is possible to legally convey the rights to land to one party while conveying the rights to the minerals therein to a different party. Any time someone buys land whose mineral rights are owned by someone else, such a land owner can only convey land rights to any subsequent buyer. The reasoning is that it is not feasible to sell what you do not own, and in this case the land owner has no ownership to the minerals the land holds.

The first-time rights to the land and the minerals are separated. Respective owners hold deeds that do not highlight the fact of right separation. This means anyone looking at the deed only sees that the land owner has the right to the land. Unless someone expressly asks the landowner or the relevant office, it is not obvious that the right to some minerals beneath the land belong to someone else.

When Mineral Rights are of no Consequence

Many times property owners do not find it necessary to determine whether rights to any minerals beneath their land are theirs or not, because even if they were, the process of mineral extraction might be too expensive for them. The process of finding out if separation of ownership exists might also be too involved.

If the parcel of land owned is in an area never known to have minerals of any kind, it is logical for property owners to assume that rights to any minerals that may exist have not been separated from the rights to land. This essentially means you own both the land and any minerals within it.

Another safeguard that makes property owners disregard any rights to minerals is that the law of the land in the US prohibits the destruction of any developments, be they homes or different structures, for the sake of mineral extraction, and their use cannot be interfered with in any way.

For this reason, people who own property in areas that are densely populated such as cities, suburbs and other such places need not be concerned about the possibility of a mineral owner disrupting their life.

When Mineral Rights are of Much Concern

It is reasonable to be concerned whether you own the rights to any minerals within your parcel of land if you own property in a region where the neighborhood has oil rigs working on a regular basis, or where oil drilling or other mineral extraction operations are evident. There is a chance the rights to land and rights to the minerals were separated many years ago when the minerals were discovered, and one day the true holder of the mineral rights might appear at your property ready to begin drilling or excavation.

The party that has rights to the minerals normally also has a right to construct roadways and any other developments that may be required in order to enable the process of extracting the minerals.

In other instances, there are restrictions put on the rights of the mineral owner. There are, for example, cases where you may own the rights to the minerals but they must be exploited within a particular period of time. Another restriction could be how deeply you can excavate the ground. There are also often restrictions meant for the protection of the owner of the land and environment, and these are regulated according to the laws of the local jurisdiction and those of the state pertaining to the activities surrounding extraction of minerals.

Best Course of Action When Doubtful About Mineral Rights

If ever someone shows up and claims to own the rights to minerals within your piece of land, the first thing you should do is find yourself a lawyer whose specialty is mineral law. The attorney is in a position to investigate and establish who the actual owner of the minerals is by tracing any deeds that date back to the time the minerals were first reserved and conveyed.

The attorney is also able to establish if there are different owners with varying rights to separate minerals on a given piece of land. One other reason it is helpful to engage a lawyer is that you may have some royalty rights attached to the profits from any minerals extracted, which are normally expressed in different documents from those that show the owner of the mineral rights.

Once it is evident that the person laying claim to the minerals does have a legal right to them, there is not much you can do to bar him/her from proceeding with extraction operations. However, your lawyer can help you negotiate a manner of operations that minimizes the impact on your land and your comfort. If nothing else, at least your attorney should be able to see to it that the owner of the minerals adheres to every restriction and regulation stipulated in the separation documents. The attorney should also be able to ensure that the party concerned adheres to all regulations that govern the extraction of minerals and the process of cleanup.

Dangers of Conveying Rights to Minerals

If you are considering selling mineral rights, there are some things you should know pertaining to potential dangers. You own the rights to both the land and the minerals before separation of those rights, and you can lease either the land or the mineral rights at will.

However, once you have sold the rights to the minerals, you only receive the one-off payment and nothing thereafter—unless there is a provision for you to earn royalties— no matter how much income the extraction and subsequent sale brings. Still, a land easement can be created between the seller and the buyer of the rights to minerals so as to facilitate the activities related to the recovery of minerals.

Easement of Rights to Minerals

An easement of rights to minerals is defined as rights held by individual persons, companies or agencies, for the use of another party's property for an identified purpose. People who buy rights to minerals ordinarily make sure they have the capacity to extract those minerals they will have owned.

Once you have sold the rights to the minerals on your land, it may become necessary for you to provide an easement on the land to enable the new mineral owner to carry out extraction work. Even if the rights to that land are still yours, you cannot interfere with the operations of the party that holds the easement.

Distinction between Selling & Leasing

Selling the rights to the minerals within your land sometimes involves selling all the commodities in mineral form that are known, as well as those below the earth's surface that are yet to be discovered. Other times it involves selling a particular mineral already known to exist beneath the earth's surface.

Often, selling the rights to minerals is tantamount to relinquishing any rights to royalties that you might have earned on a long-term basis. You should understand that once you sell your rights to the minerals, you have no control over subsequent sales of the same rights to another party. Anyone who buys the rights thereafter also acquires the rights of exploitation received by the original buyer, as well as all rights of easement. With this information, it is now incumbent upon you to evaluate the benefits to you if you sell versus if you lease those rights.

Rights to Water

It is important to understand your rights to water within the context of transactions of real estate properties. Water rights (referred to as riparian) mean the rights you legally have to use the physical water supply, whether that is on the surface of your parcel of land, beneath it or coming from a piece of land adjoining it.

Within the US, the rights to water that are linked to a piece of land are considered valuable assets. For example, whoever has riparian rights benefits a lot from accessing great water bodies within adjoining lands. This is common in the country's eastern parts.

It is important to note that although it is possible to sell water rights separately from land rights, as often happens in the states on the western side of the country, it is not feasible to de-link water rights from land rights where riparian rights are concerned.

Transactions Related to Water Rights

Rights to water often feature in real estate transactions. Water rights permit you to make use of a water mass that adjoins the land you own. For instance, if you have a property on the lakefront and you decide to sell it, the riparian rights you held are automatically transferred to the new property owner. This is to illustrate that it is not possible to sever water rights, if they are riparian rights, from the right to the adjoining land for sales purposes.

On the contrary, on the western side of the US, you may hold the rights to the subterranean streams found within your portion of land, but other times those rights may belong to another party.

Riparian rights give you authority and responsibility over any watercourses that are adjacent to or abutting your parcel of land. Good examples of such watercourses include streams and navigable rivers.

Sale of Water Rights

There are some US states, such as California, that accord owners of properties that lie above water held in underground basins the right to draw water from them. If you make use of underground water and then sell your piece of land, the person who buys it should inherit the rights to the water as well.

Nevertheless, there are instances where you can sell water rights separately from the land when it comes to subterranean streams and other waters beneath the ground. Some states, such as Texas, give landowners total ownership of the water beneath their portions of land; a right referred to as 'absolute dominion.'

One important thing to remember is that there are times you could have the right to make use of water within your parcel of land yet not have the right to own it in the traditional sense.

Rights to Air

Individuals can have air rights just as they have water rights or mineral rights. The term 'air rights' is used in reference to the right a person has to make use of, control or occupy the airspace, which is the space that exists vertically above a piece of land. It is expected that you will only exercise the right to use that space when it is necessary and also reasonable with respect to the effect it may have on your neighbors and/or other properties. A good example is the use of aircraft.

Air rights can be bought, sold or leased. This essentially means that just like you can transfer your rights to minerals and water you can also transfer your right to airspace.

The rise in the value of land and expansion of the transportation infrastructure—factors affecting the growth of urban life—has made the need for air rights that much more prominent. In the Central Business District (CBD), for example, the value of land has escalated and the transport system continues to be a concern and a focus by authorities.

For that reason, a need has arisen to construct high-rise buildings not only for retail but also to host administrative and financial centers.

Limitation of 'Cujus est Solum Ejus est Usque ad Coelum et ad Inferos'

The rights to air date way back to when common law applied as the main law. During this time, the maxim that guided air rights was the Latin 'cujus est solum ejus est usque ad coelum et ad inferos.' This translates as 'To whomever the soil belongs, he also owns to the sky and to the depths.'

Today, a person who owns land can use the airspace above it to the extent possible, subject to overriding regulations such as aviation rules.

The doctrine of 'To whomever the soil belongs, he also owns to the sky and to the depths' worked well many years ago, but with the development of aviation for commercial purposes in the 20th century, the right to unlimited airspace by individuals became a challenge. To solve the problem, Congress decided to limit how high the right to airspace can go as far as individual ownership is concerned. This limitation enabled the expansion of air travel without costly inhibitions and possible dangers.

Hence, in 1926, the Air Commerce Act was passed which gave the public the freedom to travel commercially by air, and to make use of navigable US airspace. In general, airspace that is navigable comprises airspace whose elevation is over 500 ft from the level of the land.

Today, the US government has exclusive rights to the airspace within the country though US Code 49 U.S.C. §40103(1). Subsection 2 states that the public right to use airspace is limited to the area that is high enough to be within navigable space. This means the government's right to airspace does not encroach on private ownership of airspace below navigable airspace.

It is important to note that an individual cannot be compensated for any negative impact on his/her property owing to the use of airspace by the public or the government as long as the airspace used is within navigable space. Justice Douglas ruled as such in 1946 when someone brought a suit alleging that the noise from planes, including a US bomber, had led to the death of his chickens and caused him mental agony.

The plaintiff hoped that the judge would rely on the doctrine of 'ad coelum' traditionally used in common law, which holds that if you own land you also own all that is below it as well as above it, even as high as the sky. However, the judge held that the Air Commerce Act supersedes that doctrine.

In short, it is important as a landowner to establish how high your right of airspace ownership goes before you can lease such airspace or use it yourself for development. Knowing the extent of your airspace rights is important, especially with regard to view easements and other easements such as those related to access to solar electricity, flight paths and other rights of development within the non-navigable airspace.

Before entering into any contracts regarding your airspace you need to familiarize yourself with the regulations set by your local authority including those pertaining to zoning. Normally, local authorities have additional rules guiding how individuals can utilize the navigable airspace above their portions of land, and sometimes such regulations can be so stringent that they limit development above a certain level.

Chapter 8: Government Controls in Real Estate

One major reason the government controls how land is used is to avoid a situation where developers construct properties haphazardly, leading to unsafe living conditions, unsightly structures and destruction of natural habitat. Where private control of land use is applicable, it helps to enhance order and to reduce risks that can affect residents and their neighborhood in an adverse manner.

The preservation of forests and parks is mainly the responsibility of government. In fact, the federal government has given the mandate of controlling use of land to state governments, which in turn delegate the role to respective local authorities. For this reason, land use control can vary immensely from one locality to another.

Tools for Control of Land Use

Tools used in the control of land use include government ordinances, government codes and prerequisites for acquiring a permit which ensure land in private hands is used appropriately and that natural resources are handled as per public policy.

Land use regulations are categorized variously under subdivision, zoning, codes for building and/or housing, systems of permit issuance referred to as 'curve-cut,' historic laws of resource preservation and laws pertaining to cutting down trees.

Role of US Government in Control of Land Use

The US government prevents haphazard developments from emerging through both private and public land control measures. As discussed earlier, the government also owns land, and it obviously has direct control over its property, including forests and parks.

Nevertheless, in a strict sense the US federal government has no jurisdiction over how land is used, with most of the controlling power being in the hands of the respective states. Individual states enact and enforce laws pertaining to property ownership within their jurisdiction.

Constitution of Controls on Land Use

The main control when it comes to how public land is used is in the form of zoning. Here properties of a similar type, such as those for residential and commercial use, are allocated specific geographical areas or zones. Use of private land is mainly controlled through the restrictions put on deeds which limit the developments an owner of private property can establish on a particular property. These limitations are enacted in order to restrict how far population density can rise, how much noise and other pollution can be generated and to maintain the aesthetics within a particular neighborhood.

The laws pertaining to how land may be used keep changing as the needs of society evolve, and for that reason landowners can find themselves facing big challenges as new regulations emerge. To save property owners undue pressure, laws often allow what is termed 'grandfathering' of particular provisions. This means new laws do not affect property owners who had conformed to earlier laws though their land is now within an area targeted by new laws.

On that basis, property is generally classified as legal and conforming, illegal and legal, and nonconforming. Property is considered legal and conforming when it meets the requirements of land use that are current at any given time. It is considered legal and nonconforming when it was legal under laws applicable in the past, but now is considered legal for the sole reason that it benefits from provisions that have been grandfathered in. Property that does not adhere to any provisions of the law, past or present, is illegal.

Legality With Regard to Controls on Land Use

Although the US Constitution permits enactment of laws that enhance citizens' general welfare, the 14th amendment prohibits any state from interfering with the use of property in individuals' possession or from depriving them of property unless this is done within the boundaries of the law.

The Constitution delegates power of monitoring to the respective states, giving them authority to design regulations meant to provide protection to public health and safety as well as people's overall welfare.

For effective monitoring and policing, states, on their part, find it preferable to delegate these roles to their various municipalities, because effective control of how land is used depends on how dense the population in an area is, the composition of structures of varying architectural designs and the land's general topography. These municipalities then designate ordinances which are in conformity with the laws of the state. The federal government and states carry out regulation of land use by enacting broader legislation, like the laws pertaining to the environment, management of coastlines and those on scenic easement.

A clause in the Constitution's 5th amendment, referred to as the 'takings clause,' prohibits any state from taking property in private hands and converting it for use by the public unless the private party that owns the property is duly compensated. This means if the government condemns a given property via eminent domain, it must ensure due compensation is made to the property owner.

If a piece of property is acquired from private ownership and put into public use, and the value of the adjacent property drops, the owner of that devalued land can take action referred to as 'inverse condemnation.' Such a scenario can be exemplified by the acquisition of land close to residential properties for the sake of constructing a massive highway. Owners of the residential properties can claim inverse condemnation due to the noise pollution and other inconveniences the construction is causing them.

The level of compensation is normally set through negotiations between the owner of the affected property and the government. Sometimes property owners prefer to sue the government so that a court of law can determine the amount they receive. Usually the factors considered are the value of the land before the government's interference caused a decline and the value of the land after it. This method of comparison is referred to as 'before and after.'

Zoning

Property owners cannot be restricted from making use of their property as they wish, unless the reason for the restriction is justified. For example, zoning involves locally enacted laws regulating the use of privately owned real estate, and the reason for such regulation is to enhance the orderliness in developments, regulate the population density in each area and protect resources of an environmental nature.

Unreasonable, arbitrary or destructive zoning regulations are illegal. Nor may zoning ordinances violate the Constitution or any other state law or applicable provisions.

To establish whether zoning is correctly executed, you need to consider first if it has been exercised in a manner that is reasonable, and also if it is clear enough to be understood and very specific.

Zoning should also not be discriminatory at all, and it should be applied to all pieces of property in the area in a uniform manner. Zoning should promote the health of the public, public safety and the overall public welfare as stipulated within the regulatory powers of the state.

Importance of a Master Plan

A master plan is a plan that is comprehensive, drawn prior to having the control details pertaining to land use mapped out. It helps to satisfy the set objectives while also preventing potential conflicts where future developments are concerned. The master plan provides a blueprint to aid in enhancing growth in a sustainable manner, while at the same time helping to balance social, aesthetic, economic and environmental aspirations.

Controls on land use specify not only the quantity of land parcels residents should have when it comes to zoning, but also the location of those parcels with regard to the activities carried out on the parcels— business or agriculture; recreation; transport or facilities for transit; facilities for community use; utilities; industrial use or potentially hazardous areas such as floodplains. Housing to meet present and future needs is an important consideration, even as restrictions are put in place to restrict neighborhood developments or to rehabilitate existing neighborhoods that have deteriorated.

Infrastructure for transportation such as highways and public transit must be provided, along with paths for bicycles and pedestrians, as well as parking. It is important to have a master plan to cater for utilities which include sources of water, storm drainage and sewage systems, waste treatment and its disposal, as well as flood management. Such a plan is also meant to enhance resource management, such as energy conservation. For example, how efficient transportation is depends on the decisions made pertaining to traffic signals' location, the timing of those signals, whether the traffic is one- or two-way and the direction the one-way traffic takes.

To understand zoning better, think of the comprehensive or master plan as the blueprint, and zoning as the blueprint's details. Then the laws enacted locally must adhere to the master plan, normally with particular districts designated for specific types of activities and structures like businesses and residences.

Zoning Ordinance

The term 'zoning ordinance' is used to define the different classifications of zoning comprising the uses allowed for various parts of the land. It also defines the restrictions, like the limitation of setbacks and height, just as it defines the procedures to be followed in permitting uses that are nonconforming. The zoning ordinance defines the procedures to be followed if variances, amendments or hearing appeals are to be granted. It also defines the penalties to be imposed when violations are committed.

Zoning is used to determine uses that have been permitted for respective land parcels; how big lots should be; permitted structure types and development heights and setbacks, which are denoted by the least distance between the sidewalks/streets and the property structures.

Zoning also helps in determining the density of the population or the number of structures that can be constructed for every given unit area, the style recommended, the external look of the structures and how any natural resources available are to be protected.

Zoning Map

Cities have a planning department that is charged with creating and maintaining a zoning map, which is basically a diagram showing how zoning has been classified. In particular it indicates the residential areas for single-family units, multi-units, units for mixed use, agriculture, commerce and industry.

These zones are often denoted by the use of letters like 'A' representing agriculture, 'R' denoting residential and 'C' indicating commercial. There are also 'planned units developments' (PUDs) that are zoned in order to be developed into properties for mixed use. Such properties contain units for both residential and commercial purposes.

Even after areas have been zoned for specific purposes, there is still room to subdivide them further. For example, land that has been zoned to hold residential developments can be further subdivided so that some it can be developed as single-family units and semi-detached residences with high-rise housing units not exceeding four.

You can also have 'C-1' for designated businesses like service stations and convenience stores; 'R-2' as housing developments meant for single families and 'R-4' as a residential area of high density where the construction is in the form of apartments.

Buffer Zones

The term 'buffer zone' is used in reference to an area that separates land for a specified use from land that is intended for a different use. In real estate, a buffer zone is viewed as a neutral area that is entirely vacant, often meant to remain as such without any kind of development. Though some buffer zones are left as playgrounds or parks, they still serve the purpose of separating the different zones of residence.

Special Zoning

There may be different zoning types that designate qualities of a special nature, like 'box zoning' which specifies the heights of buildings, open space percentage meant to deter overcrowding and setbacks. 'Aesthetics zoning' indicates buildings which are required to have specific architectural styles.

Incentive Zoning

The term 'incentive zoning' is used in reference to a type of zoning where ongoing development is geared towards particular desirable characteristics. In such circumstances, some restrictions may be relaxed in a bid to get developers interested in a desired type of development. For example, the local authority may prefer to have high-rise developments for mixed use as opposed to developments at street level for retail purposes.

Spot Zoning

In 'spot zoning,' a given piece of land is classified differently from other surrounding properties when the particular zone cannot be found within the comprehensive zoning plan. Alternatively, this happens when the general zoning cannot be justified owing to safety and health considerations or people's welfare in general. In short, spot zoning is tantamount to having a parcel of land zoned in its own unique way although it exists within a larger area that is zoned differently.

Zoning Permits

To confirm that a developer or property owner has adhered to the ordinances of zoning, a zoning permit is issued. This means that the owner or developer of such property has no room to alter the way the property is used without acquiring a zoning permit. A zoning permit is issued only when the property owner or developer has conformed to the set zoning ordinance, and it must be acquired before starting on large developments such as construction of housing units.

It is important to keep in mind that properties exist which were developed prior to the enactment of zoning ordinances, and so they are unlikely to conform to any current regulations. There is also the likelihood in some cases that the new zoning requirements could cause some property owners challenges due to the nature of their pieces of land or topography. Such are the circumstances that lead to exemptions, so that even as the current zoning ordinance is observed, the old developments remain as they are, even when their uses are nonconforming.

Nonconforming use normally remains as such until the purpose for which it is used is abandoned, or the property is destroyed. This means the property's nonconforming status could remain in place indefinitely, especially if it is a subject of grandfathering within the locality's zoning ordinance.

Regulations on Subdivision of Property

Regulations pertaining to subdivision of property often apply when the land is meant for use as a residential area and there is a need to specify areas designated for open spaces and to denote the pattern access roads will take.

Ultimately, these regulations help to denote the areas to be reserved as county or municipal property. The overall area density is regulated by the standards for special density zoning targeting particular subdivisions. Gross density is considered equal to the area's average count of residential development units.

Subdividers & Developers

The term 'subdivider' is used in reference to a person or party that buys land that has not been developed, then undertakes to divide it into units that are smaller in size and sells them to individuals or willing developers.

Developer

The term 'developer' is used in real estate to refer to the person or party that builds or develops structures on a given piece of land, which include housing units or business premises. Sometimes the developer also serves as the subdivider. Prior to subdividing the land, the subdivider must submit the development plan in order to confirm that it is in conformity with the municipality's comprehensive plan or master plan.

It is possible to have subdivisions whose patterns of streets vary. For example, one subdivision's streets may follow a gridiron pattern, which comprises rectangular blocks that have streets for public use on every side of the blocks, and in between the blocks are small alleys. Another subdivision may have streets that follow a curvilinear pattern, where homes are built in a cluster or within cul-de-sacs, and where there is plenty of open space and minimal use of streets. This pattern is also referred to as 'clustering.'

Plats, Lots and Blocks

After land has been subdivided, the resultant pieces are known as 'plats.' These are then subdivided to form blocks, each of which comprises a number of lots. Lots are then sold as individual units.

Borders of every individual lot and block, section, street, public easement and monument, as well as engineering data, can be seen within a plat, and the same thing applies to covenants of a restrictive nature. A plan must receive approval from the municipality before it can be put on record. It may also be necessary for the subdivider to file a report on the project's environmental impact before approval for subdivision can be given.

The subdivider decides the actual location and size of every lot, taking advantage of the natural course of drainage as well as land contours, and provides for easement of utilities, water and sewage. Sometimes a plat has an HOA association, and subdivision by-laws are maintained.

Building Codes & Permits

Building codes are used in specifying the standards used in repairs and construction of buildings, including the materials utilized, electric wiring, prevention of fire, sanitary equipment and the like.

Building Permit

It is mandatory for a property owner to request a building permit if ever he/she wants to make any changes to the property, repair it or construct anything on it. Approval of the construction plan must be received from a municipal inspector, who should continue to make inspections of the construction site from time to time.

Certificate of Occupancy

A Certificate of Occupancy (COA), also known as an occupancy permit, is issued by the municipal office after the municipal inspector has been satisfied that the construction project is fit for occupation and meets all the requirements stipulated by the municipal authority.

When issued to either the developer or property owner, a COA confirms that the development is in compliance with the public health code and building code. The certificate therefore authorizes human occupation of the structures.

It is important to realize that receiving a building permit has no impact on any restrictions the deed may have on the property. It only impacts the construction on the property, be it additions or alterations. There are some districts, such as historical ones, which have 'aesthetic ordinances.' These ordinances require that properties retain the neighborhood character or appearance. Typically, a special board is designated in such districts in order to supervise these ordinances.

Changes in Zoning: Boards/Variances/Permits of Conditional Use

Although ordinances guide how a neighborhood is developed, sometimes alterations can be made after individual owners apply for permission to the relevant authorities. Nevertheless, such changes are not taken lightly and there is a process to be followed.

Zoning Changes

Zoning changes are often required as years go by and the area needs evolve. For example, businesses may go bankrupt over the course of time or property demands may suddenly be geared towards a certain industry, especially due to competition or technological changes. Such developments may lead to unoccupied structures which were intended to house businesses. It is for this reason that some cities opt to change their zoning so that properties previously designated for businesses become residential properties.

The main point you need to understand here is that for a given property to be changed from one use to another, the authorities must first rezone the land. The specific body charged with rezoning of land is the planning commission or the zoning board, and they only do this after there has been a public hearing on the matter.

Zoning Board

The 'zoning board' is also referred to as the 'zoning board of appeal,' and before it proceeds with any changes it takes into account all applications received seeking a change in zoning. Often there are petitions seeking conditional property use, variance in property usage or exceptions.

Conditional Use Permit

The 'conditional-use permit' is also known as a 'special-use permit,' and it denotes that a property owner has permission to make use of a given property within a specified zone on a conditional basis.

Such use could be the building of a church or other such facility within an area otherwise zoned to be residential.

Variance

The authority in charge of zoning is the one that grants a variance to the owner of the property, for the sake of allowing him/her to violate a specific standard within the zoning ordinance. Often such permission is granted when it is clear the ordinance puts an unnecessary burden on the owner of the property.

You may have, for example, a variance granted to the owner of a piece of land that is just a tiny lot, because its size is unlikely to enable fulfillment of setback or open area requirements for a residential zone. Conditional use permits use of land that is related with authorized uses, while a variance permits use of land that is outright prohibited within the given zone.

Conditions for Acquiring Zoning Variance

For a zoning variance to be afforded there must be proof that the zoning of the particular area puts an unnecessary burden on that land. It must also be evident that the effect of the zoning ordinance affects the applicant in a negative way that does not affect other property owners in the same area. Additionally, it must be proven that a variance does not have the potential to change the neighborhood character or appearance as originally planned. In fact, this last condition is considered the most crucial in determining whether a variance will or will not be granted.

It costs time and money to obtain a variance or a complete change in land zoning, but success is likely if the classification you are applying to change to is similar to a property nearby. It is, for example, easier to receive approval for a change from commercial to residential if there is land in the neighborhood that has already been zoned residential.

The hearings by the board in charge of zoning and that issues permits for conditional use and variances are held publicly, and their schedules are advertised for local residents to see. This allows neighbors of the property under consideration to air their views, and those who want to contest the application can do so. Meanwhile, the owner of the property may seek that a zoning ordinance be amended in such a way that the requested modification applies to a targeted piece of land.

Amendments to the zoning ordinance require a public hearing. It is important to note that a property owner can lodge an appeal in a court of law to contest a decision made by the zoning board. However, courts do not generally take up such cases unless it is apparent there has been an abuse of power by the zoning board in making its decision.

Chapter 9: Control of Special Types of Land

There are some special uses the federal government may use land for, but for the most part it leaves individual states to regulate how land within their respective jurisdictions is used. The state government can in turn delegate some regulatory powers to local authorities.

Between 1945 and 2012, the US government invested a lot of land for rural transport, parks and wildlife, as well as for defense, industry and farming.

As far as transportation goes, the government constructed highways, other roads and railroads, and it also improved facilities in rural airports.

The government developed parks and put them under the control of the federal government and others under the respective states. This went alongside the creation of wilderness areas and wildlife refuges.

Land allocated for defense and industrial functions was used for energy development, airfields, research and development, housing and miscellaneous military-related functions. The government also set land aside for agricultural purposes.

The government subsequently declassified land uses for areas that were found to be marshy and swampy, rocky or desert-like, and other such areas considered not to have much commercial value. Most of that declassified land is under the control of the state governments.

Regulation on Flood Zones

The US government doesn't have many regulations pertaining to how areas susceptible to floods can be developed. Instead, much of that regulation is left to the state and local authorities.

In South Carolina, for example, there are many areas considered vulnerable and in the 2000s, both commercial and residential developments surged. Although FEMA has designated some areas as obvious floodplains, state authorities seem to ignore the warnings. The number of people living in areas of high flood risk rose in 2016 by 14 percent in comparison to 2000.

In comparison, the population rise in areas considered safe from floods increased only by 13 percent in the same period. One official from the Natural Resources Defense Council has been quoted as saying that the US gets what it has paid for in relation to the billions of dollars the country spends annually to evacuate and resettle people when flood-related disasters occur.

Incidentally, state governments and other local authorities have failed to prohibit construction in areas like Charleston that are considered to be floodplains, and so potential property buyers are at risk of acquiring properties that have the potential of flooding unless they deal with brokers who are great at carrying out due diligence.

As for the rules enacted under the National Flood Insurance Program, these are not only limited but also ineffective where rising sea levels are concerned. Studies conducted in recent years have indicated that the sea level has been rising off the coast of South Carolina, but this seems to be ignored by the government even as flooding is known to be a historical fact in the region. Yet there are many residents who are uncomfortable with the new developments that continue to crop up, like the 4,300 housing-unit development the local authority has sanctioned in Charleston City.

Although residents of the island have petitioned against the development, some influential members of the city council are climate-change skeptics, and so they have ignored the protests. They also think that making modifications to the zoning that was last approved in the 1990s may lead to legal suits from affected landowners, which could be very costly for the council.

In fact, there is a builders association in Charleston that is opposed to fresh zoning that would come with new restrictions, because as far as the association is concerned that would lead to the devaluation of its properties.

In the meantime, homeowners who have lived in the area for years see the new housing developments as being likely to exacerbate the risk of flooding in the region. In response to such concerns, the Obama administration required authorities at the federal level to ensure public infrastructure be constructed at elevations that are much higher, taking into consideration the risk of flooding in the respective regions.

Considering the federal government has not been proactive in regulating settlements in flood-risk areas and local authorities are not as proactive as residents would like, it is upon you as a broker or salesperson to ensure you pursue purchases that are largely safe for your clients. The Obama administration's rule, however, was overturned by the Trump administration, and coincidentally, a few days later, Hurricane Harvey hit Texas.

With the continued rescinding of rules meant to protect homeowners and residents from flooding, like the Waters of the US rule, one can only hope that FEMA will be able to encourage local authorities to raise their standards of regulation, even if it means providing discounts on flood insurance via the Community Rating System.

Without such a change, developments in areas that are primarily wetlands are likely to be on the rise, and this means an increase in the availability of buildings at affordable rates, but which are at risk of natural disasters like sinking or being hit by floods. The responsibility of brokers and salespersons in seeking out safe properties to market cannot, therefore, be overstated.

Still, some states have been protective of their residents, insisting that construction of housing developments be done on safe grounds. In Milwaukee, for example, just a third of the residential and commercial properties are on land considered to have the potential for flooding. Over time, the state has acquired the properties, and then invested in 'green infrastructure' projects, the aim being to get rid of every home that sits on what is considered a floodplain by 2035.

Restrictions on Contaminated Property

There are regulations controlling how property that is contaminated can be sold, and these include restrictions designed by the US Environmental Protection Agency (EPA). The Comprehensive Environmental Response, Compensation & Liability Act (CERCLA) was enacted in 1980. The law sought to respond to dangerous practices of disposing of hazardous waste that had been ongoing during the 1970s. There are a number of acts within CERCLA, also known as the superfund, which ensure the protection of property owners and buyers from environment-related dangers.

Any broker or salesperson who wants to ascertain the legality of buying or selling land that is thought to be unsafe can log on to the official website of the EPA and read through the legislation.

Contaminated real estate properties are restricted under the law to ensure buyers and other people are not exposed to hazardous environments. There is also legislation meant to ensure cleanup of contaminated areas and to monitor liability insofar as the selling and development of such properties is concerned.

How Contaminated Property is Controlled in Real Estate

Property owners are protected through legislation from acquiring property that is contaminated. Land that is contaminated cannot be developed into a residential or commercial property unless it is thoroughly cleaned up first, inspected and deemed habitable. Anyone who sells contaminated land to unsuspecting buyers or develops properties for sale on land that is contaminated is legally liable. The laws enforcing this help to safeguard lives, otherwise unscrupulous businesspeople might put people's lives at risk.

The Environmental Protection Agency

In the US, the EPA is the body that has been charged with ensuring that legislation enacted to protect people from environmental hazards is adhered to. The body oversees cleanup of contaminated land.

To avoid exposing potential property owners and their families to contamination and risking litigation, brokers should get useful guidance from the EPA's official, http://www.epa.gov/superfund. Property owners can also seek useful information on the same website, including the opportunities that exist for individual communities to have their environments cleaned up.

The Superfund

The superfund (CERCLA) was enacted in 1980. Its enactment was in response to increasing incidences of land contamination, which spurred Congress and the Senate to discuss the issue of how toxic waste can be disposed of to minimize potential hazards to people.

The superfund covers every aspect of environmental dangers, including how to respond to contamination-related emergencies, carry out data analysis, organize cleanups and deal with related liabilities.

Before the superfund was created, the Resource Conservation & Recovery Act (RCRA), alongside the Toxic Substances Control Act (TSCA), were the regulatory bodies charged with ensuring that individuals and organizations didn't dump toxic waste in a manner that would jeopardize people's health.

The superfund is a creation of the EPA, and through it restrictions are designed and monitored so that real estate properties are protected, whether they are meant for residential or commercial purposes.

The National Priorities List

To ensure that the superfund ran efficiently, the National Priorities List (NPL) was created in 1983. Its role was to pinpoint areas within the US that should be prioritized for thorough cleanup. The list continues to be updated on a regular basis, and brokers, just like anyone else, can access it online so as to check if a given property is a target for cleanup by the superfund.

If a property appears on the list it is a clear indication the area is not yet safe for habitation, and so the broker should not direct potential buyers to it even if other people advertise it for sale due to lack of knowledge. In fact, it would be best for brokers to avoid purchasing any properties that are near properties on the NPL list. Valuable information with regard to contaminated areas can be found at https://www.epa.gov/superfund/npl-site-status-information.

Protection Against Contamination through the RCRA & EPCRA

There were changes to the law in 1984, comprising the Hazardous & Solid Waste Amendments, whose addition to the RCRA was triggered by concerns about the dangers of gasoline plus other different chemicals seen as potentially hazardous. The materials considered under these amendments are mostly those that seep into the land and end up contaminating water sources and supplies. Overall, the law sought to prevent contamination of land and also demanded that contaminated property not be sold unless it is first thoroughly decontaminated.

To further enhance community and individual protection, the Emergency Planning and Community Right-To-Know Act (EPCRA) was passed in 1986. The aim was to offer better protection to real estate property buyers and owners against any hazards from the environment due to contamination of their property. The act assists in preparing communities for emergencies that might emerge of a chemical nature.

In this regard, companies and any parties dealing with hazardous material are expected to report to their respective local authorities and the federal government about how they store, use and dispose of hazardous materials.

The EPCRA requires that communities and anyone wishing to buy property within them be furnished with the correct information pertaining to any existing potential dangers within their environment. Brokers should, therefore, endeavor to research such details and draw potential buyers' attention to them before they enter into binding contracts with sellers. This should not be difficult as the NPLs are found on the EPA's website.

The US government has put in place several measures to ensure compliance by industry, and it has provided avenues to report any contaminated properties or cleanup undertakings. Brokers should ensure the property sellers they work with comply with every aspect of the legislation, so that as they offer property for sale they are not putting prospective buyers at risk. You can find comprehensive information on protection against hazardous material and general environmental protection at the EPCRA's official website, https://www.epa.gov/epcra.

The Superfund Amendments & Reauthorization Act

The Superfund Amendments & Reauthorization Act (SARA) brought further amendments to CERCLA in 1986. The additions to the act changed the program in certain ways, particularly putting more emphasis on establishing permanent solutions to problems of an environmental nature. States were encouraged to take into account the needs of neighboring states as they enhance protection of their own areas against hazards of an environmental nature.

The amendments also required that the EPA revise its Hazard Ranking System (HRS), so that it reflected the real risk human beings were exposed to in each case as far as their health was concerned, and in relation to the contamination within their environment.

SARA is applicable to every real estate property and not just land, and it provides room for stringent oversight, more so when it comes to selling and developing of safe property. More useful information on SARA can be accessed on the EPA webpage at https://www.epa.gov/superfund/superfund-amendments-and-reauthorizaion-act-sara.

Enforcement First Policy

In 1989, the Enforcement First policy was enacted, intended to prioritize the identification of individuals, companies or other entities responsible for contaminating given properties. The policy was also meant to ensure that any party that was culpable was made to take responsibility for cleaning up the place to the point where the level of contamination no longer constituted an environmental hazard.

This policy is still in operation and is used for the protection of property buyers, especially those who discover later on that the property they purchased has been exposed to an environmental hazard. The contamination covered under this policy includes air pollution and contamination of ground water.

Hazardous Air Pollutants

Sometimes hazardous air pollutants (HAPs) originate from power plants that use coal and other crude materials; produce chemical material and explosives; use sulfuric or nitric acid in making fertilizer; manufacture cement or glass and/or refine oil.

As for materials that cause pollution to water, they include oil, often spilled by carriers, water disposed of after use, water swept out during a storm and waste from farm animals.

Environmental Justice Plan

The pollution that has just been discussed is meant to be effectively addressed through the Enforcement First policy, where the party that is responsible for any identified pollution is taken to task and forced to clean up the mess as a matter of priority.

If a firm has caused pollution to land or water and is not willing to clean it up for the protection of residents and the environment, it can be sued under the Environmental Justice Plan. The case brought against such a firm could be either of a civil or criminal nature. Such a suit usually ends up ensuring the guilty party cleans up the mess or foots the bill for another party to clean it up.

A suit brought against an errant party is of a criminal nature if it is believed the contamination was done willingly and deliberately. There have been cases of individuals who are sent to jail for being willing participants in contaminating the environment.

In such cases, the Enforcement First policy aids in enforcing and overseeing a cleanup of chemicals or other toxic waste. The regulations contained within the policy serve to protect property owners and other members of the community against hazards of an environmental nature that result from contaminated sites, which may not necessarily belong to the members of the HOA or the local community.

There are many materials that can be considered pollutants, but this section of the book highlights those considered most hazardous to the environment, and by extension the people living around the contaminated area.

Targets of the Enforcement First Policy

Many of the contaminants that communities are protected against through the Enforcement First policy are linked to mining and subsequent processing, hazardous waste, lead-based paint and asbestos.

Mining & Processing of Minerals

By targeting mining activities and processing of minerals at the national level, the EPA seeks to prevent contamination of communities and their environments by phosphoric acid and other substances used in processing of high-risk minerals.

Hazardous Waste

Hazardous waste has contaminants targeted under the RCRA, which seeks to ensure that the material is handled in a safe manner, and that it is also treated, stored and disposed of appropriately. Such waste often contains chemical substances. The Enforcement First policy ensures concerned facilities are inspected and their records reviewed, and that action is taken to enforce conformity to required standards whenever necessary.

It is important to note that tanks that are constructed underground for storage purposes are also included under facilities requiring monitoring, authority provided in RCRA, Subtitle I.

Lead-based Paints

In the development of residential properties, many times lead-based paints are used, and these could be a health hazard to home occupants. The Residential Lead-based Paint Hazard Reduction Act protects property buyers, those who rent for occupancy, contractors involved in the use of lead-based products and other workers involved from the harmful effects of such products. The properties mainly targeted are those constructed before 1978.

Under the law, anyone selling products using lead-based paint is required to disclose the fact to potential buyers, just as owners of housing units painted with lead-based paints are required to disclose the fact to potential buyers or tenants.

In fact, the people in charge of these developments are legally required to have a pamphlet ready in print to give to anyone expressing an intention to occupy the premises, so as to provide disclosure of the fact that the paint used was lead-based. Also, any person expected to be working around an area with such buildings has a right to receive the pamphlet.

Asbestos

Property buyers are protected against the dangers of asbestos by the Asbestos Hazard Emergency Response Act (AHERA), a law that seeks to ensure that people in schools whose structures have asbestos are protected from harm. Workers working with asbestos are also protected under the Occupational Health & Safety Act (OSHA).

It is important to note that where asbestos is concerned, danger is only imminent when remodeling of buildings is being carried out. In fact, although the material has been banned in some countries, the US has not banned its use.

Chapter 10: Private Controls on Land Use

Although restrictions imposed by government on property use are most often discussed, there are also some restrictions established by owners or property developers. These may be implemented over time, becoming part of a private set of rules. Nevertheless, it is important to note that any regulation created by a developer or property owner cannot be in contravention of any law on land use created by the government.

CC & Rs limit how a specific piece of land can be used, such as a condominium or a subdivision. Restrictions like these can be written in property deeds, or they can be incorporated into by-laws to serve in property subdivision. CC & Rs are meant to maintain the appearance and feel of a given community.

Restrictive Covenants, Deed Restrictions & Latches

Restrictive covenants are meant to provide necessary standards in the development of housing units in a particular subdivision. Such standards include the structure type; size and height of the structures; the use the land is put to; the style of architecture applied; setbacks; methods used in construction and each structure's square footage.

Deed Restrictions

You can read the stipulations that control the use of land in the 'deed restriction,' which refers to either the deed or other such documents that specifies the particular limitations imposed on the use of a particular piece of property. Some deed restrictions have a time limitation, in which case after the lapse of that duration the restrictions no longer exist unless an agreement is reached to extend the time limit.

It is important to note that it is not acceptable for restrictive covenants to be illegal. For example, there cannot be a restrictive covenant banning a particular race from occupying the property. A restrictive covenant exists solely for the sake of promoting property safety and appearance. Failure to adhere to this directive could be considered interference of the free property transfer.

Land-use controls of a private nature, if acceptable in the legal sense, can impose restrictions to an even higher degree than that of public controls. Nevertheless, priority is always given to the covenant which is more limiting or restrictive.

Private controls on land use are normally enforced by owners of adjacent property, and this is because they have a right to take any person who violates their rights to court. These neighbors can thus get a court injunction that prohibits the offending activity in their neighborhood. If the plaintiff wins in court, the owner of the neighboring property will then be obliged to honor the covenant.

How Deed Restrictions Work

It is important for you to establish from the outset whether the property you want to acquire has deed restrictions. The terms 'deed restrictions' and 'deed covenants' refer to the same thing—at least in the HOA's context—and they are found in the property ownership deeds.

These deeds are meant to limit how a property owner can use his/her property, including what he/she can have built on the land. Although there are restrictions that exist by virtue of the regulations of community zoning, other restrictions are imposed by property developers.

This means even if your property is not under the authority of an HOA you can still be limited by any restrictions or rules put in place by a developer. Some of those limitations may have been imposed on property owners who first bought the property decades before you, but you still have to adhere to them.

Sometimes deed covenants are discovered when a potential property buyer or broker is carrying out a title search, and it is crucial to read the deed with great care. It is advisable to always determine whether any deed restrictions exist or not when contemplating developing a home from scratch on a given property or making additions to an existing home. This is because it is possible to have bought property without the previous owner disclosing that a deed restriction exists pertaining to property modifications or such. It's even possible the person you bought the property from had no idea it had deed restrictions.

Difference between Deed Covenants & HOA Rules

Deed restrictions or covenants are not the same as HOA rules. For one, any rule made by the HOA can be altered or dropped at any time as long as all homeowners, or the majority of them, are in agreement. For example, the board that runs the HOA to which you belong could issue a rule that no home should hang Christmas decorations on the outside where they are visible to everyone. However, if the homeowners who belong to the association object to that rule, the board will have no choice but to do away with it.

With a deed restriction, changing such regulations is much harder and takes longer. Often you'll need to go to court to try and have a deed restriction on your property lifted.

Laches

If an owner of property feels there is an infringement of his/her rights by developments occurring in the adjacent property or neighborhood but does not exercise the right to sue in good time, seeking a delayed injunction may not work. In such circumstances, the court terms the legal non-applicability of the restrictive covenant a 'lache.'

A lache can therefore be described as an undue delay or unwarranted failure on the part of the property owner to assert his legal right to seek an injunction against the neighbor. When there is such negligence, courts normally rule to have the plaintiff stopped from seeking interference with the neighbor's operations.

Nature of Deed Restrictions

Although a lot is said about deed restrictions on land and property developments, deed restrictions can be of a different nature. Sometimes a property can have a deed restriction on the color that the property's exterior is required to be, demanding that it be in conformity with other buildings. Other times the deed restriction could put a limit on the number of rental units developed on a parcel of land.

Nowadays, Vacation Rentals By Owner (VRBOs) are popular, as are Air Bed & Breakfasts (Airbnbs). More properties are having restrictions put in place to regulate rent per night or the minimum period a house can be rented for.

In general, HOAs and individual developers today make rules that are thought to be beneficial to most of the people owning property within the same neighborhood.

Main Aspects Covered in Deed Restrictions

Irrespective of who originates the deeds, they cover a number of aspects. One property may be affected by one, two or more of the ones enumerated here, but whatever do's and don'ts are contained in a deed restriction, they must be adhered to.

One restriction could be on the maximum bedrooms a housing unit should have, and this essentially restricts the number of occupants of a home. One major reason such a restriction is put in place is to restrict the volume of waste going to the sewer and the septic tank. This means that as these facilities are constructed, the developer makes their sizes correspond to the number of occupants anticipated in each property.

Another aspect of property ownership affected by deed restrictions is the height of the structures and their width, and how the structures are situated in relation to avoiding obstruction of views. Vehicle ownership may also be a subject of deed restrictions, so that there is a maximum number of vehicles property residents are permitted to have within the driveway or in the front area of a house.

Sometimes such a restriction may not just be about other property owners' convenience but also about neatness. HOAs could put in place such restrictions so that the area does not look like a junkyard where residents abandon vehicles they hardly use after they have bought new ones. They may even restrict the vehicles in terms of type such as boats, motorcycles or recreational vehicles (RVs).

Another subject of restriction could be the kind of fencing homeowners build around their units. There may be a restriction, for example, prohibiting construction of fences that are extremely high or fences made of chain-links.

There are sometimes restrictions on how many trees a property owner can eliminate. Such restrictions are sometimes enacted out of respect for the original inhabitants of the area, especially when it is a community that still has an attachment to that land.

There are also deed restrictions that focus on the architectural styles, construction and renovation materials used, the colors used on the premises and other such aspects of aesthetics. Sometimes there are deeds that restrict the construction of additional garages and swimming pools, or sheds or workshops that are detached from the main housing unit.

It is not surprising to find deed restrictions that ban running any business from within the residential properties. Such restrictions serve to keep strangers from being in very close proximity to private homes, entering and leaving a private property at will.

Some restrictions also prohibit animals within the property, such as livestock, though pets could be permitted. Pets might be limited to specific breeds.

Enforceability of a Deed

There was a time, specifically the era before WWII, when homeowners wrote restrictions that put a caveat on the religion and/or race of property occupants. However, such restrictions are now considered discriminatory and cannot be enforced. In fact, since the 1948 ruling by the Supreme Court on covenants, any attempt to enforce such deed restrictions can lead to a legal suit. Any broker trying to do due diligence on a property for prospective purchase may not even need to bother researching covenants that are not enforceable today.

All the same, it is advisable to establish first if there are deed covenants pertaining to any property you want to buy, along with whether there is still a regulatory body in existence charged with enforcing whatever covenant your research turns up.

How Deed Restrictions Can Be Altered

Making changes to existing deed covenants may not be easy, but it is not always impossible. You need to begin by visiting the local county courthouse to obtain a copy of the existing covenant. The importance of this, besides confirming that there is indeed a covenant that applies to the property, is to find out if there is a provision under which the deed can be modified.

Sometimes property owners are known to include a provision under which the deed restriction can be changed or overlooked, and there are also instances where they assign the covenant an expiration date.

Under special circumstances, you may have leeway to ignore part or all of the deed restriction, but only after seeking and being granted permission by a credible regulatory body or group such as the HOA. Depending on the kind of covenant you are seeking to break, permission from your neighboring HOA may be sufficient.

It may also be helpful to look into the regulations that operate in the state where the property is, because there are some jurisdictions that permit deed restriction modifications as long as you follow specific procedures.

In case you really want to acquire or retain a piece of property but there is a deed covenant you find bothersome, you can resort to the courts and hope your lawyer can be persuasive enough to convince the judge to eliminate the covenant. Often you are likely to win the case if the covenant put on the property is vague or impractical, or if many of the homeowners in the neighborhood have already disregarded it. If the covenant is illegal, you can be certain the judge will invalidate it.

Unalterable Deed Covenants

As a broker you need to make sure you do your research properly so that you are aware of any deed covenants that exist. If any exist, you need to find out their nature and the provisions attached to them so that you can tell, for example, if they have an expiration date or contain provisions that allow them to be altered. Property owners do not want to take up the burden of seeking permission to break covenants whether through their HOAs, the local county or the courts.

Once you know the specific deed restrictions imposed upon individual properties, you will be in a good position to know the buyers you can target who are unlikely to be affected by the relevant covenants. As a broker, if a potential buyer is discouraged from buying a piece of property because of an existing covenant, you can always look for a different property that suits him/her. This is of great importance because there are some deed restrictions that are not tenable, such as a condition which does not permit boats on a property but the potential buyer is a fisherman.

Chapter 11: Transfer of Real Estate Title

When you hold a title to your land or any other real estate property in your name, then you have proof you own the property. In fact, it is the only time you may have proper authority to transfer that title to someone else, otherwise that title may be considered either defective or outright fraudulent.

Title Insurance

There are cases where the buyer may pay for a property and be given the title, only to realize that the title is defective. It is a very costly experience to lose both the money and the property, or at the minimum legal fees and plenty of time, and that is what title insurance seeks to protect a buyer against.

Lender's & Owner's Title Insurance

As such, title insurance serves to indemnify property buyers from financial losses that they may incur from receiving defective titles to properties they have legally acquired. Some types of title insurance include lender's title insurance and the owner's title insurance. The former protects the lender or financier, and it is the person borrowing the money to finance the property who pays for it. The latter is meant for the protection of the property buyer's stake in the property, and often it is the seller who is responsible for paying for it. These two types of title insurance are issued separately.

Besides the fact that title insurance indemnifies property owners from losses of a financial nature resulting from a defective property title, most prevalent cases pertaining to financial losses linked to property titles involve back taxes. The property seller may have had accumulated unpaid taxes, mortgage loans, lines of credit against the home equity or even different wills that are in conflict with one another.

While a buyer may be working with a reputable broker while acquiring property, it is always a good idea to ensure coverage from any unforeseen hiccups in the title. Consider the cost of insurance as part of the property purchase cost, because the fee for insuring the property title is a one-off expense.

Almost every lender requires that the person being financed, or the borrower, pay for the lender's title insurance for the protection of the lending individual or institution. Among the other reasons cited for buying this type of insurance is the eventuality that the property seller is legally unable to transfer the right of property ownership to the buyer. It is crucial to keep in mind that only the lender is indemnified under the lender's insurance policy. Issuing a title insurance policy is an indication that the title search has been completed, and this serves as great assurance to the party buying the property.

When it comes to the risk new estate property owners are exposed to, it is worth noting that the title search carried out is sometimes short, especially with regard to transactions involving residential property, with some searches extending only back to one previous owner or deed. This can leave a new owner exposed to big risks that date back further but which are not turned up in such a cursory search.

This is the reason owner's title insurance is so important. It protects the property owner from losses that may crop up due to shoddy deed searches or inadvertent misses. As a property buyer, you need to be proactive in pursuing an owner's title insurance policy so that you are protected against any title defects.

Remember that although buying this policy is optional, if a defect emerges later you, as the buyer, will bear the brunt.

What to Expect of Title Insurance

For any transaction in real estate to be valid, it must involve a clean title; one that is not tied to any liabilities. Companies responsible for issuing titles are expected to carry out thorough searches on all titles so as to establish if any of them has a claim or lien against it prior to issuing it to an unsuspecting client.

Title Search

The term 'title search' is used in reference to the examination carried out on public records with the aim of establishing and confirming who the legal owner of a given property is. Besides legal ownership, a title search is also used to establish if there is any claim that has been placed on the particular property.

When erroneous surveys have been done and there are unresolved violations of the building code, it leads to the property title being considered 'dirty' or 'not clean.'

Marketable Title versus Insurable Title

A property title is said to be 'marketable' if the property ownership chain is both clear and lacking in defects. Essentially, therefore, a real estate property is said to be marketable if the buyer does not need to worry about making any amends later. It also means the seller can be confident there is no likelihood of issues of pending liabilities being raised later.

As for the term 'insurable title,' it is used to mean that the property to which the title belongs has some defects already known, which developed along the title chain. Still, the only way the insurable title will be hassle-free to the buyer and seller is if there is a title insurance firm willing to insure it against its preexisting defects.

Once the insurable title has been covered through an insurance policy, there is minimal chance of the property value dropping, which is what happens when a property has a defective title that is not insured. Thus, title ensures protects the value of the property, and ensures that property ownership is not affected even after the sale.

Example of Defect on a Title

A defect on a property title can be exemplified by a housing unit that has a mortgage that has not been paid since 1984. Considering that several decades have passed since the mortgage was first taken out, and now the property has significantly aged, chances are that the lender has written off the debt and is not expecting any further payments from anyone. For that reason, a title insurance firm could easily be prepared to insure that title against any risk, because the risk is low.

If the property in question does not have a title insurance policy that is current and valid but there is a defect somewhere along the title chain, then it is incumbent upon the property seller to ensure the particular defect is repaired before the title can be deemed marketable.

On the other hand, if the property in question has a title insurance policy that is current, the insurance firm can opt to extend the insurance to cover the defect on the title, so that it is committed to indemnifying the concerned parties from any problem that may arise at a future date owing to the defect. This latter process is sometimes less costly in terms of money and time compared to the process of trying to repair a title defect.

Unconventional Protection through Title Insurance

When contemplating buying a title insurance policy, the goal is to protect the owner of the real estate property or the financier against potential losses or damages that may occur out of liens or encumbrances not known beforehand.

The protection also covers losses that may arise from unforeseen defects in the title. Sometimes the defect is on the real ownership of the property and this has the potential for massive losses. Title insurance is different from conventional insurance in that while the latter caters for future eventualities, the former caters for dangers resulting from past happenings.

Title Insurance Basic Coverage

If as a property owner you have bought a basic title insurance policy, there are some hazards you should expect to be covered. One of them is discovering that someone else actually owns the property. Another one is a title document bearing signatures that are incorrect, whether inadvertently or through forgery, and any real fraud affecting the title document.

Another risk title insurance covers is the existence of flaws in the property ownership records which are not clear or outright defective. If the property has a restrictive covenant, meaning the property owner cannot enjoy the ownership of the property to the extent assumed when acquiring it, the title insurance covers the financial consequences of that as well.

Sometimes the restrictive covenant might be in the form of an unrecorded easement. Another hazard covered by title insurance involves encumbrances or other judgments that may exist against the property in question, good examples being pending lawsuits or liens. A mechanic's lien is another risk that interested parties often want covered by title insurance. This is the risk related to work done on the property but not yet compensated for, whether supplies, labor or both. A mechanic's lien is applicable to both personal property and real estate property.

The Real Estate Settlement Procedures Act (RESPA) prohibits property sellers from insisting on a policy being purchased from specific insurance providers or agencies. This is to avoid having the buyers harassed by unscrupulous brokers or property owners.

Title Warranty

There are instances when parties opt to do away with title insurance, and in its place rely on what is referred to as a 'warranty of title.' This title guarantees the property buyer that the property the seller is offering for sale belongs solely to him/her, and confirms that he/she owns the right of transfer of the property ownership.

When a party or parties to a real estate transaction want to purchase a title insurance policy, the starting point is the escrow agent, otherwise termed the 'closing agent.' This begins the process of acquiring title insurance after the agreement related to the purchase of the property has been completed.

In the United States, there are five major underwriters of title insurance: Fidelity National Financial, Stewart Title Guaranty Co., Old Republic National Title Insurance Co., First American Corp. and different independent companies at the regional level.

If the title insurance you are interested in buying is the owner's, then you should budget for one percent of the real estate property's buying price. Of course there are sometimes variations among states.

As a practical example, if you are buying land for half a million dollars in California, the owner's title insurance policy should cost you between $1,200-$2,000. One percent of the purchase price is $5,000, so you would be within the budget.

How Real Estate Property is Taxed

The United States has a tax code that is relatively complex, and when it comes to real estate that complexity is evident. When you want to sell real estate property you may be required to pay taxes, although how much you pay could be dependent on the kind of property you are selling, the duration it has been in your possession and other such factors.

Even when you have property to rent as an investor, you are expected to pay taxes. In this portion of the book you will learn what is required of an owner of real estate as far as taxation is concerned. This information is crucial before you can make a decision about the kind of property to buy either for personal use or for further investment.

The Capital Gains Tax

The term 'capital gains tax' is used in reference to the tax levied on capital gains. As for capital gains, they are the profits that an asset seller realizes after disposing of his/her capital asset be it land, a building or any other durable asset fit to be termed a capital asset. Sometimes the capital gains tax is set at a rate that is lower than taxes on other income.

Capital gains are sometimes taxed differently. For example, if you have held the property you want to sell for a short period, your tax rate will likely be higher than if you held it for a long period. You need to keep in mind that you can also sell your property at a loss depending on the circumstances, and you should factor this loss into your records for tax purposes as well.

When it comes to categorizing the period you have owned the property you want to sell, it is considered 'long-term' if you have had the property longer than a year and 'short-term' if you have had the property for a period shorter than one year. As for the taxation rate, you are at an advantage if you have had the property for the long-term, because then the rate on the capital gains can be as low as 20 percent. If you have had the property for the short-term the rate can be as high as 37 percent.

Tax Rate on Short-term Capital Gains

The main reason the tax-rate on short-term capital gains is higher than on long-term capital gains is that the former gains are treated like any other profit; like trading profit, for example. Just to have a better idea of how the different categories of capital gains are treated, consider: if your current tax bracket, or the level of your marginal tax rate has reached 22 percent, when you factor in your capital gains it will be taxed at that same rate of 22 percent if you have had the property for the short-term.

However, when it comes to real estate property you've held for a long term, any profit you get is categorized as long-term gain and will be treated as such. It is important for brokers and salespersons to understand the differences in the two types of capital gains and the differences in their taxation, so that they can advise their clients appropriately.

Not surprisingly, tax brackets are adjusted from time to time to factor in changes in the economic sector including inflation, but the variations are normally not drastic at any one time. As such the tax schedule for capital gains for 2019 can be relied upon to give a good idea of how long-term capital gains are taxed.

Long-term Capital Gains Tax under Each Tax Category

The US categorizes taxpayers into four groups: single filers, married couples reporting jointly, household heads and married couple reporting separately. Below a certain level of capital gains, no property seller is taxed, but the maximum varies according to individual categories.

The analysis provided next comprises income tax brackets that include capital gains for tax purposes, and not capital gains exclusively. In short, they are brackets of taxable income although our subject of discussion is capital gains.

Capital gains from single filers are subject to zero percent taxation up to $39,375, just like each of the spouses filing tax returns as individuals. The other two categories have a better benefit, because the zero percent rate of taxation for capital gains for the household head is as high as $52,750 while the married couple filing tax returns jointly has a higher threshold of $78,750.

The tax rate for the next capital gains bracket is 15 percent, and for the single filer it covers capital gains from $39,376 to $434,550. For the married couple filing tax returns separately, the bracket for 15 percent is from $39,376 to $244,425. For the head of the household, this 15 percent rate bracket is from $0 to $461,700, and for the married couple reporting taxes jointly the bracket runs from $78,751 to $488,850.

The next and last capital gains tax rate at the present time is 20 percent. For any amount of capital gain above $434,550 reported by singles, the tax rate is 20 percent, and for married couples that file tax returns separately that rate applies to all amounts above $244,425. This 20 percent tax rate for the head of the household applies to all amounts of capital gain above $461,700, while it applies to all amounts greater than $488,850 when it comes to a married couple that files tax returns jointly.

After the taxation under the given schedules is complete, individuals whose net income reaches another specified level are subjected to an extra 3.8 percent. This percentage is on an individual's net amount of investment income, and it does not matter if the capital gains posted were long or short-term; the rate remains 3.8 percent.

Chapter 12: Valuation & Real Estate Market Analysis

In all cases of buying and selling, it is crucial to be able to ascertain, or at least estimate, the value of the item you want to buy. When it comes to real estate properties, it's important that not only is the subject of sale valued, but a credible market analysis must be carried out in order to accurately assess the market situation and trends.

Appraisals

The property-buying process requires appraisals for the sake of establishing the market value of the particular property you are interested in. Only after finding out the value of the home or other such property you want to sell can you reasonably set its price. The assumption is that you will be selling your property in an open, competitive market.

Appraisals are helpful to lenders or financiers as they assess whether or not to support a particular property buyer. This is because often the property being bought serves as security for the mortgage. The results of an appraisal are used to determine whether the lender can recoup the amount the borrower needs if the property is ever sold as a result of a person's failure to repay the loan.

Differences between Appraisal & CMA

A property appraisal should not be confused with a Competitive Market Analysis (CMA), as a CMA is simply a report of sales as reflected in an MLS. A CMA analysis is used by agents in real estate to help establish a realistic asking or offering price for their property during a particular period.

Also, unlike CMAs, appraisals have many more details and are put together by a licensed appraiser. In deciding whether or not to finance the purchase of a given property, the prospective financier is only interested in the appraisal and not at all in a CMA.

Differences between Appraisal & Home Inspection

A property appraisal, including a home appraisal, is different from a property or home inspection. In inspecting a home, what is assessed are home appliances, outlets, plumbing, the heating system, cooling system and other such items to see if they are in good working condition.

As is evident, such information would not be of much interest to a financier but it would be important to a prospective home buyer or someone who intends to move in as a resident. In contrast, a home appraiser is interested in knowing the value of the entire home as a unit in the prevailing market environment.

Characteristics of Appraisals

Appraisals are conducted by licensed appraisers. To be licensed as a professional appraiser, you need to complete coursework as determined by the state in which you intend to practice, and also undergo a preset number of internship hours.

As an appraiser, you are considered a third party who is required to exercise objectivity in your appraisal work. In this regard, you are expected to have no personal or additional connection with any of the parties interested in the sales transaction.

The property being appraised is referred to as the 'subject property.' As for footing the appraisal bill, the potential property buyer sometimes pays this during the application of the financing loan, but in other cases the fee is included in the statement of settlement as the deal is being closed.

Steps Taken in Appraisals

When appraising a property, your first step should be inspecting the property to establish its realistic value. This step involves observing the physical state of that property with a view to establishing the geographical location, how many bedrooms and bathrooms the property has and other such aspects. The purpose of this assessment is to establish whether or not the property is in the state the prospective buyer imagines.

It is important to confirm that the property has the square footage reflected on the listing and that the layout is as advertised. At this juncture you need to design a sketch of the property floor plan for the prospective buyer to see. You also need to be on the lookout for any defects or property features that are likely to impact the property value.

3 Approaches to Property Valuation

There are three approaches a qualified appraiser uses after inspection to determine the property value:

1. the sales comparison approach
2. the cost approach
3. the income approach.

The income approach is particularly helpful when the property is planned for use for rental purposes.

The Sales Comparison Approach

Appraisers are expected to be already well versed with the community that they work within, in a manner that helps them understand the unique features in that market and the value one can reasonably attach to them.

An appraiser is expected to be aware of the sales that have taken place in the area within the recent past, and he/she should identify those properties that can be considered comparable to the one under appraisal. Using this method, appraisers can assign value in terms of dollars to every important feature of the property, and then value can be added or subtracted from the price at which the comparable property was sold, to arrive at the best price for the property being appraised.

The features or items that appraisers focus on include kitchens, bathrooms, types of flooring, patios or porches, and even how efficient various items are with regard to conserving energy. For example, if the property serving as the 'comparable' contains a garage and the one being appraised does not, the appraiser will subtract the garage value from the price at which the comparable was sold.

On the other hand, if the property being appraised contains an additional bathroom that is not in the comparable, the appraiser has good reason to add the value of that extra bathroom to the property price. When it comes to selling a home, this approach is popular.

The Cost Approach

In this approach, the appraiser tries to establish how much it would cost to develop the same kind of property, including the labor involved and all other resources required. Once the total amount is obtained for what would be needed to create an exact replacement of the property, that figure becomes the upper limit for the price.

Rarely is this method of property appraisal used, and when it is used it's on homes that are entirely new—new residential developments.

The Income Approach

In the income approach, the appraiser seeks to establish the level of income earned by the property within the real estate market, and with that in mind it becomes possible to compare that property with other real estate properties with similar income-generating capacity.

It is important to note that the value arrived at after property appraisal is a good indication of what a reasonable price, or highest price, should be when the transaction is completed on an open market, but it's not necessarily the figure that ends up being used as property price.

The income approach is sometimes referred to as the Income Capitalization Approach, with its main characteristic being a comparison between rate of return and property net income.

The reasons for variations between appraisal value and actual value are varied, one of them being how fast the property owner wants to vacate the particular property. Other influencing factors include property availability in the market that could cause a hike or drop in prices.

Still, the property value arrived at after the appraisal is important mainly to lenders, because they often use it to determine the amount of money they can safely lend property buyers. Lenders want to be certain that the property whose purchase they are financing can be sold on the open market for an amount sufficient to cover the money loaned to the property owner.

Role of Licensed Appraisers

As with assessors, property appraisers' role is to estimate property value whether it be buildings or land, before the property can be developed, sold, mortgaged, taxed or insured.

Typical responsibilities of a licensed appraiser include verifying the legal description of a property in the real estate public records. It is also an appraiser's duty to inspect real estate property, be it an old establishment or a newly developed property, with a view to identifying its unique features.

It is also the role of the licensed appraiser to take photographs of the property under consideration, both from its interior and exterior. Licensed appraisers are responsible for using comparables to help establish the value of the property under question. It is their role to prepare written reports regarding the value of the properties. They are also charged with preparing and maintaining up-to-date data pertaining to every property under consideration.

Both appraisers and assessors operate in locations that they are conversant with because that enables them to factor into the appraisal any concerns of an environmental nature, or other concerns that have the potential to impact the value of the respective properties.

Specialties of Appraisers

Appraisers in real estate can specialize in either of two fields—commercial or residential.

Commercial appraisers target property for commercial use, like buildings used to host offices, stores, restaurants and such.

Residential appraisers target properties which people live in, good examples being condominiums, single-family housing units and the like. This category of property appraisers concentrates on properties with the capacity to hold a minimum of one family and a maximum of four.

Part of the appraisal process is noting characteristics within the surroundings, such as proximity to a noisy highway or airport. Appraisers assess the foundation of a building and its roof, as well as apparent renovations which have been done on the property.

Appraisers photograph property exteriors to document the condition of a particular property. Beyond this, an appraiser may also choose to take photographs of particular rooms or features of the property.

When valuing a particular property, appraisers take into account recent comparable home sales, records of property lease, location of the property and the view from it, any appraisals previously done and the property's potential to generate income.

Appraisers record their own research observations and findings, as well as the specific methods they have applied in the calculation of property value.

Differences between Assessors and Appraisers

Ordinarily assessors work on behalf of their respective local authorities, where their aim is to value property so as to find a basis to assess tax.

Assessors are different from appraisers in their manner of operation because while an appraiser focuses on a single property at any one time, an assessor can assess a cluster of residential properties at one go. In a case where several homes are assessed simultaneously, the technique used is one of mass appraisal as well as other systems of mass appraisal that are facilitated by the use of computers.

An appraiser is required to state the reasons why the property under appraisal is valued at a certain amount, and because of that an appraisal report is expected to be detailed. The appraiser must look over the particular property and gather specific information to use in the valuation of the property, like the architectural features the property has, structural condition and any pertinent factors of an environmental nature.

How to Get the Property Value Right

Getting the property value right is not only good for determining the most reasonable price to buy or sell the property but is also necessary for determining the amount of insurance required and the level of property taxes. Next you will learn how to determine the best value for a real estate property, particularly for sales purposes.

From a technical perspective, the definition of property value is what the property is worth at present in terms of the benefits foreseen in the future; those that the property owner is likely to enjoy.

Although all goods are acquired for what they are worth, real property is different from consumer goods in that its value is enjoyed over a lengthy period while that of consumer goods is used up fast.

What this means is that while estimating the value of real estate property you need to consider both economic and social trends, while also taking into account government regulation. Something else that needs to be factored in is any change of an environmental nature that is likely to have an impact on property value through the major value-influencing factors of demand, utility, scarcity and transferability.

Demand

Demand is the desire to own property while being financially able to cater for that desire.

Utility

Utility relates to the capacity to fulfill the needs of the future property owner.

Scarcity

Scarcity pertains to the supply of properties that are in competition, where that supply is finite.

Transferability

Transferability is the degree of ease with which the property owner can transfer the property to someone else or another party.

Comparison of Cost to Price

It is important to understand that property cost does not automatically equal property price. The term 'cost' is used in reference to the amount spent to cover property expenses, which includes the actual amount spent to purchase materials or to pay for labor.

As for the term 'price,' it's used in reference to the actual amount paid in order to acquire ownership of the property.

It's important to note that although the value of a real estate property can be affected by the cost of the property or its price, the two are not the sole determinants of the property's value. For example, it's possible to have a house whose price is $200,000 but whose value is lower than that figure. It's also possible for the value of that house to be higher than the property price.

For example, after finding some fault with the house the new house owner could realize the value of the house is not as high as originally estimated. A weak or broken foundation is an example of a fault that could lead to a drop in the value of the house below its property price.

Real Property Market Value

To establish the market value of a given real estate property, an appraisal is carried out by an expert. The market value is the price the property is most likely to attract in a market that is not only open but competitive. The result of an appraisal is an estimate or the appraiser's opinion as to what the property value is at a particular date.

Institutions interested in reports on appraised properties include individuals and private businesses, government bodies, mortgage companies and investors of all kinds. They use the reports to help them make decisions pertaining to real property transactions.

Comparison of Market Value to Price

The market price of a real estate property is the price at which it is sold. It's worth noting that this price is not necessarily equal to the property market value. A good example is a situation where the property owner has been threatened with foreclosure and therefore wants to sell the property at the best price possible.

In such a case, the property owner may accept a price below the market value of the property just to avoid losing the property and any control over its sale. There are other such instances like when a property owner decides to sell a property privately, with the liberty to sell it below market value for personal reasons.

Factors Considered in Estimating Property Value

Brokers in real estate and their salespersons help to sell homes on behalf of the homeowners, and to acquire homes on behalf of various clients. There is, certainly, a way of circumventing the services of brokers or salespersons and for homeowners and home buyers to transact directly, but there is an advantage to engaging the services of professionals.

For one, the transactions can be much smoother with professional help, because these agents are conversant with the real estate market. They advise their clients with properties to sell on how best to present their properties on the market, and suggest the best prices they can get for those properties.

For clients wanting to buy property, brokers and salespersons can advise the best prices at which certain properties can be acquired. To do this, they use the facts they have on prevailing range of market prices, opportunities for mortgage facilities and other different factors affecting the market at any one time. They also help their clients by presenting them with a list or schedule of properties available in the market, and when it is time to view any property they accompany the potential buyer to the site. They also help to negotiate the best price for the potential buyers they are representing.

Salespersons are expected to be well versed with the respective communities within which the properties are situated, so that they can factor into the property value accessibility to schools, health care and entertainment facilities and other such social amenities.

Comparative Market Analysis

A comparative market analysis can be defined as a comparison tool for prices at which properties within the same environment were recently purchased or sold. Salespersons and brokers are known to carry out comparative market analyses on behalf of clients so that they can assist them to establish the best price at which to have their property listed as home sellers, or on which to make an offer when they are aspiring home buyers.

While assisting their clients, real estate agents also take into account the fact that individual properties may have a particular uniqueness, and so they make allowances for that when settling on a suitable price. If a property has shortcomings, they may advise that the price be adjusted downwards, and if it has an edge over other recent properties sold, they could also recommend the price be raised.

Suffice it to say, salespersons and brokers do comparative market analyses as alternatives, albeit lower in sophistication, to professional property appraisals.

If there is a need to do a comparative market analysis but there are no similar properties in the neighborhood that have been sold recently, then the real estate agent may analyze the prices of properties that sellers have listed for sale. However, it's always good to keep in mind that the prices at which properties are listed reflect the wishes of their respective owners and not necessarily the prices at which the properties will finally be sold or what they are worth.

A comparative market analysis is worthwhile although it does not count as a formal property appraisal, because the agents base their assessment on many of the same factors that professional appraisers do before determining what a given property is worth. Still, as a real estate salesperson or a broker, if you are handling a property that is unique or distinctive, which means it is not easy to find a property like it recently sold, you should consider engaging the services of a professional appraiser to determine the value of that property.

Comparative Market Analysis Illustrated

Tom and Mary had a four-bedroom, three-bathroom house, and it sat on an area 2,100 sq ft in size. The entire property on which the single-family residence sat was a quarter of an acre in size, and it had been listed at a price of $300,000.

As the couple's broker was carrying out a comparative market analysis, he identified three properties within the same subdivision which happened to be just like the home Tom and Mary wanted to sell, and these other properties had only been sold over a couple of months before.

One of the three properties was quite similar to the couple's property, with the only difference being that this one was situated along a busy road. That property was sold for $275,000.

83

Another of the three similar properties had four bedrooms, three bathrooms and sat on one quarter of an acre, but the home itself was 2,400 sq ft because it had a porch. That property sold for $315,000.

The third property also had four bedrooms, sat on a quarter of an acre and the housing unit was 2,100 sq ft. The difference between this property and Tom and Mary's was that this one had only two bathrooms and both of them were outdated. The property was sold at $265,000.

Steps to Take in the Comparative Market Analysis

(a) Begin by checking the neighborhood for quality. There are tools available online, such as Google Street View, although you may also need to do research elsewhere. Questions you should ask include:

- Are the blocks attractive?

- Does the area have schools, a hospital, shopping malls and recreational facilities?

- Is it close to a garbage dump, a noisy highway or facilities that are known for creating environmental pollution?

- Are there are a lot of rules and regulations in the area?

(b) Look at the property listings

- Check out the property photographs and go through their descriptions and try to assess how old each property is.

- Assess the property's condition and establish if it has had any upgrades in the recent past.

- Find out if there have been any issues that arose and affected the marketing of the property

(c) Establish estimates for the value of the property

If you get a good value estimate of a property recently sold, you can easily determine a close estimate of the property you have listed for your client. Such an estimate is helpful as a beginning point when it's time to calculate the cost of the property per square foot. However, you should make allowances for discrepancies in assessing other market factors that could have affected the price of the properties.

(d) Carry out a CMA on a preliminary basis

It is important to develop a general idea of what the value of the home should be by assessing recently sold properties, assessing listings that have expired with no successful sale, currently active listings and listings about to be put on the market—all within the same area and with comparable features.

Examples of Comparable Real Properties

There are some real estate properties that are comparable, and you need to recognize them so that you can incorporate them in the CMA. They include:

- Homes sold in the most recent six months

- Homes whose listings have expired within the last six months

- Homes whose listings are still pending or which have been listed for the last six months

Listings that have been sold provide information as to what properties similar to what you want have been recently successfully sold, and this information serves as an agent's primary method of assessing the market value of the property for the sake of CMA.

As for listings that have already expired, they provide information regarding pricing the market is not prepared to accept. In the meantime, listings whose sale is pending provide a pretty good image of the properties owners are currently looking to sell. Listings that are still active are a great indicator on the state of competition in the market with regards to similar properties.

- Carry out an evaluation of homes which have the same number of bedrooms and bathrooms as the property to be sold. This is because how many of these rooms a home has very often influences prospective buyers' decisions.

For example, a home with two bedrooms is less preferable to buyers than one with three bedrooms or more. Similarly, homes that have a single bathroom or which are lacking a master bathroom usually have a lower resale value than properties with more bathrooms.

- Carry out an evaluation of homes whose proximity to your property is 300 sq ft. If your home is 2,000 sq ft in area, check out homes whose floor area ranges from 1,700 sq ft to 2,300 sq ft.

- Generally speaking, the higher the number of bedrooms a home has, the higher the price it attracts. Nevertheless, the size of floor area or square footage also influences potential buyers' decisions.

- Carry out an evaluation of homes within one neighborhood. Because it can be difficult to determine the neighborhood in question, check online for details first. In particular when the home is within a gated community, it's easier to determine the neighborhood whose homes you need to assess.

- Carry out an evaluation of homes within similar school zones. Home-buyers consider school districts impOrtant, especially in big cities that have a large number of schools per district.

You may find that home properties on a particular side of the street are within a great school zone but those on the opposite side are in a lower-quality school district. How good the schools in close proximity are can have a significant impact on the price of the property you want to sell.

- Carry out an evaluation of homes whose lot size is similar. Understandably, a home property that sits on 10 acres of land is bound to have a higher value than one that sits on a single acre.

- Carry out an evaluation of homes of similar age. As expected, homes that are entirely new are often appraised at a higher value than those that are older, but there are also some homes that are older that can have a higher value because of some unique reasons such as the home being historic.

Older homes like these can have a premium well above new developments, sometimes owing to their distinct and rare design that reflects the homes of the time when they were built.

- Carry out an evaluation of home properties with similar features. An example is a home within a gated community with a clubhouse. Another example is a home that has a swimming pool or which has an oceanfront view. When evaluating the value of such a home, look for listed homes with the same unique features for comparison.

(e) Calculate an average price from listings that are comparable

Consider the sales prices of the homes you have identified as being comparable to the property you are dealing with, and then divide their respective prices with their respective areas in terms of square feet, so that you can establish the price of each property per square foot.

After establishing the price per square foot for each of the properties, find the average. The price per square foot you get will serve as the going price per square foot for similar properties in the area. As such, you can now multiply that average with the number of square feet comprising the property you want to sell, and you will get a good idea of what a reasonable market price would be for the property.

(f) Personally carry out an assessment of the home

Use the research you have done to arrive at a ballpark figure of what the property should be worth, so that you are able to advise its owner on its market value. Assessing the property in person is beneficial because you get to see firsthand the true condition of the building and can identify any additions to the property and/or upgrades that other similar properties may not have.

Also take note as to whether the property has any landscaping or unique amenities, and other factors that can raise its value or affect the value adversely. Finally, to create a CMA that is comprehensive and helpful, use this information alongside the data you have already gathered during your preliminary analysis on the listed properties.

Chapter 13: Property Financing & Definitions

Property buyers seek the cheapest means to finance their property, this often being the reason they choose one lender against others available in the real estate market. How cheap or expensive the financing is often depends not only on the rate of interest levied on the mortgage, but also other factors such as the length of the repayment period. One way home buyers try to reduce the cost of property financing is by buying mortgage points.

Mortgage Points

Mortgage points are also referred to as 'discount points,' and they represent fees paid straight to the lending institution during closing. This payment is made so that the borrower can have the interest rate on a mortgage reduced. For this reason, paying for mortgage points is referred to as 'buying down the rate.' Essentially, therefore, when you have mortgage points you should expect the amount you pay in mortgage installments to be lower than they would be otherwise.

The cost of one mortgage point is one percent of the expected mortgage payment or amount. For example, if your mortgage is $200,000 then one mortgage point will cost $2,000. So what you end up doing is paying that portion up front in anticipation of a reduction in your mortgage interest rate for the period the loan lasts.

This means that if your mortgage loan is for many years, you would benefit more if you had a higher number of mortgage points. The next section discusses how mortgage points can be beneficial.

Important Aspects of Mortgage Points

The rate of interest you receive after you buy mortgage points is not fixed, meaning it may vary from one lender to another. It may also depend on the state of the real estate market at the time of the transaction.

You may be able to get a tax break for buying mortgage points, but you need to consult a professional in tax matters to ascertain the extent to whether this is possible or not.

If you have an Adjustable Rate Mortgage (ARM), your mortgage points only cover the rate of interest on the loan for the beginning period when that rate of interest is fixed. However, customers of Bank of America benefit from mortgage points even when mortgage rate interest changes.

It's worth checking to see which is more beneficial for you: making a big down payment on the mortgage or buying mortgage points.

How to Determine if You Need Points

If you want to find out if it is worth committing to buying mortgage points, find out first if the money you have is sufficient to cater for your mortgage down payment in addition to buying mortgage points that need to be bought upfront. Also find out if, in addition, you have sufficient funds to cover your closing costs and still have some reserves. Finally, it's important for you to consider how long you plan on keeping the home.

It makes sense to buy mortgage points if the type of mortgage you want has a fixed interest rate and you intend to own the home even after you have reached the break-even point. In short, you only need to opt for mortgage points when your calculations show it makes financial sense over time.

Loan to Value Ratio

The Loan to Value ratio (LTV) is used in assessing the risk a lender bears in lending a particular amount of money. This is the ratio that potential lenders, be they mortgage financing institutions or other bodies, calculate before they approve any mortgage. Ordinarily, the greater the ratio of LTV, the higher the risk of lending, and the smaller the ratio, the lower the risk of lending.

Understandably, the higher the lending risk is found to be, the higher the cost of borrowing is and vice-versa. When the LTV, and hence the borrowing risk, is high, it's likely a borrower will be required to buy mortgage insurance, in order to mitigate the risk of lending the loan.

How to Calculate the Ratio of LTV

Anyone can calculate their home's LTV easily as long as they know the formula. You begin by confirming what the mortgage amount is in total, and then you divide that figure with the actual property price.

Suppose the home's price is $300,000 while the entire mortgage loan is $270,000. The LTV ratio in this case is $270,000:$300,000, which can be simplified to 90:100 or 90 percent. Conventional lenders usually have better terms for borrowers whose LTV does not exceed 80 percent.

Expressed differently, the LTV is simply the result of dividing the total amount of money borrowed by the value obtained after the home or property has been appraised, when it is put in percentage form.

In another example, a home's value after appraisal is found to be $200,000. The buyer makes a down payment of $20,000, which means he is left to borrow $180,000. The resulting ratio of LTV is therefore $180,000:$200,000, which is essentially 90 percent.

Important Points to Note on LTV

• The LTV is helpful in determining how big or small the required down payment is, even as the lender uses it to determine if it is worthwhile giving the required loan to the borrower.

• Most mortgage lenders offer the lowest rates of interest to applicants of home equity whose LTV is either equal to 80 percent or lower.

• There are some mortgage programs that cater for borrowers in the low-income group, which extend loans even to borrowers whose LTV is as high as 97 percent. When the LTV is 97 percent, it basically means the borrower is only required to produce a down payment of three percent of the purchase price. Examples of such programs include Fannie Mae's Home Ready and Freddie Mac's Home Possible.

Nevertheless, in this lending arrangement the home buyers are required to buy mortgage insurance until their LTV ratio drops to 80 percent.

LTV vis-à-vis Underwriting

The LTV is very important with regard to underwriting a mortgage, whether the mortgage loan is meant to purchase a home, to refinance an existing mortgage so that it becomes a renewed loan or to be used as borrowing against equity that has accumulated within a given property.

Lenders are known to assess the LTV for the sake of determining their risk in lending any amount of money as mortgage underwriters. Any time borrowers seek a loan whose amount is close to the value of the appraised property, meaning the LTV is pretty high, lenders consider the risk of default on such loans to be high.

The reason for this perception is that at the time the loan is being requested, there is minimal equity accumulated or none whatsoever within the target property. This means if there is a foreclosure, the institution that loaned the purchase money will, very likely, have difficulty finding a buyer willing to pay an amount sufficient to cover the loan balance while still leaving the lender with some profit.

Factors Influencing LTV Ratio

The major factors impacting the ratio of LTV include down payment, the price at which the property is being sold and the value established after the property has been appraised.

If your interest is to attain the lowest LTV ratio possible, which is what anyone would prefer, you need to increase your down payment while also reducing the property price.

Based on the previous example where the property was appraised at $200,000, if the selling price is now $180,000 and you make a down payment of $20,000 just as in that example, the size of mortgage you are left to settle is $160,000. This means the ratio of LTV will be $160,000:$200,000, which is 80:100 or 80 percent.

Suppose you increased your down payment up to $30,000 with all the other factors remaining the same. Your loan amount would now be $150,000, and the LTV would be $150,000:$200,000; which is 75:100 or 75 percent.

These considerations are crucial because they help you reduce the ratio of LTV and make it easier to find a lender willing to offer a manageable rate of interest on the mortgage loan. In addition, when the LTV is low, you are unlikely to be required to seek private mortgage insurance (PMI).

PMI

There are some buyers of residential properties who are required to buy PMI when they want to obtain a mortgage or home loan. It is actually typical for the borrower, who becomes the owner of a home, to pay the required part of the insurance premium as he/she makes his/her monthly loan payments. When a home buyer has PMI, the lender is more open to advancing a loan even when the LTV ratio is still high.

Buying PMI when the ratio of LTV on a property is over 80 percent is not legally required, but is, nevertheless, what the practice in real estate is for most lending institutions. Still, lenders have a tendency to make exceptions for borrowers whose income is known to be high and those with low debt levels. Sometimes, lenders also consider other factors such as a borrower with a wide range of investments.

Practical Benefits from PMI

Suppose an aspiring home buyer cannot raise the $20,000 required as the down payment for a home whose price is $100,000. By paying a PMI of $5,000, the lender finds it safe to lend the buyer $95,000 when initially the maximum to be lent would only have been $80,000.

The reason for this flexibility on the part of the lender is that once the home buyer has paid a PMI, the lender is assured the loan will be covered by the insurance firm if the lender defaults on payments. In short, insuring the loan reduces the risk on the part of the lender, and both the lender and the home buyer end up benefitting as the transaction is made possible.

PMI Features

PMI does not have to be in operation for the entire life of the loan. In fact, how long it exists depends on the loan type. Sometimes PMI might cease to be applicable when the home equity reaches the range of 20 percent to 22 percent, where the equity is the difference between the home value and the loan advanced.

It is advisable to ask the mortgage loan lender when a buyer will no longer be required to pay PMI. The lender will assess how equity is likely to build up if regular loan payments are made, and will then advise the buyer accordingly.

LTV Ratio versus Rate of Interest

Certainly, a borrower needs to cater for more than just a low LTV ratio in order to succeed in securing financing for a home or other real estate property, or to get any other line of credit. Nevertheless, the LTV is central to the decision a lender makes regarding a loan and hence determines what the overall cost to the borrower is bound to be. In actual fact, just having a high LTV ratio can hinder a borrower from securing refinancing.

The greatest ratio of LTV can be defined as the greatest ratio that is allowable for a loan size in comparison to the property value in terms of dollars. The greater the LTV, the greater the part of the property buying price which will require financing.

Considering the residential property or home being purchased serves as loan collateral, it is realistic for lenders to use the LTV to measure or assess the risk involved. Varying loan facilities come with assorted risk factors, and so each has its own maximum LTV ratio.

Types of Loan vis-à-vis LTV Ratio

When it comes to the use of LTV as a ratio to measure lending risk, different types of loans have specific rules.

LTV with Regard to FHA Loans

FHA loans initially accommodate a ratio of LTV that is as high as 96.5 percent and also require that the borrower buy a mortgage insurance premium (MIP). This insurance is expected to last for the life of the loan even when the LTV ratio drops.

What usually happens is that prospective homeowners secure mortgage financing in the form of FHA loans, and once the LTA ratio drops to the level acceptable to other financiers—which is usually 80 percent and below—they switch to conventional loans through refinancing. The logic in doing so is to eliminate further need for the MIP.

LTV with Regard to VA Loans & USDA Loans

Veterans Affairs (VA) loans are mortgage loans tailored for the benefit of veterans, who access them through the US Department of Veterans Affairs. These loans benefit not only veterans and surviving spouses of veterans, but also service members.

Like any lending facility, there are certain qualifications which determine the mortgage terms even as the VA partially guarantees the mortgage loan. The loans advanced under the VA are from the private sector, by banks and other institutions such as mortgage companies.

USDA loans are given by the United States Department of Agriculture. These are loans that do not require any down payment, and the intended beneficiaries are home buyers in both rural and suburban areas. These mortgages are designed to assist the target demographic because it is assumed they are generally not wealthy enough to be able to acquire traditional loans.

The USDA Rural Development Guaranteed Housing Loan Program helps finance home acquisitions. It is important to note that when it comes to mortgage loans under the VA or the USDA program, it does not matter even if the ratio of LTV is very high; even reaching 100 percent. The target beneficiaries will still receive the loans without being called upon to pay extra fees.

LTV with Regard to Fannie Mae & Freddie Mac Loan Programs

The Fannie Mae and Freddie Mac programs target borrowers whose incomes are low and the LTV ratio permissible can go up to 97 percent, which means only a three percent down payment will be required.

However, the borrower is required to take out mortgage insurance until the LTV ratio drops to 80 percent.

Also, refinancing the mortgage under these programs ignores the need for appraisals, which means the rate of LTV is rendered irrelevant in determining whether or not to award the loan to an aspiring homeowner. Generally, such refinancing facilities are available under the FHA, USDA and VA.

There is further good news in that any low-income earner whose position does not allow for an LTA ratio below 100 percent—meaning the borrower is 'underwater,' a term sometimes substituted with 'upside down,'—will still benefit from Fannie Mae's High Loan-to-Value Refinance Option and Freddie

Mac's Enhanced Relief Refinance. These programs are meant to be used as replacements for the HARP Refinance Program which expired December 31, 2018.

How to Rank LTV Ratio

Financiers consider a ratio of LTV that is 80 percent or below a good lending position, and thus borrowers have a good chance of having a mortgage loan approved with a low interest rate and without being required to buy mortgage insurance.

Even when home buyers are seeking refinancing under the VA or USDA, unless they are seeking cash-out refinancing, the ratio of LTV is still no hindrance. In short, under these two programs, no LTV is considered either 'good' or 'poor.' In a situation where the home buyer wants cash-out refinancing, the ratio of LTV is considered, but even a high LTV of up to 90 percent is acceptable.

LTV Ratio vis-à-vis CLTV

As already explained, the ratio of LTV takes into account a single loan's impact when one is buying a property on mortgage. As for the Combined Loan to Value Ratio (CLTV), it takes into account the impact of all the loans secured by the property, or about to be secured, when a person's capacity to repay the loan is being evaluated.

This ratio of CLTV is used by mortgage loan lenders in determining the level of default risk there is in lending money to aspiring homeowners. A good example of a property catering for multiple loans is one where the property is the security for more than one mortgage, or where it secures a mortgage and a home-equity loan or credit line (HELOC).

Overall, mortgage loan lenders are prepared to advance loans when the level of CLTV ratio is 80 percent. For borrowers whose credit rating is favorable, lenders are prepared to advance loans even when the CLTV is above 80 percent.

LTV Limitations

Although the ratio of LTV is helpful in determining the risk level of lending to a mortgage loan borrower, it also has some limitations. The major limitation is the fact that it relies solely on the state of the very first mortgage the borrower took out against the property. This means it does not take into account any subsequent mortgages or home-equity loans taken against the same property.

As such, the LTV ratio can give a false position as to the borrower's capacity to repay the new loan, unlike the CLTV ratio that considers all the loan liabilities a property has.

Possessory Interest

Possessory interest can be defined as a given party's right to take over control of a given piece of land. In fact, this interest comes to mind when you consider who owns a given piece of land—the person with the possessory interest.

Possessory interest is divided into three major categories:

- Fee simple absolute
- Life estate
- Leasehold.

Once a party has made a purchase such as buying a home, interest in ownership of that property belongs to that party. Interest in ownership of any real estate property can be held by one person or it can be shared among more than one person.

If, for instance, a group of friends decides to pool funds together and buy a piece of real property, each friend will have an interest in ownership of that property. Once a person has ownership interest in a given property, he/she has the right to make use of it or to participate in its disposition. Likewise, such a person has responsibilities with regard to that property.

Real Estate Interest

The term 'real estate' is sometimes interchanged with 'real property,' and it is used in reference to land and any buildings that may be built permanently on that land. One can claim varying interest in the ownership of real estate property, or security interest. The highest of these interests in real property is the ownership interest, and its most common form is 'fee simple absolute.'

When a person's ownership interest is in the form of fee simple absolute, it means he/she has the most rights of property ownership.

Rights of Real Estate Ownership

The interest of ownership you have on a real estate property accords you the right to make use of that property as you wish within defined boundaries. If the property you possess is damaged, or for some reason is taken from you, it is your right to be compensated.

Also, the fact that the ownership of the property is yours gives you the right to sell that property or transfer it to the person or institution you choose. It is, for instance, your right to get rid of the home you own by selling it, and that remains the case even when you have taken a mortgage on it. In a case where the property has a mortgage, often you do not require permission from your lender to sell the property.

Ownership vis-à-vis Security Interest

The most common kind of security interest with regards to real estate is the mortgage. A security interest is the benefit you give the lender who advances you the mortgage loan against the property. This security interest does not grant the lender any interest in ownership though, and the only time the lender can show intention to gain ownership interest in your property is if you violate the agreement you signed when being given the loan.

If, for instance, you cease to repay the mortgage loan installments as agreed, which means you are in default of the loan, the mortgage lender will be justified in foreclosing on and repossessing the property, thereby utilizing his/her security interest.

Multiple Ownership Interest

There are many people who have ownership in real estate together with other people, such as if you chose to buy a residential property with two of your childhood friends. To know the extent to which each of you owns the property, you need to specify each person's share of ownership interest. This means you could decide to each have equal ownership interest or not.

If the property is under joint tenancy, automatically you and the two childhood friends will have ownership interest in equal proportions. Conversely, if the three of you own the property under TIC, the shares of home ownership will not necessarily be equal.

Conveyance of Ownership Interest

If you sell your real estate property or transfer your interest in ownership to someone else, you are conveying your ownership interest.

It is important to note that although it is your right to sell your ownership interest in a property you own jointly with others, you cannot compel your co-owners to convey their interest as well by selling together with you. In the same breath, you cannot sell a home you jointly own with other people just because you want to relinquish your ownership interest. If the home is to be sold, it must be in concurrence with your other co-owners.

PITI

Principal, Interest, Taxes & Insurance (PITI) means the composition of every installment a borrower pays on a mortgage. In short, in a single installment of payment there is the principal loan lent, the interest accrued, property tax levied by government and the premium for homeowners private insurance.

It is important to note that the amount of PITI is reported on a month-by-month basis. It is handy when calculating the borrower's 'front-end' or 'back-end' ratio, both of which are based on the gross income of the borrower per month. These are ratios used to help determine the suitability of approving a mortgage loan.

In general, providers of mortgage loans have a preference for PITIs equivalent to 28 percent of the gross income of the borrower per month, and they like it better when it is below 28 percent.

PITI & Mortgage Underwriting

Considering PITI is the entire loan payment for the month, it is to the advantage of both the person taking the mortgage loan and the one providing it to establish how well the borrower can afford the mortgage. The lender normally observes PITI to try and assess if the risk of allowing the mortgage is worthwhile, and the property buyer assesses it in order to establish if he/she is in a position to buy the specific property.

Illustration: Calculation of Front-end Ratio

If the borrower of the home loan has a monthly income of $12,000 gross and the PITI is $3,000, it means the front-end ratio is $3,000:$12,000, which is 1:4 or 25 percent. For many home-loan providers, a front-end of 25 percent is good and acceptable.

Illustration: Calculation of Back-end Ratio

For the back-end ratio, not only PITI is taken into account, but the entire composition of debts the borrower is obliged to pay each month. So, the borrower's total debts are gauged against his/her gross monthly income.

Suppose the borrower has an obligation to make a car installment payment of $800 and another payment for a credit card amounting to $200, as PITI remains the same at $3,000. To find out the back-end ratio, you would need to add up all the monetary obligations the borrower has in terms of debt, and gauge the total against his/her gross income for the month.

In this example, you get the back-end by calculating: ($800+$200+$3,000):$12,000. This works to $4,000:$12,000, which is 1:3 or 33 percent.

Thirty-six percent is considered by many lenders to be the upper limit for an acceptable back-end ratio.

PITI & Reserves

PITI is also used by a number of lenders in calculating the required level of reserves. Reserves are funds required by lenders as security for home loan payments just in case the borrower is unable to pay his/her monthly installment for a while.

In many instances lenders prefer to quote the required reserve level in terms of multiples of PITI. For example, it is common to find a borrower's reserve requirement quoted as two months of PITI.

Suppose the borrower in the previous example was subject to this reserve requirement. Since his/her PITI was given as $3,000, it means the reserves would have to be $3,000 x 2, which is $6,000. As such, before the home loan can be processed, the borrower would need to have $6,000 in a reserve account first.

A Promissory Note

A 'promissory note' is a promise one makes in writing to pay a given amount of money at a given time. This document indicates the amount of money being lent, who the lender is, who is obliged to settle the debt, how often the borrower is required to make payments and how much is due per installment.

The document also shows the rate of interest charged on the principal amount lent, what the collateral is in case (if any), the date of issuing the promissory note and the venue and the borrower's signature.

When it comes to promissory notes, not only banks or companies can issue them. Businesses or individuals can issue them too if they decide to borrow from other parties.

Sometimes a promissory note can be issued without the borrower giving anything as security, meaning the loan is entirely unsecured. Often when a lender issues a loan against an unsecured promissory note, it is on the basis that the maker has an obvious capacity to repay it. As for a promissory note that is secured, the security normally is something valuable like a home or other real estate property.

The term 'maker' is used to refer to the issuer of the promissory note, the one making a promise to repay a given amount according to agreed-upon stipulations in the loan.

Promissory Note versus Mortgage

A mortgage or any other loan is generally similar to a promissory note, only there are more details in a loan process that include the course of action to be taken if the borrower defaults on repayment. A major difference between a promissory note and a mortgage is sometimes foreclosure, in the event the loan provided for a home purchase is not repaid as per agreement.

In the case of a mortgage, the document that spells out loan details including the risk of foreclosure is referred to as a 'deed of trust' and sometimes simply as a 'trust deed.'

In the course of loan repayment, the promissory note is normally kept by a lender, and once full repayment has been accomplished the lender returns the note to the party that borrowed the money and has now repaid it in full.

Promissory Note

Although individual states have varying laws to guide the use of promissory notes, the basic elements of promissory notes remain the same.

A promissory note must have:

- A payor

The term 'payor' denotes the person who has the obligation to repay the mortgage loan.

- A payee

The term 'payee' denotes the individual or entity that does the lending to the borrower.

- A date

The promissory note shows the actual date by when the payor is obligated to repay the amount owed.

- A principal

The term 'principal' denotes the cash amount the payor borrowed at face value.

- Rate of interest

The rate of interest in a promissory note indicates the rate charged on the principal debt, and it can be simple, compound or any other form agreed.

- The starting payment's due date

It could be the first of every month, for example. If that is the case, then other due dates would have to be every other first of the month that follows until the debt is fully settled.

- The payment end date

The payment end date is often the date the payor makes the final debt payment; the final installment of the amortized home loan that has been repaid over time in equal installments.

Nevertheless, there are times when the end date is marked by one 'balloon payment' set to be paid at a specified date, to cover the whole of the unpaid loan balance.

Broker Test 1: Questions

(1) Which activity when carried out by ABC Brokerage Incorporation would be considered illegal under federal law in regards to the general operations of real estate brokerage firms?

(A)   The firm advertises that once escrow is closed, it will refund $500 of the total commission it will receive to every seller and buyer the firm represents

(B)   During a golf session, DEF Brokerage Incorporation and ABC Brokerage Incorporation managing licensees divide a certain geographic territory between themselves

(C)   ABC Brokerage Incorporation decides to lay off one of its long-serving licensees who performed poorly in the previous two fiscal quarters due to illness

(D)   None of the above

(2) It is important for real estate brokers to educate their clients to ensure that the best interests of the client are protected and also to ensure that the client is negotiating from a knowledgeable position. However, there are some risks involved with client education because the information that the firm's salesperson or which a broker provides to the client must be reliable and accurate. The statements below regarding managing the risks associated with educating clients are all true except one. Which is it?

(A)   An agent should avoid giving information to clients on matters that are not within his/her authorized limits

(B)   A client can press negligence charges against an agent if the agent provided misleading information that led the client to make harmful decisions

(C)   In some cases, the client may be in a more powerful negotiating position if he/she handles contractual demands with caution

(D)   An agent should avoid discovering certain facts because learning more facts means that he/she will have to disclose more facts to a client and this increases the chances of providing inaccurate information

(3) A brokerage firm can find itself in a difficult financial period even during prosperous times. This can happen if the firm does not stay updated with the frequently changing economic direction and climate of real estate markets. Which of these statements is true regarding financial planning in real estate brokerage firms?

(A)   When other competitors reduce their commission levels, a brokerage firm may also have to lower its levels in order to keep up with competition

(B)   The economic conditions of the real estate market change once every five years, and so brokerage firms should study these conditions and use that factual assessment to plan expenditures

(C)   Advertising is an important aspect that helps a brokerage firm to become successful and so brokers should make use of every product designed to increase sales

(D)   When other competitors reduce their commission levels, a brokerage firm must employ more salespersons

(4) _____ agencies exist when authority is delegated for the undertaking of a particular act.

(A)   Special agent

(B)   Universal agent

(C)   Ostensible agent

(D)   General agent

(5) According to the law, the agency relationship between a listing broker and a seller should be of _____.

(A)   General agency

(B)   Limited power of attorney

(C)   Universal agency

(D)   Specific agency

(6) A wealthy and legally competent investor wants to sell off a large piece of commercial property and he is being represented by a successful and well-known brokerage firm in the United States. Coincidentally, the date on which the transaction will close is the same date that he will be traveling overseas for a business trip that he cannot miss and so he issues a document before leaving that authorizes his close friend to sign any documents that pertain to that commercial property. What is this document called?

(A)   Power of attorney

(B)   Listing agreement

(C)   Guardianship or conservatorship

(D)   Purchase and sale agreement

(7) Which list below contains the important elements that are found in an implementable real estate contract?

(A)   Consideration, acceptance, lawful object and performance

(B)   Competency, offer and acceptance, lawful object and consideration

(C)   Consideration, tender, performance and deposit

(D)   Considerations, signatures, competence and mutuality

(8) Which statement below is true about listing agreements that do not include the authorization to collect a deposit?

(A)   The broker should not accept any deposit

(B)   The authorization to accept deposits is implied

(C)   Should the broker accept a deposit, then he/she would be doing so acting as the buyer's agent

(D)   None of the above

(9) Which of the following is referred to as personal property?

(A)   Physical improvements

(B)   Land

(C)   A deed

(D)   Growing trees

(10)   Derrick is a homeowner whose home was recently foreclosed. In frustration, right before he received an order to vacate his home Derrick removed all the lighting and plumbing fixtures as well as the built-in appliances. What is the act of removing such fixtures termed?

(A)   Accretion

(B)   Severance

(C)   Alluvium

(D)   Annexation

(11)   A land owner who has property that touches a non-navigable river or a lake has certain rights, referred to as _____.

(A)   High-low water rights

(B)   Sub-surface rights

(C)   Riparian rights

(D)   Correlative user rights

(12)   Which statement correctly defines the prior appropriation doctrine?

(A)   The entity or person who pays more money to use the water is given the authority over that water source

(B)   First in time is first in right

(C)   The right to freely use all the lake water

(D)   The right to use the river water that is adjacent to your property

(13)   There are many similarities between a condominium owner and an apartment lessee. Which statement below represents one of those common features?

(A)   They both hold interests

(B)   They are both holders of a less than freehold estate

(C)   They are both holders of estates in real property

(D)   They are both holders of estates of inheritance

(14)   John and Emma wanted to buy their own home in a location that they felt was convenient for them. The ownership required that they adhere to certain CC & Rs and their agent informed them that for the duration of their stay, they would have to comply with all the CC & Rs or lose the home. What type of estate was this?

(A)   Determinable fee

(B)   Life estate determined by the period of stay

(C)   Fee simple absolute

(D)   Fee simple defeasible

(15)   What is severalty ownership?

(A)   Ownership by an individual

(B)   Ownership by a number of people

(C)   Ownership with the right of survivorship

(D)   Ownership by a number of stockholders from a corporation

(16) Becky, Anna and Tina bought a commercial building from a businessman. In the deed, the grantees were named as Becky Robins, Anna Stone and Tina Brown but the kind of tenancy was not specified. This means that the three ladies have _____.

(A) Severalty ownership

(B) Joint tenancy

(C) Tenancy in common

(D) Tenancy by the entirety

(17) A real property licensee shows several listings to his relatives but none of them is interested in buying any of those listed properties. After a few days, the licensee decides to write a proposal of a lease with the option to buy. Who should the licensee disclose this to?

(A) The listing broker

(B) The listing salesperson

(C) The option or/the lessor

(D) All the above

(18) When toxic mold starts to grow on a property, you can correct the defect by abating it. Which of the statements below does not explain what abatement is?

(A) Abatement occurs when the nuisance is eliminated by presenting a case to the court and having the perpetrator of the nuisance cover the cost of cleaning up

(B) Abatement occurs when the injured or offended party eliminates the nuisance

(C) A special court order must be given before abatement, and elimination of the nuisance must be carried out in an environmentally friendly way

(D) Abatement requires that the nuisance be eliminated without disturbing the peace or damaging the property

(19) Which of the following systems uses well-measured angles, directions and distances to determine the boundaries of a piece of property?

(A) Lot block and tract system

(B) Governmental survey system

(C) Rectangular survey system

(D) Metes and bounds system

(20) Which of the following statements correctly explains what a baseline is?

(A) Several townships that extend from east to west

(B) A six-mile long strip of earth that runs from north to south

(C) A latitude line that runs horizontally which is used as the starting point for all pieces of sectioned land in a particular survey area

(D) A north-south line running through the first point of the survey area

(21) Which city planning and development model is characterized by a CBD standing at the center and other developments expanding in a ring from it?

(A) A classified ring

(B) A clustered ring

(C) A traditional ring

(D) A concentric ring

(22) Which land development model runs on the theory that smaller CBDs can develop outside the city despite having the main CBD at the center of the city to shorten commutes?

(A) Wedge sector theory

(B) Central axial theory

(C) Multiple nuclei theory

(D) Zoning sector theory

(23) A certain company in the United States specializes in constructing accessory dwelling units (ADUs). This company mainly assists people who live in spacious areas to get approval for adding ADUs to their property but it also helps public entities from time to time to build small undeveloped pieces of land in the established subdivisions. What type of developments is this company involved in?

(A) Greenfield developments

(B) Infill developments

(C) Commercial developments

(D) Brownfield developments

(24) A businessman purchased his home for $620,000 and sold it for $670,000 ten years later. How much money from the sales was taxed?

(A) $50,000

(B) $60,000

(C) $55,000

(D) None

(25) What would be the adjusted basis on the residence of a taxpayer?

(A) Cost minus the improvements

(B) Cost

(C) Cost plus the improvements

(D) Cost plus the improvements minus the depreciation

(26) A wealthy businessman and an investor are about to sell off their property to one another through the 1031 exchange. This businessman owns a piece of land that has an apartment on it while the investor has a 10-acre piece of land with an office on it. The legal description given by the government survey system for the property owned by this wealthy businessman is "The southeast quarter of the southeast quarter of the northwest quarter of section 10." This legal description for the area is standard for government survey systems and the two properties have equal value. Which statement below is correct?

(A)   Capital gains tax payments will be deferred by the 1031 exchange until the property is sold

(B)   As long as the personal residence's market value is sufficient, it can apply in the 1031 exchange

(C)   You cannot use a 1031 to exchange office buildings for apartment buildings

(D)   Since the investor's land is small compared to the businessman's property, the investor has to make some allowances for the businessman

(27) What is the highest commission that a broker is allowed to charge when selling residential property?

(A)   6% of the selling price of the residence

(B)   It depends on the contract that the broker has with the principal

(C)   This is determined by tradition

(D)   It depends on the real estate laws in each state

(28) What is the name given to an agreement that is made between competitors who divide the shared market by the kind of property, geographical area, price range or other factors?

(A)   Territorial assignment

(B)   Price-fixing agreement

(C)   Commission-rigging scheme

(D)   Boycotting conspiracy

(29) When you hear the phrase 'of definite duration' when a lease is being described, the lease is most probably a/an _____ .

(A)   Estate at will

(B)   Estate at sufferance

(C)   Periodic tenancy

(D)   Estate for years

(30)   What is the term for a month-to-month lease?

(A)   Life estate

(B)   Periodic tenancy

(C)   Estate at sufferance

(D)   Estate for years

(31)   What is contained in a statement of purpose of narrative appraisal report?

(A)   Reconciliation of values

(B)   The valuation

(C)   The kind of value that is being estimated

(D)   The appraisal approach method

(32)   What does a listing price fall under in terms of the market value range?

(A)   The high end of the market value

(B)   Average market value

(C)   There is no relation between market value and listing price

(D)   The low end of the market value

(33)   Which of the following statements is false regarding the title theory versus lien theory?

(A)   In title theory, the mortgagee possesses title to the property until all mortgage payments have been settled

(B)   In a title theory state, the borrower is allowed to hold both the equitable title and the actual title to the property he has purchased during the loan term and the interest of the lender is secured using a deed of trust

(C)   In a lien theory state, the seller hands the title to the buyer and then the borrower signs a deed of trust conveying a title to the trustee

(D)   In title theory, the title to the property automatically belongs to the mortgagor once all mortgage payments have been made.

(34)   Lenders use an escrow account to avoid nonpayment issues. Which of the following payments is not paid through this account?

(A)   Insurance premiums

(B)   Loan interest payment

(C)   Property taxes

(D)   Assessments

(35)   Mr. and Mrs. Woods are 63 and 59 years old, respectively. Mr. Woods recently retired due to health complications but Mrs. Woods is still serving as a hospital nurse. Years back, they acquired a home which is clear of any liens apart from taxes from recent years. Since income is only coming in from Mrs. Woods' employment, the couple needs to look for financing which will help them to maintain their lifestyle and retain their home. The couple found a suitable loan but the lender informed them that they would receive a lower amount than they wanted due to Mrs. Woods' age. Under what circumstances is this advice from a lender accurate?

(A)   The federal Equal Credit Opportunity Act

(B)   The federal rules involving reverse mortgages

(C)   The federal rules that involve senior housing

(D)   None of the above

(36)   TILA gives some borrowers three days' right of rescission, which allows them to cancel new loans. Which of the following borrowers listed below are granted this right?

(A)   An individual who is borrowing money from an already existing lender to refinance his mortgage

(B)   An individual who is borrowing from a new lender to refinance his mortgage

(C)   An individual who is borrowing to facilitate his/her business and using real estate property as collateral

(D)   An individual who is borrowing to purchase a mortgage for a principal residence

(37)   A home owner sold his residence to Joseph for $1,000,000. Joseph paid $100,000 as the down payment and paid the balance of $800,000 with a purchase money mortgage and the other $100,000 with a seller carry-back. A month after the agreement, Joseph took out another $10,000 loan with HELOC. After a few years, Joseph found a lender who would help him refinance the $800,000 purchase money mortgage. Joseph is not willing to pay back the seller carry-back or the money purchase mortgage. However, there is no boiler-plate clause for the $100,000 carry-back mortgage like there is for the money purchase mortgage. Which document does the refinancing lender need in order to protect his lien property and who should sign it?

(A)   A Seniority Preservation Agreement with the seller's signature

(B)   A Subordination Agreement with the seller's signature

(C)   A Subordination Agreement with the buyer's signature and the lender of $800,000's signature

(D)   A Subordination Agreement with the HELOC lender

(38)   What is the monthly net income if the return rate on a $315,000 investment is   12 ½ percent?

(A) $3,937

(B) $2,520,000

(C) $3,821

(D) $39,375,000

(39)   Richard Mathews has about a million dollars that he wants to invest in an investment vehicle that will give him a 12% return. He consults his financial advisor who refers him to a real estate broker, Stephen. Stephen advises Richard to invest in real estate and even informs him of an office building which is listed for $715,000 and expected to generate $79,680 yearly gross income with a yearly maintenance and operation cost of $15,320. Stephen believes that he can help Richard achieve his 12% rate of return over a period of 10 years by negotiating a good purchase price for him. What is the highest purchase price that Stephen should negotiate to achieve this?

(A) $714,000

(B) $586,333.33

(C) $562,880.00

(D) $515,705.13

(40)   At the close of escrow, a buyer's closing cost includes an interest on loan accrued from

_____.

(A)   The settlement date up to the end of the month

(B)   The settlement date through the year end

(C)   Day one of occupancy up to the month's first payment

(D)   Day one of occupancy up to the year end

(41)   Who pays the required fees for recording the mortgage or deed of trust and the new note?

(A)   The lender

(B)   The seller

(C)   The buyer

(D)   The escrow office

(42) Some contracts of sale require that earnest money be put in an account that bears interest and that any interest earned should be handed over to the buyer. Is this acceptable?

(A) No, it's illegal

(B) Only if it's commingling

(C) No, the broker involved should resign from the listing

(D) Yes, since it's an agreement between the seller and the buyer

(43) What step should a broker take if a check bearing the purchaser's earnest money is returned due to insufficient funds once it's deposited into his trust account?

(A) The broker should tell the cooperating broker or the seller about it

(B) The broker should personally cover that bad check

(C) The broker should resign immediately

(D) The broker should alert the police

(44) Which of the following choices correctly describes how exclusive-right-to-sell listings work?

(A) The agent responsible for bringing in the buyer is the one who is compensated

(B) The agent can only receive a commission after he/she has brought in a buyer

(C) The agent can only receive a commission when the property is sold at a certain price

(D) The agent will receive a commission regardless of who brings in the ready buyer

(45) Keisha is a 16-year-old who wants to purchase a house from Anna, an adult. Which of the following statements is true about the contract that they have entered into?

(A) This contract is void since Keisha is not legally allowed to enact real estate contracts due to her age

(B) Keisha can choose to void any part of their contract before the close of the transaction

(C) Either Keisha or Anna can entirely void the contract at any point before the close of the transaction

(D) Keisha can entirely void the contract at any point before the close of the transaction

(46) Any listing contract between a broker and a principal is considered a/an _____.

(A) Breach of contract

(B) Implied contract

(C) Discharge of contract

(D) Express contract

(47) Which of the following statements is not true about a Veterans Affairs mortgage?

(A) No down payment is required

(B) There are no minimum requirements

(C) There is no maximum debt ratio

(D) No mortgage insurance is required

(48) Which of the following is true about a Veterans Affairs mortgage?

(A) It is guaranteed

(B) It is conventional

(C) It is a recourse loan

(D) It is prepaid

(49) Stella sold off her primary residence at $595,000 and made capital gains of $315,000. Given that she is single, how much can Stella exclude on her income tax?

(A) $100,000

(B) $250,000

(C) $315,000

(D) $476,000

(50) Calculate the asking price of a plot of land that measures 140 by 75 ft if the seller sells it at $130 per square foot.

(A) $1,470,000

(B) $1,050,000

(C) $1,650,000

(D) $1,365,000

Broker Test 1: Answers & Explanations

(1)The correct answer is: (B) During a golf session, DEF Brokerage Incorporation and ABC Brokerage Incorporation managing licensees divide a certain geographic territory between themselves.

Dividing territories with other brokerage firms is considered collusion and this is an activity that violates the federal Sherman Antitrust Act. Other brokerage activities that may violate this law include fixing commission fees or rates and boycotting brokerage firms with low commissions.

(2)The correct answer is: (D) An agent should avoid discovering certain facts because learning more facts means that he/she will have to disclose more facts to a client and this increases the chances of providing inaccurate information.

An agent is required to educate his/her clients on all the known facts and must also teach them how to carry out negotiations so as to ensure a client's negotiating position is strong. An agent should not avoid discovering facts for fear of having to disclose too much to the client.

(3)The correct answer is: (A) When other competitors reduce their commission levels, a brokerage firm may also have to lower its levels in order to keep up with competition.

Like any other business, a brokerage requires cash flow and income. If a brokerage firm is poorly managed, it will experience financial difficulties even when the real estate market is booming. A brokerage firm may only use a marketing product after it has carried out an evaluation of where it stands financially.

(4)The correct answer is: (A) Special agent.

Special agents have been given authority by their principals to carry out a certain deed, sign a certain contract or procure a buyer for particular real estate. An agent who has multiple listings with the same seller is still considered a special agent instead of a general agent.

(5)The correct answer is: (D) Specific agency.

Specific agency refers to a relationship whereby the licensee is only allowed to act on behalf of a principal in a limited way, for a certain period of time and for a specific transaction. General agency is where an agent has authority to act on behalf of the principal for several activities.

(6) The correct answer is: (A) The power of attorney.

A well-executed power of attorney gives an agent the authority to assume certain roles on behalf of the principal. So, the wealthy and legally competent investor is the principal while his close friend is the attorney. An attorney owes principal fiduciary duties such as duty of disclosure, obedience, confidentiality and care.

(7) The correct answer is: (B) Competency, offer and acceptance, lawful object and consideration.

When two competent parties agree to participate in a legal activity, they enter into an enforceable contract. If a party wants action to be taken against another party that has breached a contract, then the party presenting the allegations should provide evidence showing that there was an offer that was made and accepted and also that consideration was offered by the two parties.

(8) The correct answer is: (C) Should the broker accept a deposit, then he/she would be doing so acting as the buyer's agent.

If an agent is only authorized to produce a buyer for the client then the broker has no authority to accept a deposit on the seller's behalf. However, if an agent goes on to accept a deposit then the agent does so as the buyer's agent and not as the seller's agent.

(9) The correct answer is: (C) A deed.

Movable property is considered personal property. Although a deed is a document that proves ownership of a real property, it is regarded as personal property since it is movable.

(10) The correct answer is: (B) Severance.

When you cut off or remove some parts of real property which are a part of the land, you commit severance. Since the fixtures mentioned above are part of real property then the lender who is foreclosing is supposed to receive that home intact with all the fixtures in it.

(11) The correct answer is: (C) Riparian rights.

Riparian rights refer to the rights that a property owner whose property borders a water body has. The landowner owns the right to gain access to those waters but he/she does not own the waters.

(12)   The correct answer is: (B) First in time is first in right.

The prior appropriation doctrine is a doctrine giving water rights to an entity, allowing a certain amount of water flow from a particular source to be used on a specific property. These rights are assigned on a first come, first served basis whereby the entity that applied for the rights first receives first priority.

(13)   The correct answer is: (C) They are both holders of estates in real property.

Even though condominiums and apartments seem to have similar living arrangements and building structures, the only commonality between them is that they are both holders of real estate property. A person who owns a condo is in possession of a freehold estate while a lessee is a less-than-freehold estate holder.

(14)   The correct answer is: (D) Fee simple defeasible.

An estate that is capable of being defeated is known as a fee simple defeasible estate. Covenants, conditions and restrictions are conditions subsequent and this means that these conditions should be met once the title is issued and noncompliance leads to loss of ownership.

(15)   The correct answer is: (A) Ownership by an individual.

Severalty ownership refers to ownership by only one entity or person and in such types of ownership the deed bears only the name of that owner. For a survivor to inherit property that was under severalty ownership after a real estate owner's demise, the survivor's name must be in that owner's will.

(16)   The correct answer is: (C) Tenancy in common.

The transfer of ownership to more than one person automatically creates a tenancy in common-type of ownership unless it is otherwise indicated. All tenants have undivided ownership of the property and this means that they have full rights over their share and can transfer ownership without seeking consent from any other party.

(17)   The correct answer is: (C) The optionor/the lessor.

The licensee must disclose the prospective buy to all parties involved in the transaction. Here the listing salesperson and listing broker are not involved in the lease transaction since the contract involves the lessee and the optionor. Failing to disclose this information would be termed a violation of an agent's duty.

(18)   The correct answer is: (C) A special court order must be given before abatement, and elimination of the nuisance must be carried out in an environmentally friendly way.

Abatement means eliminating a nuisance which is hindering effective use of a property or which is posing a threat to the health and safety of the property. Elimination can be done through a court order by the injured party or the party that caused the nuisance. One does not need a court order before abatement.

(19)   The correct answer is: (D) Metes and bounds system.

For most states, metes and bounds is the primary system for determining boundaries. However, in the states where another system is preferred, the metes and bounds method is supplementary. This method uses the physical features on the property as well as distances and directions to establish boundaries.

(20)   The correct answer is: (C) A latitudinal line that runs horizontally which is used as the starting point for all pieces of sectioned land in a particular survey area.

A baseline is a latitudinal line that is used as the base of measurement for sectioned land in a certain survey area. This line divides the area into two halves—north and south. The point where the baseline and the principal meridian meet is known as the initial point.

(21)   The correct answer is: (D) A concentric ring.

The basic arrangement of a concentric ring model is a central business district (CBD) at the center and other developments expanding from the center in a specific arrangement. After the CBD, the first ring is the transition zone, comprising commercial and residential developments, followed by the inner suburbs, then middle-class residences and finally, commuter zones.

(22)   The correct answer is: (C) Multiple nuclei theory.

This model creates new nodes in the already developed city and that is why it is known as the multiple nuclei theory model. It was designed based upon the theory that since many people have cars, there is greater movement and this movement encourages regional centers to be specialized.

(23) The correct answer is: (B) Infill development.

The work that this company does is referred to as infill developments. This basically means that the company builds improvements on land that is underdeveloped or land that already has existing improvements. In residential developments, infill developments can either be called housing infill or suburban infill.

(24) The correct answer is: (D) None.

A total profit of $250,000 or less is not taxable. There is a tax exemption for single people who make $250,000 and a tax exemption exists for married couples that file joint returns that do not exceed $500,000. This exemption is only viable if the property has been the seller's main residence for at least two of the past five years.

(25) The correct answer is: (C) Cost plus the improvements.

Depreciation is only taken on investment property and on personal residences. The adjustable basis in this case is the cost plus the capital improvements. In the case of an investment property, it would be the cost plus the improvements minus the depreciation.

(26) The correct answer is: (A) Capital gains tax payments will be deferred by the 1031 exchange until the property is sold.

In the 1031 exchange, owners of real property investments or businesses are allowed to defer the capital gains tax on the properties that are being exchanged. Tax deferral does not, however, mean that the tax has been removed; only that taxes will be due after the sale of the newly acquired property.

(27) The correct answer is: (B) It depends on the contract that the broker has with the principal.

According to the Sherman Antitrust Act, price fixing is prohibited and so any state real estate laws that dictate the maximum commission a broker should charge when selling residential property are a violation of public policy. The seller and listing broker should be able to negotiate the listing commissions for any real estate.

(28) The correct answer is: (A) Territorial assignment.

Antitrust laws are supposed to prevent businesses from restraining trade through certain agreements. An agreement between two different brokerages to divide the market on geographical bases could be considered a violation of antitrust laws since it places limitations on consumer choice.

(29)   The correct answer is: (D) Estate for years.

Leasehold estate is a type of ownership that contains a defined start date plus a defined end date. It should not always last for years, so it can even be a six-month lease. A lease lasting a year or more should be documented; otherwise it cannot be enforced.

(30)   The correct answer is: (B) Periodic tenancy.

Periodic tenancy does not have a defined termination date and it goes on until either of the involved parties notifies the other that they want to terminate the lease. During the lease, the same terms are automatically renewed after every month and they are expected to be valid for that given month.

(31)   The correct answer is: (D) The appraisal approach method.

The statement of purpose found in research documents is used to state the reason why the research has been carried out plus the kind of research done. In a USPAP, a statement of purpose is used to state the appraisal approach method and to inform the lender about the property type.

(32)   The correct answer is: (A) The high end of the market value.

A property holder usually sets a listing price that is on the higher end of the market value based on standard market conditions while a prospective buyer of that property sets the market's value lower limit when he makes his first offer.

(33)   The correct answer is: (B) In a title theory state, the borrower is allowed to hold both the equitable title and the actual title to the property he has purchased during the loan term and the interest of the lender is secured using a deed of trust.

In a lien theory state, the buyer becomes the owner of that property and he/she holds all its rights while the grantor has a lien. In a title theory state, the borrower/buyer hypothecates his/her title to the grantor, meaning that the lender holds the actual title.

(34)   The correct answer is: (B) Loan interest payment.

Loan interest payments are a part of loan payment while insurance premiums, property taxes and assessments payments are put in a reverse account known as an impound account. The lender holds the impound account and pays the bills when the payments are due.

(35) The correct answer is: (B) The federal rules involving reverse mortgages.

According to federal law, a reverse mortgage can only be procured by a home owner who is 62 years or older and who has considerable equity on his/her home. Mrs. Woods does not qualify for this senior reverse mortgage since she is 59 years old.

(36) The correct answer is: (A) An individual who is borrowing money from an already existing lender to refinance his mortgage.

According to the Federal Truth in Lending Act, a borrower who is refinancing a mortgage with another lender qualifies for the three-day right of rescission. The other loans that qualify a borrower for the right of rescission are a home equity line of credit and a home equity loan.

(37) The correct answer is: (B) A Subordination Agreement with the seller's signature.

A subordinate agreement document requires an existing lender to subordinate or lessen the priority given to an already existing loan so as to accommodate the new loan. In this case, the $100,000 seller carry-back made the seller a junior lien holder; hence the signature of the seller is needed on the document.

(38) The correct answer is: (C) $3,821.

The first step in such calculations is to find out what the annual net income is with a capitalization rate which is 12 ½ percent, so you multiply $315,000 by $12.5 to get $39,375 as the annual income. The next step is to divide the result by 12, resulting in $39,375. The result divided by 12 will give you $3,821.25, which is the monthly income.

(39) The correct answer is: (D) $515,705.13.

Subtract the yearly operating costs from the annual gross income to get your annual net income as the first step, which is $79,680 minus $15,320 to get $64,360. The next step is to get the purchasing price by dividing the annual income, which is $64,360, by the return rate, which is 12%, to get $536,333.33. If Richard pays a commission of 4%, the highest purchase price before the commission must be ($536.333.33 ÷ 104) x 100; which is $515,705.125.

(40) The correct answer is: (A) The settlement date up to the end of month.

A lender expects the borrower to pay all the interest accrued from when a settlement is made up to when the month ends. In most loan agreements, a borrower should make the first payment at the beginning of the second month from the settlement date.

(41) The correct answer is: (C) The buyer.

In most cases, the buyer is the one who pays the fees required for recording the mortgage or deed of trust and the new note. However, in a market situation where the supply is more than the demand, the seller may decide to pay the fee.

(42) The correct answer is: (D) Yes, since it's an agreement between the seller and the buyer.

Brokers are agents and so he should follow his client's instructions provided they are all legal instructions. According to the law, a broker should have a trust bank account that does not bear interest but it does not dictate how any earned interest should be distributed.

(43) The correct answer is: (A) He should tell the cooperating broker or the seller about it.

The broker must immediately inform the seller or cooperating broker of the situation since unfunded bank checks are material facts which are also possibly fraud. A licensee is responsible for protecting the public as well as disclosing material facts regarding the transaction.

(44) The correct answer is: (D) The agent will receive a commission regardless of who brings in the ready buyer.

Once the principal has signed an exclusive right-to-sell listing, the principal is required to pay a commission to the broker even when the buyer is procured by another agent or by the principal.

(45) The correct answer is: (D) Keisha can entirely void the contract at any point before the close of the transaction.

Minors are allowed to sign real estate contracts and certain protections are given to them which are not provided to adults. In this case, Keisha has the authority to void the whole contract at any point before the close of the transaction.

(46) The correct answer is: (D) Express contract.

Listing agreements are express contracts between the broker and the principal that make the broker a fiduciary representative of that principal or the principal's agent.

(47) The correct answer is: (B) There are no property requirements.

The Veterans Affairs mortgage has minimum property requirements that ensure that the buyer receives sanitary, sound and safe property.

(48) The correct answer is: (A) It's guaranteed.

The Veterans Affairs department guarantees loans for veterans who are eligible.

(49) The correct answer is: (B) $250,000.

The maximum amount that single individuals are allowed to exclude from capital gains realized from the sales of their primary residence is $250,000, so Stella can exclude a total of $250,000 of her capital gains.

(50) The correct answer is: (D) $1,365,000.

First we need to obtain the square footage of the land, so 140 feet by 75 feet will give us 10,500 feet. If each square foot is worth $130 then $10,500 × $130 will give us $1,365,000, which is the asking price of the plot.

Broker Test 2: Questions

(1) Lucy's home is free of all encumbrances and she can legally hand her home over to her daughter. What kind of ownership does Lucy hold?

(A)   Estate at will

(B)   Leasehold

(C)   Fee simple estate

(D)   Life estate

(2) Which of the following types of deeds does not have warranties and covenants?

(A)   Warranty

(B)   Trust

(C)   Reconveyance

(D)   Quitclaim

(3) How often should independent contractors and brokers renew their contracts?

(A)   Yearly, but no later than 15 months from when the contract was last renewed

(B)   Every 3 years

(C)   Every 2 years

(D)   Every 9 months

(4)Raphael bought a house many years ago for a total of $20,500. Since he is aware that his property has appreciated in value, he tells his broker to set the selling price at $200,000 but his broker knows that the value exceeds $300,000. What should the broker do?

(A)   Tell Raphael that his house can be sold for more than he is asking

(B)   Take that listing and sell the property quickly

(C)   Buy that house using a different name

(D)   Buy the house at $200,000 and identify himself fully

(5)A seller is still responsible for defects that his/her property may have that could affect the property's value when he/she sells the property 'as is' when _____.

(A)   There are hazardous material found in the property

(B)   Repairs are likely to cost more than $20,000

(C)   The construction of the home happened before 1958

(D)   The seller knows

(6)Before a buyer signs a binding sale contract, he/she should receive a statement of disclosure from the seller disclosing the property's condition and _____.

(A)   The property seller's agent should help the buyer to fill it out

(B)   It does not matter whether the seller provides that disclosure form or not since it does not affect his liability for any undisclosed defects

(C)   The licensee should educate the seller on the legal rights and obligations that the seller has regarding filling out or ignoring the form

(D)   The seller should give a $10,000 cashier's check to the buyer at closing if the buyer does not receive this statement

(7) What amount does contract law require to be submitted as earnest money with contracts of sale?

(A)   10% of the offer

(B)   15% of selling price

(C)   You do not need any earnest money to create a contract

(D)   At least $2000

(8) After signing a contract of sale and depositing the earnest money offered by the buyer into a special account, who does the money belong to?

(A)   The buyer. It is a rebate given for the transaction

(B)   The seller. It acts as part of his capital gains

(C)   The licensee. It acts as an early payment of his/her commission

(D)   Nobody. The transaction must first be completed, breached or rescinded

(9) In a listing agreement, which contract attribute is described when a broker makes an agreement to do the best that he can to get a buyer?

(A)   Lawful purpose

(B)   Consideration

(C)   Mutual agreement

(D)   Legally competent parties

(10)   Which of the following events would not cause the termination of a listing agreement?

(A)   The broker becoming bankrupt

(B)   The seller dying

(C)   Being restricted from accessing that property

(D)   A kitchen fire occurring on the property

(11)   A broker was able to negotiate a sales price of $400,000. The buyer needs a $360,000 mortgage but the lender can only approve an 80% LTV mortgage. Because of this, the broker decides to prepare a false second contract with a purchase price of $450,000 and has the two parties sign. What can be said of this event?

(A)   The buyer, the seller and the broker are all committing fraud

(B)   The broker has rightly put the interests of the buyer first

(C)   That broker should receive a commission from the $450,000

(D)   The seller and the buyer were simply following directions from the broker and so no liability falls on them

(12)   Patricia has an amortization mortgage loan which means that _____.

(A)   She will pay a large amount of money on her final payment

(B)   What she pays every month includes interest and principal

(C)   Her loan amount is more than what FNMA requires

(D)   What she pays every month is less than the interest

(13)   Sandy and Eunice applied for Federal Housing Administration loans. Which of the following is true about this mortgage?

(A)   The federal government guarantees the mortgage without charging the borrower

(B)   Private mortgage insurance premiums pay for it

(C)   The United States government fully backs and credits the mortgage

(D)   It is insured by the Federal Housing Administration through HUD

(14) If a firm's listing is sold by an agent from a different firm for $950,000 and the 7% commission is divided equally between both companies, how much will the agent receive if she gets 60% percent of the broker's share?

(A) $19,95o

(B) $11,619.75

(C) $10,850

(D) $13,237.50

(15) King leased four apartments in a nearby state for a sum of $4,500 per month. If this amount represents an 8% yearly return on his investment, calculate the initial cost of this property.

(A) $450,000

(B) $675,000

(C) $56,250

(D) $54,000

(16) Which description best describes capitalizing of income in real property?

(A) Price

(B) Cost

(C) Location and attractiveness

(D) Current value of the property based on its future benefit

(17) According to the Real Estate Settlement Procedures Act, when should good faith estimates indicating the borrower's closing costs be issued to that borrower?

(A) Within two days of closing

(B) Within three business days or when applying for the loan

(C) When closing

(D) Within 72 hours of closing

(18) When the Johnsons bought a house from their parents, they only received a quitclaim deed. What could have been the reason for that?

(A)   The Johnson are tenants by the entirety

(B)   There was a mortgage involved

(C)   Transactions within families mostly use a quitclaim deed

(D)   Mr. Johnson will only own the house during Mrs. Johnson's lifetime

(19) Which document do property managers use to predict expected expenses and revenues?

(A)   The operating budget

(B)   The prospectus

(C)   The offering memorandum

(D)   The management agreement

(20) Which of the following features will be excluded from real property when Kim sells off his farm?

(A)   Farm equipment

(B)   Fences

(C)   Growing trees

(D)   Permanent buildings

(21) Kevin bought a vacation house that borders a river. What kinds of rights does he have to the river?

(A)   Littoral rights

(B)   Riparian rights

(C)   Reversionary rights

(D)   Laches rights

(22) Samson, an agent who works under a broker called Keith, was recently hired as an agent for another broker, Tom. Before the transfer, Samson had brought five listings to Keith. What will happen to the listings?

(A)   They will be terminated

(B)   They will be transferred to Tom

(C)   They will be divided between Keith and Tom

(D)   They will remain with Keith

(23) Real estate brokers are required to report cash deposits that exceed _____.

(A) $10,000

(B) $5,000

(C) $20,000

(D) $15,000

(24) Rachael signed a four-month listing with Dreams Realty, but after 70 days she decides that she doesn't want to sell her property and informs Dreams Realty of her decision. When will the contract be terminated?

(A)   When the listing expires

(B)   On the 71st day

(C)   On the last day of the four months

(D)   After an agreed-upon period of time

(25) The principle of caveat emptor states that if a buyer buys a title that is faulty, the party responsible for it is _____ .

(A) The broker

(B) The abstractor

(C) The seller

(D) The buyer

(26) Which of these would be affected by the Americans with Disabilities Act of 1990?

(A) Multifamily houses consisting of three units

(B) Third-floor apartments that are constructed in a new apartment complex

(C) Single-family homes

(D) A business that has 30 employees

(27) Joseph is a developer and has retained agent Maggie to sell apartments. Stella, who is also an agent, presents an offer asking to purchase unit 1605 for $14,000 and they execute a sale of contract. However, typographical errors occur and the contract identifies unit 1604, which is listed for $20,000. What is the state of the contract at this point?

(A) Enforceable

(B) Void

(C) Invalid

(D) Voidable

(28) Ken has submitted an offer seeking to buy a condo from Nick. Nick would like to keep his silver chandelier so on the contract he adds that the silver chandelier is not included, then signs and returns the document to Ken. Is this a binding contract?

(A) No, Nick has rejected Ken's offer and so for the contract to be binding, Ken must accept Nick's counteroffer without changing anything else

(B) Yes, the change Nick made was insignificant

(C) For the contract to be binding, Ken will have to accept the counteroffer without any further changes

(D) No, Nick has rejected Ken's offer

(29) Julie entered into a contract with the aim of selling her property. The contract states that the broker who sells the property is the one who will receive a commission. This agency agreement is best described as a/n _____ agreement.

(A) Open listing

(B) Exclusive agency listing

(C) Net listing

(D) Exclusive right-to-sell

(30) Tim is an agent who had a representation agreement in writing with a willing buyer. At closing, the seller paid Tim 4% of what the seller received from the sale. What was the position of the broker?

(A) The seller's agent

(B) Dual agent

(C) The buyer's agent

(D) None of the above are correct. The broker was in violation of real estate laws and he risked license revocation or suspension

(31) According to the Federal Housing Administration, which of the following statements is correct?

(A) You do not need to make a down payment

(B) You can make a down payment of 3%

(C) You are required to make a down payment of 10%

(D) You are required to make a down payment of 20%

(32) What do we call bank letters sent to borrowers to inform them that the bank will provide funding for their mortgage loans?

(A) Preapproval

(B) Rate lock

(C) Mortgage commitment

(D) Prequalification

(33) Steve is a broker who received a 6% commission from the sale of a house. Calculate the sales price if the 6% commission is an equivalent of $21,600.

(A) $225,000

(B) $290,000

(C) $360,000

(D) $315,000

(34) Calculate the cost per square foot of land that measures 50 by 125 feet if the total selling price was $455,000.

(A) $69.70

(B) $72.80

(C) $70.25

(D) $75.75

(35) Household and per capita income greatly determine the value of land. Under what category does this factor that affects the value of real estate fall under?

(A) Physical and environmental

(B) Economic-financial

(C) Sociological

(D) Political-governmental-legal

(36) Which valuation approach used in real estate does the comparative market analysis resemble?

(A) Sales comparison

(B) Income

(C) Guesstimate

(D) Cost

(37) What do we call the document that is signed by the seller at closing as a requirement by the title-issuing company to ensure that the seller has not been involved in any bankruptcies, judgments or divorce cases since the title examination?

(A) Title insurance policy

(B) Evidence of title

(C) Affidavit of the title

(D) Abstract of the title

(38) A property management company receives 10% of the rental income that is collected from an apartment every month and the rent roll per month for this property is $55,000. One tenant paid $250 out of the $1,000 dollar while three others skipped out on their entire rent for that month. How much money is the company owed?

(A) $5,400

(B) $5,125

(C) $4,825

(D) $5,200

(39) Where does a property manager maintain abstracts of every tenant's lease as well as the property's curb appeal description?

(A) Prospectus

(B) Market analysis

(C) Property analysis

(D) Management agreement

(40) Lisa's property has been encroached by his neighbor's garage which sits on her property line but she is not asserting her rights. This is a _____.

(A) Parole evidence rule

(B) General obligations law

(C) Statute of limitations

(D) Doctrine of laches

(41) Which of the following is not considered chattel?

(A) Curtains

(B) A trade fixture

(C) A barn

(D) A tractor

(42) A licensed broker is legally allowed to pay part or all of the commission from real estate to _____.

(A) His own agent

(B) The buyer

(C) The seller

(D) His friend who gave him listing leads

(43) Pattie is not a licensed broker but she communicates with homeowners via phone to find out if they may have an interest in selling off their homes. Mercy is licensed and she pays Pattie $200 for the leads that she gives her. Is this a violation of licensing law?

(A) Yes, because Pattie is using her home telephone without a broker's sign put up outside the house

(B) No, since the compensation is less than $250

(C) No, because Pattie does not sell or list property

(D) Yes, because Mercy is paying for a service that should be provided by a licensed agent

(44) When are commissions earned?

(A) When a seller accepts a buyer's offer with no conditions

(B) When a buyer gives his purchase offer

(C) When a lender makes his commitment to fund a loan

(D) When a title to a property has been searched

(45) For an owner to get innocent landowner immunity, he/she should not have any previous knowledge, whether constructive or actual, of the damage than is on his/her property. When buying the property, the owner should also have _____.

(A) Received a phase one assessment for the property

(B) Shown his due diligence to ensure that this property is in good condition

(C) Owned the property for a period of only one year

(D) Requested the mortgage lender carry out an environmental survey

(46) Sam is an agent. He declined to show several Muslims the houses in a neighborhood he believed was not Muslim-friendly. What do we call this type of action?

(A) Steering

(B) Blockbusting

(C) Good faith expression

(D) Redlining

(47) In cases where earnest money is offered, the broker is the one who receives it when a contract of sale is required by the property seller and given to the ready buyer. If no specific instructions are included in the sale contract, what legal responsibility does the broker have?

(A) He should keep that check in his transaction file and leave it there until closing

(B) He should deposit it in his special account

(C) He should keep it in his secure safe

(D) He should deposit it in his operating account

(48) What does an option do?

(A) It gives the optionor permission to carry out a purchase

(B) It ensures that the seller becomes responsible for paying a commission

(C) It allows an offer to remain open until a specified period

(D) It gives the optionee ownership of the property

(49) Sam is not capable of making sound decisions due to his mental condition and so he has a guardian who was appointed for him by the court. Which of the following statements is true if Sam enters a contract with the aim of purchasing a home from Ken?

(A)   The contract is void

(B)   Sam or Ken can decide to void the contract at any point before the close of the contract

(C)   Sam can decide to void part of that contract at any point before the close of the contract

(D)   Sam can decide to void the whole contract at any point before the close of the contract

(50) Any enforceable agreement made between competent parties and in which every party acquires benefits or rights is known as a _____.

(A)   Clause

(B)   Certiorari

(C)   Consideration

(D)   Contract

Broker Test 2: Answers & Explanations

(1) The correct answer is: (C) Fee simple estate.

In a fee simple estate, the owner has the right to pass on wealth to his/her heirs upon his/her demise.

(2) The correct answer is: (D) Quitclaim.

You cannot find warranties or covenants in a quitclaim.

(3) The correct answer is: (A) Yearly, but it should not be later than 15 months from when the contract was last renewed.

A contract between a broker and a salesman, an associate broker or an independent contractor must be renewed on a yearly basis in order to update the terms of the contract.

(4) The correct answer is: (A) Tell Raphael that his house can be sold for more than he is asking.

It is the responsibility of the broker to transact any business with reasonable care and ensure that he values properties at reasonable prices.

(5) The correct answer is: (D) The seller knows.

Even if the seller is selling the property 'as is,' if he/she knows about the undisclosed defects which may affect the property's value, he/she is still responsible and liable.

(6) The correct answer is: (B) It does not matter whether the seller provides that disclosure form or not since it does not affect his liability for any undisclosed defects.

Providing a disclosure form does not affect the liability that the seller has for defects that are not disclosed. Some states, however, require that a seller provide a property condition disclosure statement to the buyer before signing any contract of sale.

(7) The correct answer is: (C) You do not need any earnest money to create a contract.

One does not need earnest money in order to create binding contracts. However, in some cases the buyer offers earnest money or the seller requires it to be included in the transaction. In such situations both parties can negotiate the amount.

(8) The correct answer is: (D) Nobody. The transaction must first be completed, breached or rescinded.

Upon the completion of the transaction, either of the parties may receive or fail to receive the money and because the money is placed in trust, it does not belong to the broker. However, the involved parties can decide what to do with the earnest money.

(9) The correct answer is: (B) Consideration.

Consideration refers to the shared benefit that the involved parties enjoy when they enter into a contract. The benefit that a principal enjoys when he/she commissions a broker is the agreement by the broker to do the best he can to get a buyer once the property is listed.

(10) The correct answer is: (D) A kitchen fire occurring on the property.

A kitchen fire is not likely to terminate a listing agreement unless the fire destroys the property. Factors that may cause the termination of a listing include the bankruptcy or demise of one of the involved parties or the fulfillment or completion of the agency's agenda.

(11) The correct answer is: (A) The buyer, the seller and the broker are all committing fraud.

In such a case, the three parties involved are all committing fraud and such a contract should not be submitted to receive financing.

(12) The correct answer is: (B) What she pays every month includes interest and principal.

Amortizing mortgage loans have monthly payments that include interest and principal. Once Patricia pays her final installment, her loan will be considered fully paid.

(13) The correct answer is: (D) It is insured by the Federal Housing Administration through HUD.

The Federal Housing Administration works under HUD to insure the mortgage loans that are taken by lenders against any loss.

(14) The correct answer is: (A) $19,950.00.

For you to get the agent's total commission you should multiply the sales price, which is $950,000, by 7%, which is the commission percentage. So $950,000 × 0.07 = $66,500. After that, divide the commission by two to get every broker's share, then multiply that by the share the agent gets. $66,500 ÷ 2 = $33,250 × 0.06 = $19,950.

(15) The correct answer is: (B) $675,000.

To get the value of King's property you should first determine the yearly rent by multiplying the monthly rent by 12, so $4,500×12 will give you $54,000. Divide the yearly rent by returns per year, which is 8%, so, $54,000÷8/100 = $675,000.

(16) The correct answer is: (D) Current value of the property based on its future benefit.

In real property, capitalization of income is best explained as the current value of the future benefits that are attributed to the property.

(17) The correct answer is: (B) Within three business days or when applying for the loan.

The lender is required to provide a GFE when the borrower applies for the loan or within three business days. The GFE is used to indicate the closing costs that a borrower will incur.

(18) The correct answer is: (C) Transactions within families mostly use a quitclaim deed.

Simple transactions within known parties or family members commonly use a quitclaim deed. Since the transaction between the Johnsons and their parents is a family transaction, the likely deed to be used is the quitclaim deed.

(19) The correct answer is: (A) In the operating budget.

Property managers are required to forecast anticipated expenses and revenues in the operating budget.

(20) The correct answer is: (A) Farm equipment.

Farm equipment is not considered part of real property since it is a trade fixture. Trade fixtures are personal property and that means that farm equipment still belongs to Kim.

(21) The correct answer is: (B) Riparian rights.

The owner of property that borders a stream or river has riparian rights that allow him/her to use the property accordingly.

(22) The correct answer is: (D) They will remain with Keith.

Samson created the five listings when he was working for Keith which means that the listings will remain with Keith since he is still the agent representing the sellers.

(23) The correct answer is: (A) $10,000.

It is the responsibility of the broker to report any cash deposits that exceed $10,000 to the IRS.

(24) The correct answer is: (B) On the 71st day.

Agency relationships can be terminated whenever the agency will no longer be needed.

(25) The correct answer is: (D) The buyer.

Caveat emptor, which implies that the buyer should be aware, holds lenders and buyers responsible for carrying out their due diligence on title records.

(26) The correct answer is: (D) A business that has 30 employees.

The Americans with Disabilities Act of 1990 advocates for inclusion of people with disabilities in the business community. Existing businesses that have 15 or more workers are required to update their businesses to conform to ADA rules.

(27) The correct answer is: (D) Voidable.

In a transaction, all parties including agents are required to read through the binding agreements carefully. A mutual and unintentional mistake which is free of negligence is likely to make the contract voidable.

(28) The correct answer is: (A) No, Nick has rejected Ken's offer and so for the contract to be binding, Ken must accept Nick's counteroffer without changing anything else.

For a contract to be created there should be no variation in the terms provided in the deal. Essentially, a counteroffer means that the initial offer was rejected and either a change in the existing offer has been made or an entirely new offer has been issued.

(29) The correct answer is: (B) Exclusive agency listing.

In this kind of listing agreement, the broker who receives a commission from the principal is the one who procures the able and willing buyer.

(30) The correct answer is: (C) The buyer's agent.

You cannot determine an agency relationship by identifying who is giving the compensation. In some cases, the broker is not representing the party paying the commission.

(31) The correct answer is: (B) You can make a down payment of 3%.

The Federal Housing Administration is under the U.S Department of Housing and Urban Development. This institution insures mortgages for multifamily homes, single-family homes, nursing homes and mobile homes. Down payments as small as 3% are accepted.

(32) The correct answer is: (C) Mortgage commitment.

When the lender agrees to provide funding for a mortgage loan, he must provide a written document, which is referred to as a loan or mortgage commitment letter, to the borrower.

(33) The correct answer is: (C) $360,000.

If Steve received a commission of 6% of the total sales price, which is $21,600. We need to get the value of 1% of the sales price, so if 6% =21,600 then 1%= $21,600 ÷ 6/100 = $36,000. If 1% is $36,000 then 100%, which is our sales price, will be $36,000 × 100 = $360,000.

(34) The correct answer is: (B) $72.80.

To get the price per square foot, first determine the square footage of the plot then divide that figure by the total sales price. 50 × 125 feet = 6,250 square feet and the total sales price was $455,000. So $455,000 ÷ $6,250 is $72.80 for every square foot.

(35) The correct answer is: (B) Economical-financial.

The value of land is greatly determined by its location. Some of the major determinants include the kind of industries located in that area, stability, interest rates and unemployment rates.

(36) The correct answer is: (A) Sales comparison.

A CMA works in a similar manner to a sales comparison valuation method because it involves examining recent sales made for comparable property.

(37) The correct answer is: (C) Affidavit of the title.

At closing, the seller must sign a document known as an affidavit of title which assures the company that no judgment, divorce or bankruptcy cases have been linked to the seller since the title was examined.

(38) The correct answer is: (B) $5,125.

One tenant paid his rent partially while three paid nothing so first calculate the total deficit. The first tenant owes $1,000 - $250= $750. The other three combined owe $1,000 × 3 =$3,000. So the total deficit is $750+$3,000=$3,750. The roll-out is usually $55,000, so $55,000 - $3,750$=51,250 and 10% of $51,250 is $5,125.

(39) The correct answer is: (C) Property analysis.

Property analysis looks at the existing leases that tenants have as well as the curb appeal of the property.

(40) The correct answer is: (D) Doctrine of laches.

In a doctrine of laches the property owner does not assert his/her rights.

(41) The correct answer is: (C) A barn.

Chattel includes things such as drapes, refrigerators, money and clothing.

(42) The correct answer is: (A) His own agent.

Brokers can share their commissions with their salespersons, other licensed brokers or associate brokers.

(43) The correct answer is: (D) Yes, because Mercy is paying for a service that should be provided by a licensed agent.

Unlicensed assistants are not allowed to scout for prospective listings.

(44) The correct answer is: (A) When a seller accepts a buyer's offer with no conditions.

Commissions are only earned after the seller has accepted an offer given by a willing and ready buyer.

(45) The correct answer is: (B) Shown his due diligence to ensure that this property is in good condition.

For the owner of the property to be eligible for innocent landowner immunity, he/she must have carried out due diligence to ensure that the property was in good condition when purchasing it.

(46) The correct answer is: (A) Steering.

Steering is an act that involves directing or failing to direct certain clients to an area with consideration to their race, sex, religion, national origin, familial status or handicap and this practice violates the Fair Housing Act.

(47) The correct answer is: (B) He should deposit it in his special account.

The broker is required to follow all the legal instructions given to him by the client. In cases where special instructions have not been given, the broker should immediately place the earnest money in a special account in the brokerage.

(48) The correct answer is: (A) It gives the optionor permission to carry out a purchase.

A seller is bound to pay a commission by a listing agreement while an offer simply refers to a proposal. An option can be referred to as a contract which allows a person to carry out a certain task such as purchasing property, but it does not necessarily represent ownership.

(49) The correct answer is: (A) The contract is void.

Since Sam is not mentally competent and he has an appointed guardian, the contract he has entered into is considered void. If he did not have a guardian appointed for him, he could enter into any contract.

(50) The correct answer is: (D) Contract.

A contract can be described as an agreement that is voluntarily made between competent parties with the aim to carry out or avoid certain legal acts.

Broker Test 3: Questions

(1) James, a broker, is preparing the 'Exclusive Authorization & Right to Sell' pertaining to John, who wants his property sold. John has requested that there be a clause added to indicate that the property buyer is to assume the major liability with regards to an existent loan. In fulfilling this request, James should insert the following clause in paragraph 2 _____.

(A)   Buyer taking over property possession 'subject to' loan liability

(B)   Buyer expected to 'assume' the loan liability

(C)   Buyer expected to pay entirely in cash

(D)   Buyer expected to pay a massive down payment so as to avoid the risk of foreclosure

(2) There is a mortgage payment arrangement where you make payments fortnightly, and at the end of the year you will have made 13 and not 12 payments, meaning your loan will clear faster. The term used for this arrangement is _____.

(A)   Bimonthly mortgage

(B)   Accelerating mortgage payment

(C)   Biweekly mortgage

(D)   None of the above

(3) Real property boundaries can be defined as _____.

(A)   Surface area represented on the map

(B)   Fair utilization of airspace that also extends to the earth's center

(C)   Fair distance beneath the earth and unlimited area within the airspace

(D)   Utilization of the earth in a practical way and unlimited use of the airspace

(4)For a homestead to be considered valid, which of the following is needed?

(A)   A statement indicating that the claimant resides within the particular premises and wishes to have it termed a homestead

(B)   A statement that indicates the precise amount the homestead cost to acquire

(C)   Description of the property that shows any improvements it has undergone

(D)   The signatures of the couple who own the property

(5)With regard to a piece of property that has not been listed anywhere for sale, if someone wishes to acquire it and proceeds to make an offer through a broker to whom he gives a $5,000 deposit, this broker _____.

(A)   Is permitted to receive the check on the property owner's behalf as long as he proceeds to present the given offer to the property seller directly; hence acting as the agent of the property seller.

(B)   Is not permitted to receive the check

(C)   Is permitted to receive the check when acting exclusively as the buyer's agent

(D)   None of the above

(6)Susan is selling her house and looks forward to moving into a new house, but that new house is yet to be completed. As such, Susan enters into an agreement with the person buying her house to allow her to continue staying in the house for some time after the sale has been sealed. That agreement is referred to as _____.

(A)   An agreement on lease without rent

(B)   An agreement for purchaser to delay possession

(C)   A sale leaseback

(D)   A single-year lease after closing

(7)An installment plan obligation of a financial nature is liquidated through _____.

(A) Conveyancing

(B) Amortization

(C) Conversion

(D) Acceleration

(8)Any agreement of an oral or written nature that is legally binding is referred to as _____.

(A) A promissory note

(B) A contract

(C) A gentleman's agreement

(D) A business deal

(9)If one of the parties involved in a real estate transaction offers to execute the part of the contract relevant to him/her, this offer is referred to as _____.

(A) Satisfaction

(B) Recourse

(C) Gratuity

(D) Tender

(10) A property buyer can use which of the following options as a genuine monetary deposit in the purchase of real estate property?

(A) A promissory note whose security is a trust deed

(B) A check that is postdated

(C) A promissory note that is unsecured

(D) All of the above

(11) A form is required to denote that a licensee in real estate is acting as agent to both the major parties—the seller and the buyer. That form is referred to as a/an _____.

(A) Statement of securities

(B) Exchange agreement

(C) Sale agreement

(D) Statement of the loan broker

(12) Which of the following choices pertains to an assessment?

(A) It puts a certain value on the property to facilitate a sale in real estate

(B) It means an analysis of a competitive market situation

(C) It puts a certain value on the property to facilitate taxation

(D) It is performed by the town mayor

(13) There are times when a property title ceases to be marketable. Which of the following has a minimal chance of leading to such an eventuality?

(A) A title being imperfect owing to a breach from a previous owner's adverse possession

(B) A lis pendens being filed by the record owner's husband

(C) Restrictions put in place by someone privately via a deed notation

(D) A public restriction that is within the zoning ordinances and building codes

(14) The party that decides what the property value is for the sake of taxation is referred to as the _____.

(A) Tax appraiser for government

(B) Assessor

(C) Appraiser

(D) All of the above

(15) Which of the following has the capacity to carry out conduit installation?

(A)   A carpenter

(B)   An electrician

(C)   A roofer

(D)   A plumber

(16) 'Note rate' is a term used in reference to _____.

(A)   A musician's rate of playing scales

(B)   Rate of interest as indicated on a mortgage note

(C)   Rate of interest as indicated on a personal loan

(D)   Amortization rate of a given note

(17) Among the real estate syndicates listed below, one requires 100 investors or more. Which is it?

(A)   A corporation

(B)   A limited partnership

(C)   A joint venture

(D)   A real estate investment trust

(18) A mortgagor pays for government or private mortgage insurance. This is referred to as a _____.

(A)   Mortgage insurance premium

(B)   VA insurance premium

(C)   Private mortgage insurance premium

(D)   FHA insurance premium

(19) Hussein is a real estate salesman, and after receiving a deposit and a well-written purchase offer from a client he delivers both of them to the broker under whom he works. The broker forwards the deposit and the offer to the property seller who then appends his signature and accepts the offer. Thereafter, without involving Hussein, the property buyer, together with the seller, instructs the broker to refund the deposit. Which of the following is correct about this scenario?

(A)   It is fine for the broker to retain half of the original deposit while leaving the other half with the property seller

(B)   The broker is required to give back the entire deposit but it is within his right to institute a legal suit against the property seller

(C)   It is fine for the broker to retain half of the original deposit while returning the other half to the potential property buyer

(D)   It is within the broker's right to retain the entire deposit as compensation for the effort he put into the transaction process

(20) Which of the following serves only minimally in protecting a residential area from blights that may affect potential development?

(A)   Barriers that are either natural or even artificial

(B)   A neighborhood that is only partially developed or built

(C)   An upcoming neighborhood within the path of the city's direction of growth

(D)   Families being within the same income group

(21) Which of the following is untrue regarding the word 'depreciation'?

(A)   It denotes a drop in the property value

(B)   It's used in matters of accounting to indicate a drop in an asset's value in monetary terms

(C)   It represents a real expense involving money spent

(D)   When the borrower is self-employed, the lender adds back the amount indicated as depreciation for inclusion in calculating income

(22) Any loan where the rate of interest does not vary over the loan repayment period is referred to as a/an_____ mortgage.

(A) Fixed rate

(B) Owner financing

(C) Marketable

(D) Conventional fixed rate

(23) Whenever a description of a legal nature makes use of sections and townships as well as ranges, those lines involved pertain to _____.

(A) Lines of survey used by government

(B) Descriptions of metes and bounds

(C) A tract map that has been recorded

(D) Contour lines

(24) There is a law for the protection of consumers that regulates consumer credit report disclosures by the agencies dealing with credit reporting. This law provides the procedures that are required to be followed in correcting any mistakes appearing on a person's credit report or record. This law is referred to as the _____.

(A) Truth as You Lend Act

(B) Fair Credit Reporting Act

(C) Credit Reporting Act

(D) Consumer Protection Act

(25) When a lender is speaking of the process followed in acquiring a fresh loan, he/she uses the term
_____.

(A) Lender's challenge

(B) Loan origination

(C) Product sale

(D) Borrower's feat

(26) Any time a person has not made a mortgage payment within a period of 30 days following the due
date, the particular mortgage is said to be in _____.

(A) A state of bankruptcy

(B) Default

(C) Trouble

(D) Arrears

(27) The type of loan people apply for when they visit a mortgage firm or a bank seeking to acquire a
home is referred to as a/an _____.

(A) Variable rate loan

(B) Conventional loan

(C) Government loan

(D) American loan

(28) When a veteran is eligible to receive a loan, the VA issues him/her with a document referred to as
a/an_____.

(A) Met requirements certificate

(B) Certificate of authenticity

(C) Approval certificate

(D) Certificate of eligibility

(29) A loan security issued in the form of real estate property depends on _____.

(A) The amount of credit being sought

(B) The property value

(C) Currency value and stability

(D) All of the above

(30) When the party lending money agrees to issue a loan against a particular real estate property, the borrower and the lender will _____.

(A) Declare a statement indicating the buyer and his/her property have passed inspection

(B) Become equal business partners

(C) Enter into a firm commitment

(D) Make the decision to have the loan issued

(31) When a property title search is carried out, _____ is confirmed as true.

(A) The person selling has legal ownership of the property

(B) Any claim to the property is of little monetary value

(C) The property was previously owned by a corporation

(D) The previous loan against the property was completed a year before

(32) The schedule showing the amount of money to be added to the principal loan and towards the interest amount over the period of the loan repayment is referred to as an _____.

(A) Amortization schedule

(B) Assumption

(C) Annual rate as a percentage

(D) None of the above

(33) When a certain amount of money is borrowed, referred to as the principal, and then it is repaid together with the interest levied on it, the term for this money is _____.

(A) Alternative form of mortgage

(B) A loan

(C) A form of conventional loan

(D) A mortgage

(34) When a property seller hires a broker, the expectation is that the broker will disclose to the principal all information that is significant or considered material. Which of the following options is material information that needs to be disclosed to the principal?

(A) The potential buyer comes from Asia

(B) There is a great likelihood of receiving another offer that is much better

(C) The lender will ultimately demand that an impound account be opened

(D) None of the above

(35) When a contract is being created, one of the elements listed below is not necessary. Which one is it?

(A) Consideration

(B) Acceptance

(C) Offer

(D) Performance

(36) Which of the following describes community property?

(A) Property which a whole condominium owns

(B) Property which a whole subdivision within single-family homes owns

(C) Property taken to be in joint ownership after spouses have acquired it in the course of their marriage

(D) None of the above

(37) Which of the following is normally considered a cost of home ownership?

(A) Amenity value

(B) Depreciation of land

(C) Appreciation from improvement

(D) Interest on owner's equity that gets lost

(38) Once mortgage ownership has been transferred to one party from another, be it a company or an individual, this is termed_____.

(A) Assumption

(B) Assignment

(C) Assessment

(D) None of the above

(39) When your insurance policy is a combination of personal liability and hazard insurance for your home and its belongings, the policy is termed _____.

(A) Homeowners insurance

(B) Insurance on errors and omissions

(C) Buyer's insurance

(D) None of the above

(40) _____ represents a right of way that accords other people who are not necessarily property owners the means to access a property.

(A)   Easement

(B)   Egress

(C)   Ingress

(D)   None of the above

(41)   Which of the following areas is largest?

(A)   5,280 by 10,560

(B)   Two sections

(C)   2 miles square

(D) $^1/_{10}$ of one township

(42)   One lumber piece is 2 x 12 x 24. How many board feet can you get from this piece of lumber?

(A)   98

(B)   48

(C)   72

(D)   36

(43)   If the lumber piece you have is 4 x 4 x 9, calculate the number of board feet you can get from it.

(A)   10

(B)   4

(C)   8

(D)   12

(44) Which of the following is true of a dual agency?

(A) It's not legal

(B) It requires utmost care

(C) The broker still works for a single principal

(D) It's impractical

(45) Bradshaw is an appraiser and the home he wants to begin appraising was constructed in 1912. Which of the following should Bradshaw use to start carrying out his appraisal?

(A) 1912's cost of living index

(B) The cost of the materials in 1912

(C) Cost of living index that has risen from 95 – 128

(D) Current reproduction cost minus depreciation

(46) Mary is a property owner within one project of cooperative apartments, and she continues to make payments on a monthly basis that cover the principal amount, interest, insurance and taxes. Which of the following is not true, based on this scenario?

(A) Mary should expect a personal tax bill separate from other owners' bills

(B) Costs incurred on the assessment bond will be shared among all property owners

(C) Mary can deduct her portion of taxes from her income when filing tax returns

(D) In case not all owners make payments, Mary can end up losing her equity during a foreclosure, the basis being the first trust deed

(47) _____ is the type of lien meant to cover all of a debtor's real properties.

(A) Blanket encumbrance

(B) General obligation

(C) General loan

(D) Specific lien

(48) If you act on behalf of two or more parties in a single transaction and you fail to disclose the fact to all the parties involved or to secure their consent, there is a penalty for that. What is that penalty?

(A)   License suspension or revocation

(B)   Increase in license fee

(C)   Inactivation of license

(D)   License restriction

(49) In a limited partnership, a general partner can be removed through written consent or a vote by the limited partners whose total shareholding has reached _____.

(A)   51%

(B)   60%

(C)   67%

(D)   75%

(50) When one person or party holds a piece of property on behalf of another, this is termed _____.

(A)   Joint tenancy

(B)   Leasehold

(C)   Trust

(D)   None of the above

Broker Test 3: Answers & Explanations

(1) The correct answer is: (B) Buyer expected to 'assume' the loan liability.

Whenever someone buys property that has a loan liability attached to it, he/she accepts being the person primarily responsible for the repayment of the loan.

(2) The correct answer is: (C) Biweekly mortgage.

This mortgage payment arrangement is referred to as a biweekly mortgage, where the prefix 'bi' means two.

(3) The correct answer is: (B) Fair utilization of airspace that also extends to the earth's center.

The area below the earth's surface up to the earth's center forms part of the owner's real property, in addition to the area on the earth's surface. As for the airspace; it is meant for public use, and so its use is limited to heights considered reasonable.

(4) The correct answer is: (A) A statement indicating that the claimant resides within the particular premises and wishes to have it termed a homestead.

If you want to file a homestead it is a requirement that you be residing on the premises during the time of filing, and that you append your signature to a statement which shows your wish to make the claim.

(5) The correct answer is: (C) Is permitted to receive the check when acting exclusively as the buyer's agent.

The broker accepts that check as the buyer's agent exclusively, with no listing at all with the property seller.

(6) The correct answer is: (C) A sale leaseback.

The term 'sale leaseback' is used in reference to a method used to have the seller transfer a property deed to the buyer in exchange for some consideration, while at the same time leasing that property from the buyer.

(7) The correct answer is: (B) Amortization.

The term 'amortization' is used in reference to the payment of the principal sum plus the interest accrued over the period the loan exists.

(8) The correct answer is: (B) A contract.

It is acceptable for a contract to be either written or oral, and it is recognized to be legally binding.

(9) The correct answer is: (D) Tender.

A tender is normally made right at the end of the transaction process, being an offer to fulfill the terms given or to which the party offering is in agreement. If other parties involved cannot fulfill the terms required, the party that presented the tender is in a position to assert that the other parties have defaulted.

(10) The correct answer is: (D) All of the above.

It is acceptable to make a deposit in the form of a secured or unsecured promissory note, or even a postdated check, as long as a disclosure of such a deposit is made to the property seller before the deposit has actually been accepted.

(11) The correct answer is: (B) Exchange agreement.

Under an exchange agreement, the licensee in real estate operates as the agent for both the buyer and seller, and there is a chance of earning a commission from both parties for the same transaction.

(12) The correct answer is: (C) It puts a certain value on the property to facilitate taxation.

When an assessment of real estate property is carried out, the purpose is to facilitate calculation of taxes.

(13) The correct answer is: (D) A public restriction that is within the zoning ordinances and building codes.

Restrictions of a public nature rarely lead to a title becoming unmarketable, unlike a private restriction that has a bigger chance of adversely affecting marketability.

(14)   The correct answer is: (B) Assessor.

An assessor is a public officer tasked with establishing the value of a given piece of property in order to facilitate taxation.

(15)   The correct answer is: (B) Electrician.

An electrician is qualified to place electrical wiring within a metallic pipe, known as a conduit.

(16)   The correct answer is: (B) Rate of interest as indicated one a mortgage note.

The term 'note rate' is used in reference to a rate of interest as indicated on a given mortgage note.

(17)   The correct answer is: (D) A real estate investment trust.

A real estate investment trust happens to be established under federal law, and the investors involved go up to 100 and sometimes beyond.

(18)   The correct answer is: (A) Mortgage insurance premium.

A government agency like the Federal Housing Administration, or a private mortgage firm like the Mortgage Insurance Company, receives money meant to cover mortgage insurance in the form of mortgage insurance premiums from mortgagors.

(19)   The correct answer is: (B) The broker is required to give back the entire deposit but it is within his right to institute a legal suit against the property seller.

The moment the property seller accepts the offer, the deposit becomes his. However, because the broker will have earned a commission, if the seller subsequently decides the deposit should be returned, the broker can sue him to the extent of that commission even as he refunds the entire deposit.

(20)   The correct answer is: (B) A neighborhood that is only partially developed or built.

For a neighborhood that is only partially developed, blighting is a definite possibility considering how likely it is for vandalism to take place on the incomplete buildings.

(21) The correct answer is: (C) It represents a real expense involving money spent.

The term 'depreciation' does not represent a true monetary expense and is only an indication of how far the property value may have declined.

(22) The correct answer is: (A) Fixed rate.

Any loan where the loan interest remains unchanged over the full period the loan is being paid is termed a 'fixed-rate mortgage.'

(23) The correct answer is: (A) Lines of survey used by government.

Sections and townships as well as ranges are made use of as the government conducts its surveys to provide descriptions for land locations. Metes and bounds provide a general description of a given area.

(24) The correct answer is: (B) Fair Credit Reporting Act.

This Fair Credit Reporting Act legally protects consumers by regulating the disclosures made by credit reporting firms, and by providing procedures to be adhered to when rectifying mistakes reflecting on a person's credit report or record.

(25) The correct answer is: (B) Loan origination.

The appropriate term used by a lender in reference to issuance of a loan that is entirely new is 'loan origination.'

(26) The correct answer is: (B) Default.

A mortgage or loan is said to be in default if the borrower fails to pay any installment within 30 days of the due date, or within any other specified time.

(27) The correct answer is: (B) Conventional loan.

Any loan that does not fall under either the FHA or VA is termed conventional.

(28) The correct answer is: (D) Certificate of eligibility.

A certificate of eligibility is a document the Veterans Administration issues to any veteran who is eligible for a loan as per the VA.

(29) The correct answer is: (B) The property value.

Since the real estate property serves as security against the loan being advanced, it matters what the property's value is at the time of borrowing.

(30) The correct answer is: (C) Enter into a firm commitment.

When there is a lender's agreement giving assent to loan issuance to a specified borrower and against a specified piece of property, the agreement is said to be a 'firm commitment.'

(31) The correct answer is: (A) The person selling has legal ownership of the property.

Title searches are used to establish legal ownership of the property, among other things such as ensuring the property doesn't have any liens against it.

(32) The correct answer is: (A) Amortization schedule.

The term 'amortization schedule' is used in reference to a particular table that shows the proportion of every payment that goes towards payment of the principal and interest. It also shows the decline in the loan until this is zeroed out.

(33) The correct answer is: (B) A loan.

Simply speaking, any money borrowed and expected to be repaid with some interest on it is a loan.

(34) The correct answer is: (B) There is a great likelihood of receiving another offer that is much better.

The likelihood that an offer that is better than the current one is in the offing can have an impact on the decision the property seller is about to make. As such, it is imperative that the broker discloses the information to the seller before he/she makes any serious decisions.

(35)   The correct answer is: (D) Performance.

The fact that two different parties are bound by a contract does not guarantee performance or fulfillment of the obligations each of them has. On the contrary, for a contract to be effective, the other three elements of offer, acceptance and consideration must be present.

(36)   The correct answer is: (C) Property taken to be in joint ownership after spouses have acquired it in the course of their marriage.

'Community property' is one a couple has acquired in their relationship as a couple.

(37)   The correct answer is: (D) Interest on owner's equity that gets lost.

The interest on owner's equity ends up getting lost because the property owner cannot make use of those funds for the sake of investment. That particular interest is termed 'lock-in' equity.

(38)   The correct answer is: (B) Assignment.

To say mortgage ownership has been transferred to a different party actually means it has been assigned to a different party, hence the term 'assignment.'

(39)   The correct answer is: (A) Homeowners insurance.

Homeowners insurance is a combination of insurance on personal liability and hazard coverage of your dwelling and whatever is in it.

(40)   The correct answer is: (A) Easement.

Easement legally provides people who are not property-owners access to the property, otherwise termed 'right of way,'

(41)   The correct answer is: (C) 2 miles square.

2 miles square means that every side is 2 miles long, and so the area formed is 4 square miles. Option (A) is equivalent to 2 square miles, option (B) the same and option (D) is equivalent to 3.6 sq mi.

(42)   The correct answer is: (B) 48.

2 x 12 x 24 is the same as 2 x 12 x 288. To get 288, 24 is multiplied by 12. To get the board feet possible, you need to divide the length by 144, meaning 6,912÷144, which is 48.

(43)   The correct answer is: (D) 12.

You need to convert feet into inches so you can work with like terms: 4" x 4" x (9' x 12) or 4" x 4" x 108", and then divide the product with 144. 1,728÷144 = 12.

(44)   The correct answer is: (B) It requires utmost care.

If a listing broker begins to act on behalf of a potential buyer, he/she assumes the role of dual agency because by listing a property, he/she has already become that owner's agent. The broker therefore has to be very careful to ensure fairness to both the seller and the buyer.

(45)   The correct answer is: (D) Current reproduction cost minus depreciation.

The appraiser's best method is the approach that uses the reproduction cost and then takes into account the depreciation which has accrued during the life of the structure.

(46)   The correct answer is: (A) Mary should expect a personal tax bill separate from other owners' bills.

Mary is a tenant in common and should not expect a separate tax bill. A single tax bill is received by the manager and he/she prorates the amounts to individual unit owners.

(47)   The correct answer is: (A) Blanket encumbrance.

Examples of 'blanket encumbrance' include blanket mortgages and blanket trust deeds.

(48)   The correct answer is: (A) License suspension or revocation.

The penalty of a license suspension or revocation is imposed because you will have violated your fiduciary duty to make relevant disclosures to the parties for whom you are acting.

(49) The correct answer is: (A) 51%.

Only a simple majority is required to remove a general partner in a limited partnership.

(50) The correct answer is: (C) Trust.

A broker sometimes holds money in trust for his/her client, and it is important that such money be deposited in a trust account.

Broker Test 4: Questions

(1) Without considering taxes, selling costs or any other costs, how much money will a seller pay for a piece of land selling at $163,000 if the land appreciates at 14% compounded yearly and the property seller decides to keep it for a total of seven years?

(A) $70,500

(B) $65,000

(C) $55,000

(D) $72,000

(2) The Smiths sold their residential house and the deal is set to close on July 1. Which statement accurately explains what will happen at closing if they fully paid their yearly town taxes at the beginning of the year?

(A)   The Smiths will owe their buyer the tax due

(B)   The buyer will owe them the tax from the remaining part of the year

(C)   The Smiths will owe their buyer half of that tax due

(D)   Nothing will happen

(3) Andrew is John's grantee to a deed. He signs the deed and gets it acknowledged, then receives a payment from him. The next day, Andrew plans a meeting with John where he hands over the title of the deed to him. At what stage does John become the owner of that property?

(A)   After he records that deed

(B)   Immediately, since he has made the payment

(C)   As soon as he signs that deed

(D)   The next day when he receives his copy of the deed

(4)How does the Section 8 program of the Federal Housing Administration help low- to moderate-income earners?

(A)   It partly pays their rent

(B)   It insures their mortgage loan

(C)   It pays off their mortgage loan

(D)   It pays the maintenance cost on their purchased homes

(5)According to coinsurance clauses, how much of a structure's replacement value should be covered with fire insurance?

(A)   80%

(B)   50%

(C)   60%

(D)   70%

(6)Under what clause of a deed can you find the metes and bounds and monuments of the property?

(A)   The defense clause

(B)   The demising clause

(C)   The habendum clause

(D)   The description clause

(7)When is a deed valid?

(A)   After it's signed

(B)   After it's recorded

(C)   After it's delivered and accepted

(D)   After it's notarized

(8) Milly has just joined a brokerage firm after receiving her salesperson's license. What title is she likely to hold for tax reasons?

(A) Salaried employee

(B) Realtor

(C) Associate broker

(D) Independent contractor

(9) What are license laws in real estate designed to do?

(A) Raise operating revenue and tax for local and state governments

(B) Ensure that the market is not flooded with salespersons and brokers

(C) Maintain high market standards and protect people

(D) Match the requirements of the federal government

(10) When a buyer retains a broker, what should the broker owe the seller?

(A) Undivided loyalty

(B) Honest and straightforward treatment

(C) Obedience to all lawful instructions

(D) Confidentiality regarding the seller's financial situation

(11) Which of the following information should a seller's broker disclose to the prospective buyer?

(A) That the seller has HIV

(B) That the house is haunted

(C) That the previous owner was killed in the house

(D) That the heating system is faulty

(12) Steve wanted to purchase Sam's home and so he used Nancy as his agent. He sent her with a purchase offer that had a time limit of 48 hours in which Sam was supposed to accept the offer. Sam rejected his offer after 36 hours. Which of the following is true?

(A) The offer was terminated the minute that Sam rejected it

(B) The offer is still valid since Sam changed his decision before the 48-hour deadline

(C) The offer is still valid since Steve has not withdrawn his offer formally

(D) Since Sam has accepted Steve's offer, they have a binding contract

(13) John is a broker and he has sent an offer to Bridget, an agent. The offer made by his client is a purchase offer for a 300-acre piece of land for $500,000, two farming machines and 300 goats. The consideration that is offered is _____.

(A) Inadequate

(B) Good

(C) Valuable

(D) Valuable and good

(14) What determines how much commission brokers should give their agents?

(A) The National Association of Realtors dictates commissions

(B) The federal law dictates commissions

(C) The commission should be split equally between the agent and the broker

(D) The agent and the broker should negotiate between themselves

(15)   What do we call a listing agreement where the principal has listed his property with several brokers?

(A)   A Net listing

(B)   An exclusive agency

(C)   An exclusive right-to-sell

(D)   An open listing

(16)   An agreement between two parties that is demonstrated through their conduct and actions is called a/an _____ contract.

(A)   Implied

(B)   Express

(C)   Unilateral

(D)   Voidable

(17)   Which kind of loan is not insured by the Federal Housing Administration to facilitate housing?

(A)   A construction loan

(B)   A nursing home mortgage loan

(C)   A mobile home loan

(D)   A multifamily housing loan

(18)   Which term best describes a mortgage that requires you to pay a large principal payment at the end?

(A)   An open mortgage

(B)   A blanket mortgage

(C)   A variable-rate mortgage

(D)   A balloon mortgage

(19)   What must a seller's minimum sales price be if he wants his net amount to be $362,000 after paying his broker a 6% commission?

(A) $364,208

(B) $332,180

(C) $385,106

(D) $371,280

(20)   How much money will a broker receive if he gets a 7% commission from selling a home that was worth $750,000?

(A) $52,500

(B) $45,000

(C) $26,250

(D) $5,250

(21)   Which of the following valuation approaches is used to appraise single-use properties when there are no comparable properties on sale to compare to?

(A)   Cap rate approach

(B)   Anticipation factor

(C)   Cost approach

(D)   Income approach

(22)   According to the Real Estate Settlement Procedures Act, agents are not allowed to pay unearned fees or kickbacks. However, the act does not prohibit _____.

(A)   Brokerage referral fees

(B)   Paying fees to moving companies

(C)   Paying fees to furniture suppliers

(D)   Receiving referral fees from insurance agents

(23) When is it necessary for a notary to acknowledge a signature on a deed?

(A) Before the payment of transfer tax

(B) Before the deed is recorded

(C) When the deed needs to be made valid

(D) When giving notification of the deed's transfer

(24) Beatrice was looking at some vacant houses in an apartment where she was interested in becoming a tenant when she accidentally slipped and fell. Which insurance plan belonging to the property's owner will cover the expenses Beatrice incurred due to her injuries sustained in the fall?

(A) Liability insurance

(B) Casualty insurance

(C) Contents and personal property insurance

(D) Fire and hazard insurance

(25) There are six categories in real property and these are commercial, residential, special purpose, agricultural, industrial and _____.

(A) Multifamily

(B) Mixed use

(C) Farmland

(D) Government property

(26) Under what circumstance is private mortgage insurance required in a conventional loan?

(A) When loan-to-value amounts are more than 80%

(B) When providing conforming loans

(C) When loan-to-value amounts are lower than 80%

(D) When giving interest-only loans

(27) Which of the following instruments is used as security when repaying home loans?

(A) Lease

(B) Bond

(C) Mortgage

(D) Deed

(28) Calculate Liz's profit rate if she bought a house at $330,000 and later sold it at $425,000.

(A) 78.78%

(B) 28.78%

(C) 21.21%

(D) 61.32%

(29) Calculate the commission rate that a broker charged if he made $30,800 from the sale of a house that was bought for $385,000.

(A) 10%

(B) 8%

(C) 14%

(D) 8.5%

(30) Calculate the value estimate of a building if its gross income is $122,000 and the operating expenses amount to $70,000 with a capitalization rate of 10%.

(A) $420,000

(B) $520,000

(C) $720,000

(D) $1,220,000

(31) There are several forces that affect the value of real estate. Both deed restrictions and zoning fall under one of these forces. Which of the following is that force?

(A) Political-governmental-legal

(B) Sociological

(C) Physical and environmental

(D) Economic-financial

(32) Brian sold a piece of land to Kevin but Kevin has yet to clear the outstanding balance they had agreed upon. Which of these can Brian use to obtain payment if Kevin fails to pay the arrears?

(A) A vendor's lien

(B) A mortgage lien

(C) A vendee's lien

(D) A lis pendens

(33) Property managers are tasked with maintaining a property's value while _____.

(A) Maximizing occupancy

(B) Minimizing turnover

(C) Minimizing the capital expenses

(D) Maximizing income

(34) What is curb appeal?

(A) How a property appears externally

(B) The drainage and sewer systems found along the property

(C) The state of the streets and curbs along the property

(D) The square footage that is usable on the property

(35) A deed is used to _____.

(A) Pledge property to use as collateral when taking out mortgage loans

(B) Remove vendors' liens from the property

(C) Convey the ownership of property from one party to another

(D) Acknowledge contractual agreements

(36) Which is the highest kind of ownership in the real property market?

(A) Life estate

(B) Fee simple

(C) Leasehold

(D) Qualified fee

(37) What type of agency is an agent engaged in when he/she represents the purchaser instead of the property seller?

(A) Good faith

(B) Buyer protection

(C) Seller protection

(D) Buyer agency

(38) Charity has listed her house with Stella, who is a licensed broker, and has also offered $500 as a bonus commission to whoever brings in the right buyer before August. Richard, who is also a licensed agent, is associated with a firm owned by Mr. Smith and he manages to make the sale by July 1. Who receives the promised broker commission?

(A) Mr. Smith

(B) Stella

(C) Richard

(D) None of the above

(39) Kate has just gotten an offer for her seller client but she believes that her client will not seriously consider the offer since it is 15% lower than the amount on the listing. What should this licensed broker do?

(A) Persuade the prospective buyer to raise his offer

(B) Try and convince the prospective buyer not to make that offer

(C) Submit the offer to her client

(D) Wait for more offers and then present them together

(40) If a buyer wants to sue a broker on the grounds of misrepresentation, he/she must be in a position to prove _____.

(A) That the misinformation was documented

(B) That the seller was aware of the misleading statement

(C) That the buyer requested verification of the information from the broker

(D) That the buyer incurred damages as a result of the misinformation

(41) Which of these advertisements is acceptable according to the standards of HUD?

(A) Traditional living

(B) Senior housing

(C) A bachelor community

(D) An exclusive neighborhood

(42) Which of the characteristics listed below is not associated with easement?

(A) Interest that a third party cannot interfere with

(B) The capacity to be created through conveyance

(C) Interest that is not possessory

(D) Interest that the land processor can terminate if he/she wishes

(43) A judgment abstract for an amount of cash that a court has awarded is recorded within the county that the judgment debtor's property is situated in. This becomes a/an _____.

(A) Involuntary lien

(B) Voluntary lien

(C) Attachment lien

(D) Equitable lien

(44) 'Periodic rate cap' is a term used in reference to _____.

(A) A rate of mortgage that is adjustable

(B) A limit that indicates the extent to which a hike or reduction in rate of interest can be effected in a single period of adjustment

(C) A conventional loan that has a fixed rate

(D) A limit that indicates the extent to which a hike or reduction in rate of interest can be made in a single period of adjustment, which also means the rate of mortgage is adjustable

(45) One characteristic that makes an option in real estate distinct from a sales contract of a conventional nature is ____.

(A) Its obligation lacks mutuality

(B) It is irrevocable

(C) Its contract has mutuality

(D) Not only is it irrevocable but its obligation lacks mutuality

(46) There is justification for hiring a property management specialist _____.

(A) When the property owner is absent

(B) Owing to advances in technology involving building-related concepts

(C) When there are more vacancies than normal

(D) Due to urbanization

(47) If you decide to purchase property that another person on the property title has a loan on, the particular person with the obligation is referred to as _____.

(A)   A spouse

(B)   A friend ready to share the property and down payment with you

(C)   A co-borrower

(D)   None of the above

(48) The main factor that justifies zoning ordinances is _____.

(A)   Their capacity to enhance conformity in how structures look externally

(B)   Their capacity to limit particular businesses in the area that has been zoned

(C)   Their capacity to enhance the community's health, safety and general welfare

(D)   Their capacity to widen the formal tax base for the local authority

(49) A lender must consider _____ when undertaking risk management of any property portfolio.

(A)   How diversified the portfolio is

(B)   The state of liquidity

(C)   The level of reserves

(D)   Portfolio diversification, liquidity and reserve level.

(50) Which of the following is true of condominiums?

(A)   They are about ownership and not construction or development

(B)   All owners have a right to everyone else's interior units

(C)   They are about ownership, with the property owners having rights not only to their respective properties but also to the common areas together.

(D)   They are about ownership and not construction or development, with the property owners having rights not only to their respective properties but also to the common areas together.

Broker Test 4: Answers & Explanations

(1) The correct answer is: (B) $65,000.

When we use V=P (1+r/n)^nt as our formula, whereby V is the investment's future value, which is $163,000; P is the principal investment; r is the yearly interest rate, which is 14%; n is the total compounding time; and t is the years invested, which is 7 years. We get P. $163,000=P(1+0.14/1)^1×7, which is $65,000.

(2) The correct answer is: (B) The buyer will owe them the tax from the remaining part of that year.

When closing, the buyer will refund the property taxes that were paid in advance by the Smiths.

(3) The correct answer is: (D) The next day when he receives his deed.

Once the deed has been delivered and accepted, the property becomes rightfully owned by the deed holder.

(4) The correct answer is: (A) It partially pays their rent.

The Federal Housing Administration's Section 8 program helps to partially pay the rent of low- to moderate-income earners.

(5) The correct answer is: (A) 80%

Insurance policies have coinsurance clauses which state that at least 80% of the replacement value of a building should be covered.

(6) The correct answer is: (D) The description clause.

In deeds, the description clause provides the metes and bounds and monuments of property and this legal description of the real estate can be presented in a court of law.

(7) The correct answer is: (C) After it's delivered and accepted.

After the grantor delivers the deed, the grantee accepts it and the transfer of the title takes place.

(8)The correct answer is: (D) Independent contractor.

According to a survey conducted by the National Association of Realtors, in 90% of real estate companies, sales associates are treated as independent contractors to avoid the bookkeeping that comes with social security payments, withholding taxes and unemployment insurance.

(9)The correct answer is: (C) Maintain high market standards and protect people.

The role of real estate license laws is to protect people from dishonest and incompetent salespersons and brokers and maintain a high standard in the industry.

(10) The correct answer is: (B) Honest and straightforward treatment.

When a broker is retained by a buyer, he should provide honest and straightforward treatment to the prospective seller.

(11) The correct answer is: (D) That the heating system is faulty.

The broker has a responsibility to the prospective buyer to inform him of latent defects such as a faulty heating system but he should not disclose facts that can stigmatize the seller or the property.

(12) The correct answer is: (A) The offer was terminated the minute that Sam rejected it.

An offer is automatically terminated once it is rejected and it does not need to be revoked or formally withdrawn. Termination can also occur when an offer reaches its expiration date, when a counteroffer is accepted or when either the offeree or offeror dies.

(13) The correct answer is: (C) Valuable.

Contracts are usually bound by consideration which is offered to a party in order to induce it into entering a contract. Anything that is valuable such as goods, money, property exchange, personal services or a promise to produce or deliver valuable items is termed valuable consideration.

(14) The correct answer is: (D) The agent and the broker should negotiate between themselves.

The broker and the agent should negotiate among themselves and decide how to share the commission.

(15)   The correct answer is: (D) An open listing.

An open listing allows the principal to list his property for sale with several brokers and only pay a commission to the broker who successfully procures a willing, able and ready buyer.

(16)   The correct answer is: (A) Implied.

Implied contracts are characterized by the parties demonstrating their commitment through their conduct or actions.

(17)   The correct answer is: (A) Construction loans.

The Federal Housing Administration does not provide insurance for construction loans.

(18)   The correct answer is: (D) A balloon mortgage.

In balloon mortgages, the final payment usually consists of a larger amount than what you have been paying in the previous installments on your loan. This type of loan is not fully amortized.

(19)   The correct answer is: (C) $385,106.

The seller is left with 94% of the proceeds from the sale after paying a 6% commission to the brokerage firm. When you divide $362,000, which is the net amount, by 0.94, which is the final sale proceeds, you will get $385,106, and that is the minimum sales price.

(20)   The correct answer is: (A) $52,500.

For you to know how much the broker received in commission you should multiply the figure given as the sales amount by 7%. So $750,000 $\times$ 0.007 will give you $52,500.

(21)   The correct answer is: (C) Cost approach.

We use cost approach to determine appraisal in cases where a single-purpose property has very few or no comparable properties to use.

(22) The correct answer is: (A) Brokerage referral fees.

The Real Estate Settlement Procedures Act prohibits payment of unearned fees and kickbacks but it doesn't prohibit a brokerage referral fee.

(23) The correct answer is: (B) Before the deed is recorded.

Before recording mortgages, deeds or any documents of a similar nature, they must first be acknowledged.

(24) The correct answer is: (A) Liability insurance.

Public liability insurance is used to cover any risk that the property owner assumes once people are in the building. These risks may include medical expenses incurred when a person is injured inside the building as a result of a landlord's negligence.

(25) The correct answer is: (B) Mixed use.

The six categories of real estate are commercial, residential, special purpose, agricultural, mixed use and industrial.

(26) The correct answer is: (A) When loan-to-value amounts are more than 80%.

PMI is needed when a loan amount is more than 80% of the value of the property after appraisal or more than 80% of the selling price of that property, whichever one has a lower amount. A high loan-to-value amount translates to a higher PMI cost.

(27) The correct answer is: (C) Mortgage.

The borrower gives the lender a mortgage pledge which acts as security or collateral for the loan.

(28) The correct answer is: (B) 28.78%.

First we need to know how much profit Liz made from the sale so we subtract the selling price, which is $425,000, from the buying price, which is $330,000. So $425,000 - $330,000 = $95,000. To get the percentage, take the total profit and divide it by the buying price, then multiply by 100. So, $95,000 ÷ 330,000 × 100 is 28.78%.

(29) The correct answer is: (B) 8%.

To get the commission rate you need to divide the indicated commission received, which was $30,800, by the sales price, which was $385,000, then multiply by 100. So $30,800 ÷ $385,000 × 100 will give you 8%.

(30) The correct answer is: (B) $520,000.

In this case, you need to first calculate the net income, which is the gross income minus the operating expenses. So, $122,000 - $70,000 will give you $52,000. Once you have your net income, divide it by 10% to get $520,000.

(31) The correct answer is: (C) Physical and environmental.

Some of the physical and environmental factors include shape, dimension, topography, area and drainage, as well as soil conditions. Utilities, streets, sidewalks, curbs, gutters and landscaping are also part of physical and environmental forces.

(32) The correct answer is: (A) A vendor's lien.

The vendor's lien should be used by the seller to claim the unpaid amount that was agreed upon during the purchase.

(33) The correct answer is: (D) Maximizing income.

Property managers should maintain the property's value and also maximize income.

(34) The correct answer is: (A) How a property appears externally.

Curb appeal is the appearance that a property has externally.

(35) The correct answer is: (C) To convey the ownership of property from one party to another.

Deeds are used to convey the ownership of property from one party to another. This written instrument is used by the owner of a real estate to convey a title, interest or right in a piece of real property.

(36) The correct answer is: (B) Fee simple.

Fee simple is the highest form of ownership found in real property since the owner has all the rights to his/her property.

(37) The correct answer is: (D) Buyer agency.

In real estate, the term agency is used to mean representation. In such a case, the buyer is the principal and he gives legal rights to his agent, who is supposed to act in place of the buyer when working with the third party, who is the seller.

(38) The correct answer is: (A) Mr. Smith.

Like many salespersons, Richard is likely to accept commissions only from his supervising broker.

(39) The correct answer is: (C) Submit the offer to her client.

An agent is required to submit all offers immediately to the client or principal.

(40) The correct answer is: (D) That the buyer incurred damages as a result of the misinformation.

For a buyer to build a successful suit against a broker on the grounds of misrepresentation, he must show proof that damages were caused by the misinformation.

(41) The correct answer is: (B) Senior housing.

Words that imply discrimination by race, color, religion, familial status, national origin, sex or handicap are unacceptable. Other words such as restrictive, exclusive, board-approved and traditional are also considered to be discriminatory according to HUD standards.

(42) The correct answer is: (D) Interest that the land processor can terminate if he/she wishes.

The land possessor is the person who owns the particular piece of land, and when it comes to easement, he/she does not have the capacity to terminate it on a whim.

(43) The correct answer is: (A) Involuntary lien.

The term 'lien' is used in reference to an encumbrance in monetary value. You can, for example, have an encumbrance put on a property even when the property owner has not provided consent, which means such a lien would be involuntary.

(44)   The correct answer is: (D) A limit that indicates the extent to which a hike or reduction in rate of interest can be made in a single period of adjustment, which also means the rate of mortgage is adjustable.

Whether the index provided is high or low, when there is a rate of mortgage that is adjustable, the limit stipulated as the amount of interest that can be added or reduced in one period of adjustment is referred to as the 'periodic rate cap.'

(45)   The correct answer is: (A) Its obligation lacks mutuality.

When it comes to an option in real estate, just a single party is bound, with the optionee having the full right to make the purchase or reject it.

(46)   The correct answer is: (A) when the property owner is absent.

A property owner is considered absent if he/she does not live within the property, or is not close enough to properly manage its supervision.

(47)   The correct answer is: (C) A co-borrower.

Whenever there is someone else on the property title that has a loan against it, once you purchase that property that person is referred to as 'co-borrower.'

(48)   The correct answer is: (C) Their capacity to enhance the community's health, safety and general welfare.

It is a prerequisite before any zoning ordinance can be legally enacted that it be confirmed as something that will enhance the community's health and safety as well as its general welfare.

(49) The correct answer is: (D) Portfolio diversification, liquidity and reserve level.

A lender must always consider the category of loans within the portfolio, and also take into account how fast it can take to sell out the loans, the reserves available, how diversified the loans are, whether all the loans are business-related, residential or a mix of both.

(50) The correct answer is: (D) They are about ownership and not construction or development, with the property owners having rights not only to their respective properties but also to the common areas together.

Where condominiums are concerned, the property owners collectively own the common areas and the entire building, and the only part they do not own collectively is each owner's interior side of the housing unit. In short, condominiums are not construction types but ownership types.

Salesperson Test 1: Questions

(1) What do we call personal property which is attached to real property in such a way that it is considered to be real estate?

(A)   A fixture

(B)   An appliance

(C)   Personalty

(D)   An emblement

(2) Which of the following gives the correct description of the economic and physical qualities of real property?

(A)   Unique, abundant, indestructible and immovable

(B)   Immovable, unique, scarce and indestructible

(C)   Indestructible, movable, unique and scarce

(D)   Scarce, unique, indestructible and depreciable

(3) What type of interest does a property owner who has full control over the property and an indefeasible title have in that property?

(A)   Life estate

(B)   Fee conditional estate

(C)   Defeasible fee estate

(D)   Fee simple estate

(4)John and Smith own contiguous properties that sit on the shores of a river and John's property is located upstream from Smith's property. Over the years, dirt and silt from the shore where John's property is situated has been deposited downstream on Smith's property. Which of the following describes what is happening on Smith's property?

(A)   Accession, standing water and littoral

(B)   Alienation, alluvium and attachment

(C)   Accession, accretion and alluvium

(D)   Assemblage, increased value and plottage

(5)What is the difference between a property's value and the sum total of liens attached to that property?

(A)   Down payment

(B)   Equity

(C)   Bases

(D)   Investment

(6)Lisa is the life tenant in a residential home that she owns under a life estate agreement and her niece Amanda is her remainderman. Which of the following is correct if Lisa decides to use the residential home as collateral for a loan?

(A)   Amanda's signature on loan documents will not help to secure the interests of the lender

(B)   Lisa holds non-freehold estate since she is the life tenant

(C)   It will not be possible to find a lender since the collateral being used is property that is held under a life estate agreement

(D)   Both Lisa and Amanda will have to sign the loan documents which will protect the security interests of the lender

(7)A few months ago, four different real estate properties were sold by different owners. One of the properties was sold by an investment company to the state; the second one was held by three brothers who conveyed ownership to their mother; while the third piece of real estate was held by three corporations until two of those corporations sold their ownership to the remaining one. Finally, the last piece of real estate was held by a couple who sold it to a businesswoman. What is the common characteristic shared among these buyers?

(A)   Ownership in severalty

(B)   Right of survivorship

(C)   Concurrent ownership

(D)   Fractional yet undivided ownership

(8)Which of the following statements is true about the metes and bounds system?

(A)   It must start and end at a given point

(B)   The system can only be used in areas that are not included in the rectangular survey system

(C)   It is not allowed in courts in many jurisdictions

(D)   It is only used in cases where a recorded subdivision plat is not available

(9)Your neighbor walks through your property in order to get to his house which sits on his own property. To correct this issue, you consult your attorney on how to prevent your neighbor from accessing your property but the attorney informs you that your neighbor has an easement appurtenant right included in his ownership that allows him to use a certain part of the property. Your property can be referred to as the _____.

(A)   Servient tenement

(B)   Leasehold interest

(C)   License property

(D)   Dominant tenement

(10) Mr. Thompson owned a large piece of land which he then divided into two parcels. The southern parcel is situated to the south of the northern parcel and the only available road in that area borders the southern parcel. To prevent the northern parcel from being landlocked after selling the southern parcel, Mr. Thompson kept a nonexclusive easement that granted him ingress and egress rights over the southern parcel. A few years later both pieces were bought by new owners and the owner of the southern parcel fenced his parcel, which barred the owner of the southern parcel from having access. In a court case between the two new owners, which argument would stand a winning chance?

(A) It's not possible for an easement appurtenant to be terminated by a servient tenement and so the holder of the northern parcel would win

(B) It's not possible for an easement in gross to be brought to an end by a servient tenement and so the holder of the northern parcel would win

(C) Since there is only one access road, the easement is an easement by necessity and so the holder of the northern parcel would win

(D) Excluding non-owners from accessing your property is an important property ownership right and so the owner of the southern parcel would win

(11) The county government wanted to widen a highway and this meant that it would have to demolish some residential houses as well as commercial properties. After legal proceedings, they began to demolish the earmarked properties but some residents refused to relocate to the point that one elderly lady had to be dragged out of her home where she had lived for years. What do we call this kind of government power?

(A) Police power

(B) Condemnation

(C) Escheat

(D) Eminent domain

(12) You cannot find any statewide or nationwide zoning laws. Is this statement true or false?

(A) False

(B) True

(C) It is true only sometimes

(D) It used to be true in the 1940s but not today

(13) What is the name given to the discriminatory and illegal practice that persuades a person to sell his real estate after he has been convinced by another that the market value in the neighborhood is set to decline because members of a certain protected class have bought property in the neighborhood?

(A)   Redlining

(B)   Blockbusting

(C)   Neighborhood canvassing

(D)   Boycotting

(14) Police power is mainly used to _____.

(A)   Extinguish fire

(B)   Prevent civilians from participating in criminal activities

(C)   Protect the safety, welfare and health of the entire community

(D)   Ensure that citizens and property owners know their rightful place

(15) Which of the following statements explains the differences between a general lien and a specific lien?

(A)   Specific liens require collateral while general liens do not

(B)   General liens require collateral while specific liens do not

(C)   You can secure specific liens using collective assets but you can only secure general liens using a specific asset

(D)   Specific liens can be secured using a specific asset while general liens can be secured using collective assets

(16) Brooke Williams has decided to sell her three-bedroom house and has entered into an agreement with one of the local licensees in the state. This written agreement is an exclusive right-to-sell listing agreement. Which of the following terms correctly describes the type of agency created?

(A) General agency

(B) Express agency

(C) Implied agency

(D) Universal agency

(17) Which of the following does not represent an agency relationship?

(A) A real estate broker and seller relationship

(B) An attorney and client relationship

(C) A listing broker and seller relationship

(D) A real estate salesperson and buyer relationship

(18) According to real estate brokerage firms, what does the company dollar stand for?

(A) Sect 1031 tax-deferred exchanges

(B) Office exchanges that are divided among brokerage associates

(C) The brokerage firm's income before deducting licensee commissions

(D) The brokerage firm's income after deducting licensee commissions

(19) The nonrefundable fee that a broker receives from a seller to cover advertisement costs after signing the listing is a trust fund referred to as an advance fee. Is this statement true or false?

(A) False

(B) True

(C) It depends on the term the broker prefers

(D) It depends on the term the broker and seller agree on

(20) The listing agreement between a real estate licensee and the seller of a prime property in a prestigious neighborhood is a type of bilateral contract which includes a defined end date. If the seller finds a buyer, then the licensee shall not receive any commission. This listing agreement is referred to as _____.

(A) Exclusive agency

(B) Exclusive right-to-sell

(C) Exclusive right-to-buy

(D) Open

(21) What do you call a listing whereby the seller lists his property with three different brokerage firms and agrees to pay a commission to the agency that will find an able, willing and ready buyer?

(A) An MLS listing

(B) An exclusive agency listing

(C) An open listing

(D) An exclusive right-to-sell listing

(22) A land owner and a willing buyer have entered into a documented agreement that states that the buyer pays the land owner a nonrefundable amount of money and in exchange the land owner holds the property for the buyer for an agreed time. If that buyer buys the land, the two parties have an agreed-upon purchase price and if the buyer fails to buy the land then the land owner retains the fee received when signing the contract. What is the name given to this kind of contractual agreement?

(A) Unenforceable contract

(B) Bilateral contract

(C) Option contract

(D) Purchase contract

(23) What is the law used in all the states that mandates that a real estate sale contract, or a contract that states an interest in the real estate, is not enforceable unless the contract is written and bears the signatures of both parties?

(A) The statute of frauds

(B) The statute of limitations

(C) The statute of estoppels

(D) The statute of real estate

(24) A wealthy businesswoman owned a large piece of land that she planned to leave to her daughter after her death. She executed a deed in which she made the daughter the legal grantee of the property. She then explained to her daughter that she had placed the deed inside a safe in her room and that once she was gone, she would be the sole heir to the land. After the lady's death, her daughter found the deed exactly where she had been told it would be. This pattern shows _____.

(A) Improper delivery

(B) Lack of capacity

(C) Invalid deed

(D) Concurrent ownership

(25) What aspect in the deed process indicates the transfer of ownership and the intention of making the deed effective and operative?

(A) Acceptance of the title deed

(B) Delivery of the deed

(C) Recording of the deed

(D) Notary of the deed

(26) A loan-to-value ratio refers to the highest amount that a lender is willing to lend for the financing of a loan whose collateral is real estate. This amount is arrived at by using a fraction of the appraisal or purchase price, whichever value is less than the other. Lenders traditionally used to ask for a 20% down payment and this made homeownership difficult for many Americans. The FHA came in and ensured that this down payment was significantly lowered by minimizing the lender's risk of loss in case a borrower defaults on payment. Which statement is true about the FHA?

(A) The FHA lends jointly with institutional lenders who are HUD approved

(B) The FHA lends directly

(C) Loans insured by the FHA have an LTV ratio that is lower than that of a conventional loan

(D) The insurance premiums owed to the FHA can either be added onto the loan or paid during the end of the transaction

(27) What do we call lenders in a security instrument used to hypothecate real estate that constitutes three parties?

(A) Mortgagees

(B) Trustors

(C) Mortgagors

(D) Beneficiaries

(28) According to the Truth in Lending Act or regulation Z, a lender should issue a loan applicant with a certain document before that borrower begins to pay the loan. Which document is this?

(A) A deed

(B) A financial statement

(C) An amortization schedule

(D) A disclosure statement

(29) Which of these activities when carried out by real estate brokerage firms whose specialty is managing property can be considered illegal?

(A) Racial profiling of potential tenants to achieve a diverse tenant population

(B) Rejecting the applications of families who have minor children in favor of senior housing

(C) Failing to issue a warning that a 1987 building may contain lead

(D) Rejecting tenants who are hardworking simply because of their history or credit score

(30) Which of the following is not the responsibility of a property manager?

(A) Honesty and fairness

(B) Staying updated on the vacancies in an area

(C) Staying updated on rental rates within an area

(D) Informing a property owner of the property's market value

(31) Amanda is a lessee of an apartment. One cold day, the heat suddenly goes out and so she calls Mathew, who is the lessor, and reports the issue. Mathew promises that the heater will be fixed but he does not give a specific time frame. Amanda continually calls Mathew but he takes no action. Amanda leaves the apartment and refuses to make payments for the lease and so Mathew sues her for defaulting on payment. Who is likely to win the lawsuit?

(A) Amanda, since Mathew breached the contract of quiet enjoyment

(B) Mathew, since Amanda is in breach of contract since she failed to pay the required rent

(C) Amanda, since Mathew is in breach of the implied warranty of habitability

(D) Mathew, since maintenance of necessities like heat should be done by the lessee

(32) If Christine rents an apartment from Joshua, who is the owner of the apartment, then
_____.

(A)   Joshua is a lessor while Christine is the lessee

(B)   Joshua is a lessee while Christine is a lessor

(C)   Christine is a lessor while Joshua is the landlord

(D)   Christine is the tenant while Joshua is a lessee

(33)   An appraiser has been hired to carry out an evaluation of a family residential home that has five bedrooms and five bathrooms. For him to complete that appraisal, he needs comparables and so he finds three properties in the subdivision that have been recently sold. The first house has five bedrooms and five bathrooms, the next one has five bedrooms and four bathrooms, while the last property has four bedrooms and five bathrooms. Which of the following statements regarding the market data approach is true?

(A)   The comparables must consist of a similar number of bathrooms and bedrooms as the ones in the property that is being appraised

(B)   Some adjustments should be made on the property in order for it to match the available comparables

(C)   You must add the value of one bathroom to the sales price given for your second comparable

(D)   You must subtract the value of one bedroom from the sales price of your third comparable

(34)   Which principle of appraisal dictates that the value of a home increases when the demand increases?

(A)   The principle of progression

(B)   The principle of substitution

(C)   The principle of regression

(D)   The principle of supply and demand

(35) Kim buys single-family homes and then uses them as rental properties. Currently, he owns four properties and he wants to buy his fifth single-family home within the same geographical area. He does not want to incur appraisal costs and so he plans on using a Gross Rent Multiplier to get an appropriate offer. His four current properties have a monthly GRM of $200 and so for him to maintain that GRM for property whose monthly rent is $2,500, what should his offer read?

(A) $500,000

(B) $400,000

(C) $700,000

(D) $600,000

(36) Which statement defines investing?

(A)   Saving to consume in the future

(B)   Sacrificing present spending to enjoy future benefits

(C)   Revenue that exceeds cost

(D)   Buying of real estate in cash

(37) A family home was constructed from June 1, 1977, to January 1, 1978. The owner, Joseph Brown, acquired this property from the developers and the house has never been rebuilt or remodeled since. Joseph is now working with a licensee to sell the house. Which of the following statements regarding the lead-based paint disclosure is correct?

(A)   The seller should have the house inspected by professionals for any lead-based paint

(B)   Since the construction of the house was completed on the first day of 1978, this federal disclosure requirement is not necessary

(C)   The licensee is required to comply with the lead-based paint disclosure

(D)   The seller is required to alert any potential buyers of lead-based paint on the property

(38) What is the process of covering landfills with two to four feet of soil and then planting some grass on top?

(A) Chipping

(B) Soiling

(C) Remediation

(D) Capping

(39) John wants to sell his apartment to Sally for $450,000 and he has already paid an entire year's worth of property taxes on that property. Sally plans on moving in four months before the tax year end. John has a pending mortgage of $350,000, mechanic's arrears of $2,500 and a brokerage fee. When a closing statement is prepared, which of these credits will go to John?

(A) The brokerage fee

(B) Prepaid property taxes

(C) Payoff of the $2,500 mechanic's lien

(D) Payoff of the $350,000 mortgage lien

(40) Which settlement form is used in real estate for mortgage loans that are federally related?

(A) Truth in lending disclosure statement

(B) Good faith estimate settlement statement

(C) Regulation Z settlement statement

(D) HUD-1 settlement statement

(41) A wealthy developer bought unimproved property at a cost of $3,542.45 per acre in order to construct a subdivision. The legal description given for that property is 'the Northwest Quarter of the Southeast Quarter of sect twenty six ...' What is the total amount that the developer paid for that property?

(A) $141,698

(B) $106,273.50

(C) $566,792

(D) $212,547

(42) A deed that does not give specific details on the type of estate that is being conveyed is most likely to be used for transferring a/an _____.

(A) Life estate

(B) Fee simple absolute estate

(C) Defeasible fee estate

(D) Estate for years

(43) The rights of control, enjoyment and possession are in_____.

(A) The statute of frauds

(B) Deed restrictions

(C) An appurtenance

(D) The bundle of rights

(44) If Alex deeds real property to Cassie and sets a condition that states that if Cassie does not leave any heirs to the property then that property will go to Sandra, what kind of real estate does Sandra hold?

(A)   Contingent remainder fee

(B)   Reversionary interest

(C)   Contingent life estate

(D)   Contingent reversion fee

(45) What kind of interest does a grantor have if a deed states that certain property belongs to Eunice for life?

(A)   Remainder

(B)   Life estate

(C)   Right of reentry

(D)   Reversion

(46) You can grant life estate _____.

(A)   For a defined term

(B)   Only if it is to last through the grantee's lifetime

(C)   Only if the grantee is above the majority age

(D)   Based on the lifetime of someone else instead of that of the grantee

(47) Which of the following is not a freehold?

(A)   Fee simple estates

(B)   Defeasible fee estates

(C)   Life estates

(D)   Estate for years

(48) Which of the following is not fee simple?

(A) Freehold estates

(B) Estate by inheritance

(C) Indefinite duration

(D) Less-than-freehold estate

(49) Miss Smith is an elderly lady who has life estate ownership of a real property. She decides to give the real property to Bethel Church as a gift. In this case the church can be referred to as the _____.

(A) Remainderman

(B) Grantor

(C) Donor

(D) Reversionary party

(50) Which of the following activities cannot be carried out by life estate owners?

(A) Lease

(B) Devise

(C) Mortgage

(D) Sell

Salesperson Test 1: Answers & Explanations

(1) The correct answer is: (A) A fixture.

When you can't detach personal property from real property without causing damage to the real property because the personal property is significantly attached to it, then that personal property is referred to as a fixture.

(2) The correct answer is: (B) Immovable, unique, scarce and indestructible.

Land is immovable and indestructible since you can neither move an entire piece of real property nor destroy it entirely. Land is also considered to be scarce and unique since it cannot be created or manufactured and each piece is in a distinct location.

(3) The correct answer is: (D) Fee simple estate.

Fee simple estate refers to ownership whereby an entity or person is given complete control over the land.

(4) The correct answer is: (C) Accession, accretion and alluvium.

In real estate, the term 'accession' means acquiring more land, be it a large or small amount, while accretion means accession brought about by natural causes. Alluvium is the term used for the dirt and silt that was deposited on Smith's property.

(5) The correct answer is: (B) Equity.

The sales price of a property and the down payment made during the purchase does not directly affect equity.

(6) The correct answer is: (D) Both Lisa and Amanda will have to sign the loan documents which will protect the security interests of the lender.

The remainderman does not have to put her signature on the loan documents when a life tenant is taking a loan. However, the remainderman's signature helps to safeguard the security interests of the lender in case the life tenant dies.

(7)The correct answer is: (A) Ownership in severalty.

Ownership in severalty refers to ownership whereby only one person, corporation, trust or government entity owns a piece of real estate.

(8)The correct answer is: (A) It must start and end at a given point.

The metes and bounds description starts at a defined point which is known as the point of beginning and follows along the land's boundaries using distances and directions around the plot. It then ends at the same starting point.

(9)The correct answer is: (A) Servient tenement.

An easement appurtenant is a right that allows one property owner to partly benefit from another property owner. In this case, your property can be referred to as servient since it is affected by the easement, and that of your neighbor is dominant because it is benefiting from that easement.

(10) The correct answer is: (A) It's not possible for an easement appurtenant to be terminated by a servient tenement and so the owner of the northern parcel would win.

The question refers to an 'easement appurtenant,' whereby the original property owner split the big parcel he owned into two smaller parcels and retained the easement within the deed provided to the person who purchased the southern parcel first.

(11) The correct answer is: (D) Eminent domain.

According to the 5th Amendment of the United States Constitution, a government entity has the power to take any private property to be used for the benefit of the public. This power is known as eminent domain.

(12) The correct answer is: (B) True.

There are no statewide or nationwide zoning laws but the government can use special legislation like wildlife preserves, national park regulations, environmental laws and coastal management to regulate the use of land. Zoning laws in counties and cities identify how each piece of land should be used.

(13)   The correct answer is: (B) Blockbusting.

Even though blockbusting is not commonly practiced anymore, it may still happen indirectly. This practice is used to persuade homeowners into selling their property at deflated prices after which the property is sold to members of minority groups at inflated prices.

(14)   The correct answer is: (C) Protect the safety, welfare and health of the entire community.

Police power refers to the power that the state has to enforce rules and laws that protect community members.

(15)   The correct answer is: (D) Specific liens can be secured using a specific asset while general liens can be secured using collective assets.

A specific lien is secured using a particular piece of a debtor's property while a general lien is secured using a debtor's collective assets. Many times borrowers assume that no collateral is needed to secure general liens but that is not the case.

(16)   The correct answer is: (B) Express agency.

The agreement described tells us that there was a written agreement involved. Express agency refers to an agency that is formalized either in writing or verbally.

(17)   The correct answer is: (D) Real estate salesperson and buyer relationship.

A salesperson has a fiduciary duty to the principal or client. However, a broker must supervise all the activities carried out by the salesperson.

(18)   The correct answer is: (D) The brokerage firm's income after deducting licensee commissions.

The company dollar refers to the amount of money that a brokerage firm is left with after paying all licensee commissions.

(19) The correct answer is: (B) True.

The nonrefundable fee that a broker receives from a seller to cater for advertisement costs is regarded as a trust fund and should be used for the intended purpose or returned to the seller.

(20) The correct answer is: (A) Exclusive agency.

In exclusive agency agreements, if the seller gets a buyer, the licensee does not earn any commission. But if a buyer is found through the licensee, then the licensee earns a commission. In this kind of agreement, the licensee is given a clearly stated time frame in which he should find a suitable buyer.

(21) The correct answer is: (C) Open listing.

The open listing allows a seller to establish as many listing contracts as possible with different brokerage firms and only pay commission to whichever brokerage firm delivers a buyer. The firms that had also listed the property but did not get a buyer do not receive a commission.

(22) The correct answer is: (C) Option contract.

The type of agreement described is referred to as an option. This unilateral contract ensures that the land owner does not sell off the property during the specified time agreed upon in the agreement.

(23) The correct answer is: (A) The statute of frauds.

Statute of frauds prevents fraudulent parties from trying to enforce contracts that were never made but the statute was not created to prevent verbal contracts. However, there is an exception to the rule: oral leases that do not exceed a year are enforceable.

(24) The correct answer is: (A) Improper delivery.

The facts described show an improper deed delivery. To transfer a title, you need to have a valid title deed and ensure proper delivery and acceptance of that deed. Deeds are delivered when the property needs to be conveyed.

(25) The correct answer is: (B) Delivery of the deed.

The intention to transfer the deed is manifested when the deed is delivered. For a deed to become valid, it must go through the process of delivery and acceptance as well as notification.

(26) The correct answer is: (D) The insurance premiums owed to the FHA can either be added onto the loan or paid at the end of the transaction.

The insurance premiums owed to FHA mortgage can either be paid in the end or added on to the loan and paid on a monthly basis. FHA mortgage insurance ensures that a lender is protected in case a borrower defaults on payment.

(27) The correct answer is: (D) Beneficiary.

The three parties found in such a trust deed include the borrower, also called the trustor; the lender, who is the beneficiary; and the trustee, who receives the legal title from the borrower and holds it for the period of that loan.

(28) The correct answer is: (D) A disclosure statement.

The Truth in Lending Act requires that the lender issue a disclosure statement to the borrower which indicates an annual percentage rate that the borrower is required to pay as well as the sum amount inclusive of interest that the borrower must repay by the end of the loan.

(29) The correct answer is: (A) Racial profiling of potential tenants to achieve a diverse tenant population.

Racial discrimination in leasing or purchase of real estate has always been considered illegal even in cases where the racial profiling is done to bring about racial diversity in the area.

(30) The correct answer is: (D) Informing a property owner of the property's market value.

Property managers are required to stay updated on the rental rates within the area and also should know how many vacancies are in their building. It is, however, not their responsibility to stay updated on the market values of the properties.

(31) The correct answer is: (C) Amanda, since Mathew is in breach of the implied warranty of habitability.

Mathew, who in this case is the landlord, breached the warranty of habitability. In the US, many jurisdictions treat the assurance of providing a habitable living environment as an implied law which does not have to be written down or discussed verbally in a lease agreement.

(32) The correct answer is: (A) Joshua is a lessor while Christine is the lessee.

The owner of the property or the landlord is the one who gives lease rights and is known as the lessor while the tenant receiving those lease rights is known as the lessee.

(33) The correct answer is: (C) You must add the value of one bathroom to the sales price given for your second comparable.

When compared to the family residence home that is being appraised, the second home that is used as a comparable is lacking one bathroom. For you to get an accurate market value for your subject property you should add the value of one bathroom into the sales price of that second comparable.

(34) The correct answer is: (D) The principle of supply and demand.

Among the principles of economics, the principle of supply and demand is the oldest and most predictable. The value of homes tends to increase when the demand, which is caused by national economic factors, increases.

(35) The correct answer is: (A) $500,000.

Kim's GRM for the four properties is $200 and the monthly rent for the property is currently $2,500. For him to maintain the GRM of $200, he should multiply the GRM, which is $200, by $2,500, which is the current rent, to get $500,000.

(36) The correct answer is: (B) Sacrificing present spending to enjoy future benefits.

In real estate, investing refers to sacrificing money that can otherwise be spent on other expenses in exchange for creating a potentially profitable gain for the future.

(37)   The correct answer is: (D) The seller is required to alert any potential buyer of lead-based paint on that property.

Any housing projects that took place before January 1, 1978, could contain lead-based paint. Since the construction began in 1977 and ended on the first day of 1978, the warning should be issued to all potential buyers.

(38)   The correct answer is: (D) Capping.

The soil used in capping is clay-like and so very little water filters past the barrier that the soil creates. This prevents groundwater contamination since the larger part of that water remains on the top levels of the ground.

(39)   The correct answer is: (B) Prepaid property taxes.

When Sally owns the property, John will receive his money back for the four months of prepaid property taxes.

(40)   The correct answer is: (D) HUD-1 settlement statement.

The standardized HUD-1 settlement statement form is used to list the services and fees charged by a broker or lender when the borrower is applying for loans. The buyer should receive the final statement a day before signing any documentation.

(41)   The correct answer is: (A) $141,698.

A square mile is equivalent to 640 acres, so a quarter of the section is 640÷4 = 160. A quarter of the quarter section is 160÷4, which is 40. If 40 acres of land were purchased at a price of $3,542.45 per acre then $3,542.45 ×40 will give us the cost: $141,698.

(42)   The correct answer is: (B) Fee simple absolute estate.

Fee simple absolute estates are not conditional or qualified and the deed does not specify what estate is being conveyed. However, in life estates and defeasible fee estates the deed should have clear specifications.

(43)   The correct answer is: (D) The bundle of rights.

When you own real property, you are afforded the bundle of legal rights which includes the right to possession, exclusion, control, disposition and enjoyment.

(44)   The correct answer is: (A) Contingent remainder fee.

A remainder can either be a vested or contingent remainder and in this case, the real property shall 'remain' away from Alex, who is the grantor, while Sandra will become a fee owner if Cassie dies with no heirs.

(45)   The correct answer is: (D) Reversion.

When Eunice dies, her life estate will end and the real property will revert back to her grantor. A right of reentry can be found in a lease or in fee simple estates where a condition has been violated.

(46)   The correct answer is: (D) Based on the lifetime of someone else instead of that of the grantee.

In life estate, you can use someone else as your measuring life instead of the grantee. In the event that the person who was used as the measure of life dies, the property is reverted to the grantor.

(47)   The correct answer is: (D) Estate for years.

If you are a holder of an estate for years, you have a leasehold estate which is ownership that is leased for an indefinite duration. Fee simple absolute, defeasible fee and life estates are currently the most known forms of freehold estate.

(48)   The correct answer is: (D) Less-than-freehold estate.

One major characteristic of fee simple estates is that property can be passed from one family member to another through inheritance, which causes the property to remain in one family for ages. Life estate and fee simple estate are the most common types of freehold estate.

(49)   The correct answer is: (A) Remainderman.

Upon the demise of Miss Smith, her life estate shall come to an end but the ownership will still remain away from her grantor's estate and the church's remainder interest will then become a fee simple absolute estate.

(50) The correct answer is: (B) Devise.

A devise refers to a transfer of ownership through a will. In a life estate, the interest of the life tenant ceases when he/she dies; therefore, a life tenant cannot appoint heirs to the estate.

Salesperson Test 2: Questions

(1) Land appropriated for public use by the land owner and received on the public's behalf is known as _____.

(A)   A public grant

(B)   An easement

(C)   A condemnation

(D)   A dedication

(2) Which document should a real property owner review to confirm if he/she has riparian rights included for the property?

(A)   The grant deed

(B)   The appropriate state laws

(C)   The title policy

(D)   The water department's records of the deed's registry

(3) A property's boundary can be changed through _____.

(A)   Avulsion

(B)   Encroachment

(C)   Accretion

(D)   Fence construction

(4) Riparian owners have property which bounds on _____.

(A)   A waterway

(B)   National forest areas

(C)   Public land that is not surveyed

(D)   Municipal property

(5) Physically, real estate includes all of the following except _____.

(A)   Personal property

(B)   The earth's surface

(C)   The subsurface

(D)   The air that is above the land's surface

(6) Who possesses riparian rights?

(A)   The owner of property located in a rural area

(B)   The owner of property located near a certain waterway

(C)   A property owner who is entitled to fruit from his crops

(D)   Property owners granting easement for watering pipes

(7) What term describes the removal of a part of land caused by a sudden change of a stream's channel?

(A)   Breach

(B)   Adverse possession

(C)   Accretion

(D)   Avulsion

(8) When selling an acre of land, the owner must_____.

(A)   Release riparian rights if there are any

(B)   Hand over air rights by signing the quitclaim deed

(C)   Give a specific description of the available air rights so that the buyer can gain title to them

(D)   Reserve mineral rights so that they do not automatically go to the buyer

(9) What title does a woman hold when she receives real property as a gift in a will?

(A)   Probate

(B)   Intestate

(C)   Chattel

(D)   Devisee

(10)   What is the term used to describe an activity whereby the soil gradually wears away due to natural processes and causes the loss of real property?

(A)   Escheat

(B)   Curtilage

(C)   Obsolescence

(D)   Erosion

(11)   Land can be improved or modified to increase real estate's value. All of the following are improvements except _____.

(A)   A house

(B)   An access road

(C)   Planted crops

(D)   Utilities

(12)   The following properties are all considered real property except _____.

(A)   Appurtenances

(B)   Furniture

(C)   Water rights

(D)   Airspace rights

(13)   Which statement best describes riparian rights?

(A)   Rights granted when a property owner purchases fixtures

(B)   Rights that are granted for a specific water source

(C)   Rights that a property owner gets when a natural waterway crosses his/her land

(D)   Rights that are kept on record at the office of the county recorder

(14)   Which of these is a privilege, right or improvement that is also passed on with the property?

(A)   A restriction

(B)   An emblement

(C)   An encroachment

(D)   An appurtenance

(15)   In real property, the word 'fee' is used to mean _____.

(A)   Leased land

(B)   The money that a broker charges for his services

(C)   An estate obtained through inheritance

(D)   The cost of researching a title

(16) The right to space that is above a property's ground within a vertical plane is known as
_____.

(A)   Solar rights

(B)   Air rights

(C)   Bundle of rights

(D)   Riparian rights

(17) Crops which are planted and cultivated annually on land can be referred to as _____.

(A)   Real property

(B)   Fixtures

(C)   Emblements

(D)   Fructus naturales

(18) What are rights that are automatically passed on when land is conveyed known as?

(A)   Warranties

(B)   Reversion interests

(C)   Reservation interests

(D)   Tenements

(19) All of the following except one are considered real property since they are affixed to land as appurtenances. Which is the exception?

(A)   Trade fixtures

(B)   Growing trees

(C)   Buildings

(D)   A buried water tank

(20) Samuel left a valid will before his death which named his son as his heir. Since the son is a minor, his wife claimed an elective share through the Uniform Probate Code. Samuel's property was _____.

(A)   All given to his wife

(B)   Given to his son

(C)   Divided between Samuel's wife and their son

(D)   Not given to Samuel's wife

(21) What is the term for a man who creates a will?

(A)   An executor

(B)   A testator

(C)   An administrator

(D)   A testatrix

(22) In buildings, the ceiling tiles dropping into a metallic frame can be considered _____.

(A)   Fixtures

(B)   Real property

(C)   Personal property

(D)   Trade fixtures

(23) What does a devisee receive?

(A)   Personal property through a bill of sale

(B)   Real property through a will

(C)   Property through escheat

(D)   Property by foreclosure

(24) The word intestate is used to mean that a man has died _____.

(A) Leaving no will

(B) Before naming an heir

(C) Without making a will

(D) Leaving his property to the state

(25) How is real property that is transferred through a codicil to the will conveyed?

(A) By decree

(B) By demise

(C) By degree

(D) By devise

(26) The term 'probate' is used to mean the act of _____.

(A) Processing a will so as to make it valid

(B) Curing a defect through the quitclaim deed

(C) Processing the partitioning of a property

(D) Proving title through adverse possessions

(27) What is a devise?

(A) A development scheme or plan

(B) A real estate gift

(C) A perpetual trust

(D) A gift of real estate by a last will and testament

(28) When a person dies intestate, his property is passed over by _____.

(A) Accretion

(B) Succession

(C) Prescription

(D) Acquisition

(29) When someone dies intestate, without heirs to inherit the property through intestate succession, his/her property is reverted to the government through _____.

(A) Reversion

(B) Escheat

(C) Succession

(D) Re-conveyance

(30) What happens to a person's real property if he/she dies testate?

(A) His next of kin get the property

(B) The devisee gets the property

(C) The administrator gets the property

(D) Escheat and the property is auctioned

(31) Which of the following does not represent personal property that is conferred by a will?

(A) A gift

(B) A legacy

(C) A codicil

(D) A bequest

(32) You can transfer title to real estate upon the demise of the property's owner using _____.

(A)   A warranty deed

(B)   A trustee's deed

(C)   A will

(D)   A special warranty deed

(33) What does the term 'escheat' mean?

(A)   The right that a government has to acquire title upon the demise of a property owner who left no will or heir

(B)   Acquiring title through adverse possession

(C)   Feudal law whereby the king seizes land

(D)   The right that a government has to take property that is privately owned for public use upon payment

(34) Who receives payment last after an estate has been probated?

(A)   Heirs

(B)   The government

(C)   Creditors

(D)   Second mortgage holder

(35) Which of these words does not relate to the other words?

(A)   Devise

(B)   Testator

(C)   Will

(D)   Intestate

(36) Which document acts as evidence to show that certain personal property will be used as security for a certain loan?

(A) Chattel mortgage

(B) Bill of sale

(C) Partial release

(D) Bargain/sale deed

(37) In real property, which instrument is not used to transfer interest?

(A) A lease

(B) An option

(C) An agreement of sale

(D) A bill of sale

(38) After the death of a man, the probate court determined that the will that the man had executed was invalid since it failed to meet the state's legal requirements. In this case, who will the title go to?

(A) The people who had previously owned the property

(B) The property will revert to the government

(C) The devisees who are named in that will

(D) Those entitled to the property through the intestate succession law

(39) An estate's executor is selected by _____.

(A) The administrator

(B) The testator

(C) The probate court

(D) The heirs

(40) If a person dies without leaving a last will and there are no relatives who survived him, the five acres of land that he owned will _____.

(A) Go to the testatrix

(B) Go to his devisees

(C) Revert to the initial grantor

(D) Escheat to government

(41) A real property owner is eligible for riparian rights when _____.

(A) A discovery of minerals on the land is made

(B) The land borders an ocean

(C) The land borders a stream

(D) The land is located in a geothermal field

(42) What happens to a person's real property when he/she dies testate?

(A) It is passed on to his/her next of kin

(B) It is taken by the government

(C) It descends to his/her survivors

(D) It is passed on to his/her devisees

(43) Which of the following statements is not true regarding party walls that are built on a property line that is between two plots?

(A) It is the responsibility of only one of the owners to maintain the wall

(B) It is the responsibility of each owner to pay a maintenance fee for their part of the wall

(C) Each one owns the wall that lies on their side and has easement rights on the other half

(D) There must be an agreement between both owners before taking down the wall

(44) The Uniform Commercial Code was created to _____.

(A) Provide regulations for commercial leasing

(B) Ensure that there is no fraud in oral sale contracts

(C) Create a uniformity in real estate transactions

(D) Regulate the personal property pieces that are pledged in sale contracts

(45) Which of the following statements best differentiates an executor and an administrator?

(A) Administrators are devisees while executors are not

(B) Administrators are testators while executors are not

(C) Administrators are assigned by a court to manage a decedent's estate but executors are named in the will of the decedent to execute that decedent's will

(D) Executors have riparian rights but administrators do not

(46) A baker found an ideal location to set up her cake shop. The location allowed customers to drive through and it was on a major highway that led to a populated employment city. Which economic concept did the baker use in order to locate this shop?

(A) Immobility

(B) Uniqueness

(C) Indestructibility

(D) Situs

(47) Irene has a structure whose interior dimensions are 24' by 30,'and its walls are 6". What area of land, in square footage, does this building cover?

(A) 744

(B) 803.25

(C) 775

(D) 747.25

(48) Ownership of a mobile home that is already in use can typically be transferred through _____.

(A)   A warranty deed

(B)   A grant deed

(C)   A certificate of ownership

(D)   A bill of sale

(49) If you want to find out how long ago a development improvement was made, the best source of information is _____.

(A)   The office of the tax assessor at the county level

(B)   The office of the state secretary

(C)   The records of the builder

(D)   The treasurer's office at the county level

(50) It is possible to find a type of roof whose surface is level, such as _____.

(A)   A flat roof

(B)   A gambrel roof

(C)   A hip roof

(D)   A gable roof

Salesperson Test 2: Answers & Explanations

(1)   The correct answer is: (D) A dedication.

A dedication refers to a grant that the public is given which can either be an easement or a fee simple, while condemnation refers to when the government takes private property to be used for the public and provides compensation.

(2) The correct answer is: (B) The appropriate state laws.

Riparian rights are granted to those with property that adjoins non-navigable water the state is responsible for creating these rights. A local real estate attorney can help you check these rights if you are in doubt.

(3) The correct answer is: (C) Accretion.

Accretion is said to occur when soil is gradually added to a shoreline or to land that borders a stream and becomes the acquired property of that shoreline or streamside owner.

(4) The correct answer is: (A) A waterway.

A riparian owner has property that borders a waterway and is often granted riparian rights that enable him/her to use the waters.

(5) The correct answer is: (A) Personal property.

Personal property can be removed from the real property but the surface of the earth, the subsurface and the air above the surface cannot be removed and are all part of real property.

(6) The correct answer is: (B) The owner of property located near a waterway.

A person who has property that is located near a waterway is granted riparian rights which enable him/her to use the water source for personal use and also enjoy increased land caused by accretion.

(7) The correct answer is: (D) Avulsion.

Avulsion occurs when a stream suddenly changes its course causing the removal of a part of the land.

(8) The correct answer is: (D) Reserve mineral rights so that they do not automatically go to the buyer.

Air rights and mineral rights are a part of real estate and they are passed down together with the property when it is being sold unless the grantor reserves the rights.

(9) The correct answer is: (D) A devisee.

The woman is referred to as a devisee since she has acquired the property as a gift in a will.

(10) The correct answer is: (D) Erosion.

Erosion is a process whereby soil gradually wears away as a result of natural processes and causes loss of property.

(11) The correct answer is: (C) Planted crops.

Improvements are manmade constructed developments or additions to property and include buildings, roads and fences which become part of real estate. Crops, in this case, are an example of personal property.

(12) The correct answer is: (B) Furniture.

Appurtenances, water rights and airspace rights are all real property but furniture is considered personal property unless it is built-in.

(13) The correct answer is: (C) Rights that a property owner gets when a natural waterway crosses his/her land.

Riparian rights are granted to property owners whose property borders a non-navigable stream.

(14) The correct answer is: (D) An appurtenance.

An appurtenance is a right to land which is passed on to the current owner together with the property.

(15) The correct answer is: (C) An estate obtained through inheritance.

The term 'fee' is used to refer to freehold estate acquired through inheritance.

(16) The correct answer is: (B) Air rights.

Air rights involve the right to the space above the ground that is within the vertical plane.

(17) The correct answer is: (C) Emblements.

Crops that require annual cultivation are known as emblements while shrubs and trees that do not require annual cultivation are considered real property.

(18) The correct answer is: (D) Tenements.

The term 'tenement' is used to refer to the rights that a new owner gets which include the rights to fences, buildings, rents and easements available on the property.

(19) The correct answer is: (A) Trade fixtures.

The tenant can remove trade fixtures like storage systems, barber chairs and display cabinets from the property once the lease expires since such items are personal property.

(20) The correct answer is: (C) Divided between Samuel's wife and their son.

In a state that uses the Uniform Probate Code, Samuel's wife can get a third of her husband's property as an absolute interest estate.

(21)   The correct answer is: (B) A testator.

A man who makes a will is known as a testator while a woman who makes a will is called a testatrix. Executors are those who are named in the will and an administrator is appointed by a court to administer the estate of the deceased.

(22)   The correct answer is: (A) Fixtures.

The intention determines whether an item will be considered a fixture or not. In this case, the ceiling tiles are a movable object and they have been incorporated into the building, therefore, they are fixtures.

(23)   The correct answer is: (B) Real property through a will.

A devisee receives real property through a will made by the property owner.

(24)   The correct answer is: (A) Leaving no will.

When a man dies without leaving a will, he is considered to have died intestate and at that point the state applies the intestate succession law.

(25)   The correct answer is: (D) By devise.

A codicil refers to an addition made to the will and the execution process should be the same as that of executing an original will.

(26)   The correct answer is: (A) Processing a will so as to make it valid.

Upon the death of a testator, the will is checked to ensure that it is valid and the creditors are notified so that they can file any claims before the title is transferred to the heirs.

(27)   The correct answer is: (D) A gift of real estate by a last will and testament.

A devisee is a person who has received real property as a gift through a will. He/she can only obtain the title after a probate process has been completed and the estate has been settled.

(28) The correct answer is: (B) Succession.

Different states have different rules regarding who receives the property that was owned by the deceased, so the successor is determined by the state.

(29) The correct answer is: (B) Escheat.

Before the government can take the deceased's property, it allows sufficient time in order for next of kin to come forth and claim the property after which escheat takes place if no one claims it.

(30) The correct answer is: (B) The devisee gets the property.

When a person dies testate, it means that he/she left behind a will which identified who their property would go to, so the property is handed over to the devisees.

(31) The correct answer is: (C) A codicil.

A codicil refers to an addition made to the original will to transfer some real property or personal property.

(32) The correct answer is: (C) A will.

A will is written at any point when the testator is alive but it is only effective after the death of the testator and the successful completion of a probate process.

(33) The correct answer is: (A) The rights that a government has to acquire title upon the demise of a property owner who left no will or heir.

The government has the authority to take the property of an owner who did not leave a will or have heirs upon his/her death.

(34) The correct answer is: (A) Heirs.

The government, unsecured creditors and secured creditors receive payment before the property's heirs do.

(35)   The correct answer is: (D) Intestate.

Intestate is a term used when a person dies without leaving a will or heirs to his/her property.

(36)   The correct answer is: (A) Chattel mortgage.

A state that has the Uniform Commercial Code uses a security agreement document called the chattel mortgage to secure loans.

(37)   The correct answer is: (D) Bill of sale.

Bills of sale are used for transferring title of personal property but sometimes they are also used for real estate transactions.

(38)   The correct answer is: (D) Those entitled to the property through the intestate succession law.

If a will is proven to be invalid, the state has a responsibility to identify the relatives who are entitled to the deceased's personal property and real property.

(39)   The correct answer is: (B) The testator.

The executor is usually identified in a will by the testator, but in cases where the testator did not designate one then a probate court appoints an administrator.

(40)   The correct answer is: (D) Escheat to government.

If a person dies without leaving a will and no relatives come forth to claim the property, then the government has the authority to take the property.

(41)   The correct answer is: (C) The land borders a stream.

Riparian rights are granted to people whose property borders a stream or waterway.

(42)   The correct answer is: (D) It is passed on to his devisees.

When someone dies testate, it means that he/she left a will in place and so the property is devised to the people named in that will.

(43)   The correct answer is: (A) It is the responsibility of only one of the owners to maintain the wall.

In big city tenements, it is very common to find party walls and both owners are responsible for the maintenance of the wall that lies on their side.

(44)   The correct answer is: (D) Regulate the personal property pieces that are pledged in sale contracts.

The uniform Commercial Code regulates personal property that is pledged in a sale contract.

(45)   The correct answer is: (C) Administrators are assigned by a court to manage the decedent's estate but executors are named in the will of the decedent to execute that decedent's will.

Administrators are assigned by a court to manage the decedent's estate but executors are named in the will of the decedent to execute that decedent's will

(46)   The correct answer is: (D) Situs.

Situs refers to an economical characteristic whereby an owner prefers a particular area over another.

(47)   The correct answer is: (C) 775.

The way to do this is to first convert the wall dimensions into feet so that you have 0.5'. Then add that measurement to each of the other dimensions and multiply to find the area covered. (24+0.5+0.5) x (30+0.5+0.5) = 25 x 31 = 775.

(48)   The correct answer is: (C) A certificate of ownership.

In transactions involving mobile homes already in use or which have been previously used, title to the property is confirmed once the certificate of ownership is properly dated, endorsed and delivered.

(49) The correct answer is: (A) The office of the tax assessor at the county level.

The county office of the tax assessor is the best place to source information on improvements' age because when improvements have been completed there is normally a completion notice filed at the county tax office, which is meant to be used to establish the tax base.

(50) The correct answer is: (A) Flat roof.

It should be noted that a flat roof still has a slope, but one that is extremely low. Its pitch is usually below a quarter of an inch for every foot.

Salesperson Test 3: Questions

(1) What do we call the initial cash payment that a buyer makes to partially cover the buying price of certain property without using a mortgage to finance it?

(A)   A down payment

(B)   A deposit

(C)   A deed of trust

(D)   A second mortgage

(2) A female who is identified in a last will as the administrator of an estate can be referred to as a/an _____.

(A)   Able inheritor

(B)   Individual representative

(C)   Executor

(D)   Executrix

(3) Which is the highest possible interest that one can hold in real estate?

(A)   No additional fees

(B)   Ownership

(C)   Fee simple

(D)   Fee complex

(4) What kind of insurance is a property owner required to have whose property is located in a federally designated flood area?

(A) Hurricane insurance

(B) Flood insurance

(C) Water damage insurance

(D) None of the above

(5) Which statement is true regarding government loans?

(A) Government loans are insured by the Federal Housing Administration

(B) The Department of Veterans Affairs guarantees the loans

(C) The Rural Housing Service guarantees the loans

(D) All of the above

(6) What is the name given to a person conveying interest in a real property?

(A) The grantor

(B) The grantee

(C) The mortgagor

(D) The buyer

(7) Which insurance covers property against physical damage that is caused by fire, vandalism, wind or any other hazard?

(A) Hazard insurance

(B) Act of God insurance

(C) Hazardous insurance

(D) None of the above

(8) What are liquid assets?

(A)   Assets that are not in a solid state

(B)   Assets that one cannot freeze

(C)   Assets that are hard to acquire

(D)   Cash assets or assets that can be easily converted into cash

(9) What term is used to refer to a lender in the mortgage agreement?

(A)   Mortgagor

(B)   Private mortgage firm

(C)   Mortgagee

(D)   Banker

(10)   If a house buyer asks the property seller to partly or fully provide financing, what kind of financing is he/she asking for?

(A)   Personal financing

(B)   Non-bank financing

(C)   Special financing

(D)   Owner financing

(11)   What is a point?

(A)   A baseball game score

(B)   The moral of a story

(C)   One percent of the total mortgage amount

(D)   The sharp end of a pen used to sign contracts

(12) What can a person with power of attorney do?

(A) Partially or completely make decisions on someone else's behalf

(B) Enter law school

(C) Inherit a certain estate

(D) Decide the medical facility that someone will use

(13) What does the term 'principal' refer to?

(A) A value or ethic

(B) An unpaid or borrowed amount

(C) A monthly mortgage payment made to reduce the remaining mortgage balance

(D) Both B and C

(14) The term 'promissory note' refers to _____.

(A) A note that is passed around in class

(B) A note one sends to another person informing them of one's intentions

(C) A promise made in writing to pay a certain amount of money over a certain time period

(D) A promise made orally to repay money at a certain time period

(15) Which of the following statements correctly describes a salesperson in real estate?

(A) A person who owns real estate firms

(B) A person who is licensed to negotiate and transact real estate sales

(C) An insurance and property seller

(D) Someone who transacts and negotiates real estate sales but has no license

(16) An assumption occurs when _____.

(A) The purchaser assumes a seller's mortgage

(B) A seller assumes a purchaser's mortgage

(C) Someone assumes something and the assumption ends up being true

(D) All of the above

(17) What is the name given to the legal document used to convey title to property?

(A) Option of purchase

(B) Contract for deed

(C) Sales contract

(D) Deed

(18) Which clause contained in the mortgage enables a lender to demand the payment of a loan balance in the event that the borrower transfers title to someone else without alerting the lender?

(A) Amortization schedule

(B) Due on demand clause

(C) Acceleration clause

(D) Both B and C

(19) The most common form of bankruptcy is _____.

(A) Chapter 7

(B) Chapter 11

(C) Chapter 7 no-asset

(D) Chapter 11 no-asset

(20) A broker is best described by which of the following statements?

(A) Brokers are owners of real estate firms

(B) An agent whose role is to bring two interested parties together in order for transactions to take place and who is paid for it through a fee

(C) A real estate agent who works for brokers

(D) All of the above

(21) In real estate contracts, normal contingencies are those whereby _____.

(A) The buyer gets a home inspection done by a qualified inspector

(B) The seller has permission to spend two weeks each year in that house

(C) The buyer can occupy the house immediately after the signing of the sales contract

(D) The seller can carry away some landscaping from the home

(22) What do we call a report prepared by the credit bureau that gives information on a person's credit history and is used by lenders to determine if that person qualifies for a loan?

(A) Credit card history

(B) Savings account history

(C) Credit report

(D) Personal affidavit

(23) Which term do appraisers use when estimating a building's physical condition?

(A) Preferred age

(B) Estimated age

(C) Effective age

(D) Longevity

(24) The total difference between a property's market value and the outstanding mortgage loan and liens is a property holder's financial interest. What is the term used to refer to this interest?

(A) Balance due

(B) Equity

(C) None of these choices

(D) Indebtedness

(25) When putting up a new fence, Mr. Smith realized that the fence crosses his property line and edges onto his neighbor's property by several inches. Such an action is known as _____.

(A) Easement

(B) Illegal driveway

(C) Extra benefits

(D) Encroachment

(26) What is the name given to government loans that are not VA loans?

(A) FDA mortgage

(B) ARM mortgage

(C) FHA mortgage

(D) Such loans do not exist

(27) When interest in some real property is conveyed to a family member, the family member becomes the _____.

(A) Grantee

(B) Receiver

(C) Lucky relative

(D) Mortgagor

(28) Supposing you decide to purchase a car and borrow a loan against equity on your house. You receive a specific mortgage loan amount. This arrangement can be referred to as a _____.

(A) Line of credit that is for personal use

(B) Perfect way to purchase a car

(C) Leverage against the house

(D) Home equity line of credit

(29) Mary and Rachel are sisters and the joint heirs of a piece of land which their deceased mother left them. Mary has two children while Rachel has one. If Mary dies before Rachael, who will the piece of land belong to?

(A) The land will be divided equally among Mary's two children

(B) The land will go entirely to Rachel

(C) The land will go to Mary's estate

(D) The land will be divided equally among Mary and Rachel's children

(30) Liens can best be described as _____.

(A) Illegal activities

(B) Legal claims against property which are required to be paid up once the property is sold

(C) Items in the house that are not valuable

(D) No choice above

(31) The term 'lock-in' is used to refer to _____.

(A) A type of punishment that parents give their wayward children

(B) Communities which lock their gates at midnight

(C) A certain key that is sold in hardware stores

(D) An agreement given by the lender that guarantees a certain interest rate over a certain period of time

(32)   What do we call the right that a government holds which allows it to take certain private property to be used by the public after paying the property's market value?

(A)   Encroachment

(B)   Legal possession

(C)   Eminent domain

(D)   Governmental domain

(33)   What do we call a mortgage that has a lien position which is subordinate to an initial mortgage taken on a certain property?

(A)   An illegal mortgage

(B)   A second mortgage

(C)   A lien position mortgage

(D)   A first subordinate mortgage

(34)   What is an adjustable-rate mortgage (ARM)?

(A)   A mortgage that has a fixed interest rate

(B)   A mortgage whose interest rate periodically changes based on the stock market

(C)   A mortgage whose interest rate periodically changes based on the index

(D)   A mortgage that can be adjusted by the mortgagor

(35)   Which term is used to refer to a schedule used to show how loan payments are distributed towards the principal and the interest during the loan period?

(A)   An assumption

(B)   An amortization schedule

(C)   A yearly percentage rate

(D)   None

(36) Upon the sale of a property, a lender demands that he be paid in full. The provision included in the mortgage for such a demand is called the _____ provision.

(A) Buyer pays all

(B) Due-on-sale

(C) Seller pays all

(D) None

(37) The collective personal and real property that a person owns by the time he/she is dying is known as the _____.

(A) Probate

(B) Will

(C) Estate

(D) There is no correct answer

(38) When a property owner lists his property with one agent then signs an agreement stating that no one else is entitled to that listing up to a certain time, the listing is an _____.

(A) Exclusive right to advertise

(B) Inclusive listing

(C) Exclusive listing

(D) Exclusive right to show

(39) When a lender makes an agreement to provide a certain borrower with a loan on a certain property, the lender is said to have _____.

(A) Decided to provide that loan

(B) Made a firm commitment

(C) Made a statement declaring that the property and the buyer have passed inspection

(D) None of the above

(40) Serena bought a home and decided to build some shelves into the walls. When she sold the house, she left the shelves behind. This is because the shelves were _____.

(A) Part of that house

(B) An attachment

(C) A fixture

(D) None of the above

(41) A legally recognized property description that is sufficient for locating and identifying property without the need for verbal testimony is referred to as the _____.

(A) Property's address

(B) Property's identifying information

(C) Property's 911 address

(D) Property's legal description

(42) The day the unpaid principal of a bond, loan or any other financial instruments becomes due or payable, this is said to be the _____.

(A) Delivery date

(B) Due date

(C) Maturity date

(D) End-of-paper trail

(43) What is the name given to the borrower in the mortgage agreement?

(A) Borrower

(B) Mortgagee

(C) Lessee

(D) Mortgagor

(44) Which of the following items is personal property?

(A) Windows in the home

(B) A couch

(C) A garage that is attached to the house

(D) The front lawn of the home

(45) Sometimes a borrower may receive a penalty if he/she makes an early payment on a loan that is not due. This penalty is known as _____.

(A) The loan-to-value penalty

(B) An early withdrawal penalty

(C) There is no penalty for an early payment

(D) A prepayment penalty

(46) Which of the following statements is correct about the term 'preapproval'?

(A) It only applies to property

(B) This is a term that is used loosely

(C) It is carried out before the completion of a loan application

(D) None of the above

(47) What is a PITI reserve?

(A) An amount of money that is financed by a mortgage

(B) The cash amount that a borrower should have for closing costs and down payments

(C) Both A and B

(D) None of the above

(48) Public auctions are designed to _____.

(A) Sell property so as to repay defaulted mortgages

(B) Help people buy property

(C) Inform people about property that is on sale

(D) Provide employment for auctioneers

(49) The term 'realtor' is used to mean _____.

(A) An agent in real estate who has successfully passed his/her state exams

(B) An agent in real estate who has an active license

(C) An agent in real estate who is on a local board that is an affiliate of the National Association of Realtors

(D) An agent in real estate who is a member of a local board

(50) What does a 'remaining term' mean?

(A) The school term that is remaining

(B) The remaining months in a woman's pregnancy

(C) The difference between the initial amortization term and the payments made

(D) None of the above

Salesperson Test 3: Answers & Explanations

(1)   The correct answer is: (A) Down payment.

A down payment refers to the initial payment that is made in cash as soon as a transaction is finalized and it covers part of the amount due.

(2) The correct answer is: (D) Executrix.

A female executor who is identified in a last will and testament as the administrator of the deceased's estate is referred to as an executrix.

(3) The correct answer is: (C) Fee simple.

Fee simple interest is the greatest interest that one can possibly hold in real estate.

(4) The correct answer is: (B) Flood insurance.

A property owner whose property is in a designated flood area is required to have flood insurance coverage.

(5) The correct answer is: (D) All of the above.

A government loan can either be insured by the Federal Housing Administration or guaranteed by the Department of Veterans Affairs or the Rural Housing Service.

(6) The correct answer is: (A) The grantor.

A person conveying interest to another is referred to as the grantor.

(7) The correct answer is: (A) Hazard insurance.

Hazard insurance covers physical damage on property caused by wind, fire, vandalism and other hazards.

(8) The correct answer is: (D) Cash assets or assets that can be easily converted into cash.

Liquid assets are either cash or can be easily converted into cash.

(9) The correct answer is: (C) Mortgagee.

In mortgage agreements, the lender is referred to as a mortgagee.

(10)   The correct answer is: (D) Owner financing.

When the property owner partially or fully provides financing, we call it owner financing.

(11)   The correct answer is: (C) One percent of the total mortgage amount.

A point refers to one percent of the total mortgage amount.

(12)   The correct answer is: (A) Partially or completely make decisions on someone else's behalf.

The power of attorney grants a person limited or complete authority on someone else's behalf through a legal document.

(13)   The correct answer is: (D) Both B and C.

The term 'principal' refers to the borrowed or unpaid amount or the monthly mortgage payment made to reduce the remaining mortgage balance.

(14)   The correct answer is: (C) A promise you make in writing to repay a certain amount of money over a certain time period.

The term 'promissory note' refers to a promise you make in writing to refund a certain amount of money over a certain time period

(15)   The correct answer is: (B) An individual who is licensed to negotiate and transact real estate sales.

Real estate agents are licensed people who negotiate and transact real estate sales.

(16) The correct answer is: (A) The purchaser assumes a seller's mortgage.

A transaction is referred to as an assumption when a buyer assumes a seller's mortgage.

(17) The correct answer is: (D) Deed.

The legal document that is used to convey title to property is called a deed.

(18) The correct answer is: (C) Acceleration clause.

In the event that the borrower transfers title or defaults on payment without alerting the lender, the acceleration clause grants the lender the right to demand the payment that is due.

(19) The correct answer is: (C) Chapter 7 no-asset.

For individuals, Chapter 7 no-asset bankruptcy is most common and it relieves a borrower of many kinds of debts.

(20) The correct answer is: (D) All of the above.

Brokers can own real estate, work for other brokers who own brokerage firms and be loan brokers in mortgage industries, but basically a broker is an agent who brings two willing parties together with the aim of initiating a transaction between them so as to earn a fee from the transaction.

(21) The correct answer is: (A) The buyer gets a home inspection done by an inspector who is qualified.

In sales contracts, a normal contingency is one where the buyer can get a satisfactory property inspection from a qualified inspector and this condition should be met prior to creating a legally binding contract.

(22) The correct answer is: (C) Credit report.

Credit reports contain a person's credit history and they are prepared by the credit bureau. Lenders are able to determine an applicant's creditworthiness using this report.

(23) The correct answer is: (C) Effective age.

Effective age is a term used to refer to the appraiser's estimation of a building's physical condition. The actual age of the building can sometimes be longer or shorter than the effective age.

(24) The correct answer is: (B) Equity.

The financial interest that a homeowner has in his/her property is known as equity. This is the total difference between the market value of the home and the outstanding mortgage loan as well as other liens.

(25) The correct answer is: (D) Encroachment.

Encroachment happens when an improvement illegally intrudes on someone else's property while an easement is a legally allowed intrusion.

(26) The correct answer is: (C) FHA mortgage.

 A Veterans Affairs loan and a Federal Housing Administration mortgage can be insured by the FHA.

(27) The correct answer is: (A) Grantee.

A grantee is a person who receives real property interest from the owner of the property.

(28) The correct answer is: (D) Home equity line of credit.

Home equity line of credit refers to mortgage loans that allow a borrower to get a predetermined cash amount which is borrowed against his home's equity.

(29) The correct answer is: (B) The land will go entirely to Rachel.

In a joint tenancy agreement, the survivor becomes the owner of the property entirely.

(30)   The correct answer is: (B) Legal claims against property which are required to be paid up once the property is sold.

Liens such as first trust deeds or mortgages are legal claims against property that should be paid when that property is sold.

(31)   The correct answer is: (D) An agreement given by the lender that guarantees a certain interest rate over a certain period of time.

The term 'lock-in' refers to a rate that is guaranteed by a lender for a specified amount of time and at a given cost to a buyer.

(32)   The correct answer is: (C) Eminent domain.

Eminent domain refers to the right the government has to buy certain private property to be used by the public.

(33)   The correct answer is: (B) Second mortgage.

A mortgage that has a lien position that is subordinate to an initial mortgage is known as a second mortgage.

(34)   The correct answer is: (C) A mortgage whose interest rate periodically changes based on the index.

Adjustable rate mortgages are mortgages whose interest rates change periodically due to fluctuations in the index.

(35)   The correct answer is: (B) Amortization schedule.

The amortization schedule shows how the money given toward a loan repayment is distributed. This schedule is recorded in the form of a table and it shows what portion goes to the principal and what portion goes to the interest.

(36) The correct answer is: (B) Due-on-sale.

The due-on-sale provision is a provision found in some mortgages and it gives the lender the right to demand full repayment once a borrower sells off the property which was serving as the mortgage security.

(37) The correct answer is: (C) Estate.

The collective property that a person has at the time of death is referred to as that person's estate.

(38) The correct answer is: (C) Exclusive listing.

When an agent is given exclusive rights through a signed contract, making him/her the only agent allowed to sell certain property for a specified time, this is considered an exclusive listing.

(39) The correct answer is: (B) Made a firm commitment.

When a lender makes an agreement to provide a certain borrower with a loan on a certain property, the lender is said to have made a firm commitment.

(40) The correct answer is: (C) A fixture.

When personal property is attached permanently to real estate, it becomes part of real property since it becomes a fixture.

(41) The correct answer is: (D) Property's legal description.

With the legal description, you do not need oral testimony to identify and locate property since it gives a clear description.

(42) The correct answer is: (C) Maturity date.

The day when an outstanding principal balance becomes due or payable is referred to as the maturity date.

(43) The correct answer is: (D) Mortgagor.

In mortgage agreements, the borrower is also known as the mortgagor.

(44) The correct answer is: (B) A couch.

Personal property refers to any property which is not classified under real property. In this case, windows, a garage and the front lawn are all real property since they are affixed to the home.

(45) The correct answer is: (D) Prepayment penalty.

A borrower may be charged a fee, referred to as the prepayment penalty, for paying off his/her loan before its due date.

(46) The correct answer is: (B) This is a term that is used loosely.

The term 'preapproval' can be loosely used to mean that the borrower has successfully completed his application for a loan and provided savings, income and debt documentation which has been reviewed and approved by an underwriter.

(47) The correct answer is: (B) The cash amount that a borrower should have for closing costs and down payments.

PITI reserves should hold an amount of cash that is equal to the expected payment amount that a borrower must make for principal, taxes, interests and insurance over a certain period of time.

(48) The correct answer is: (A) Sell property so as to repay defaulted mortgages.

Public auctions are held in a public location and the property that is sold at these auctions facilitates the repayment of defaulted loans.

(49) The correct answer is: (C) An agent in real estate who belongs to a local board that is an affiliate of the National Association of Realtors.

A realtor can be defined as a broker, associate or agent who is an active member of a local board that is an affiliate of the National Association of Realtors.

(50) The correct answer is: (C) The difference between the initial amortization and the payments made.

A remaining term is the initial amortization term minus the applied payments.

Salesperson Test 4: Questions

(1)   In a will, a widow is declared the owner of a residential home for as long as she is alive and her child is to receive the title upon her demise. What type of estate does the widow hold?

(A)   An easement

(B)   Fee simple estate

(C)   Life estate

(D)   A leasehold

(2) Which of these statements about life estate is true?

(A)   It can be created either by deed or will

(B)   Only one person can be used as the measurement of life

(C)   The holder is required to make principal payments for any encumbrances

(D)   The holder may not encumber it since it is life-based

(3) The quantity or degree of interest that a person has in a real property refers to his _____.

(A)   Dower

(B)   Estate

(C)   Possession

(D)   Courtesy

(4) What best describes the returning of real estate to a grantor's heirs or to the grantor at the end of the grant?

(A) Kickback

(B) Remainder

(C) Surrender

(D) Reversion

(5) What type of estate does a woman hold if she has been granted ownership of land until she gets married?

(A) Estate in equity

(B) Life estate

(C) Defeasible fee estate

(D) Less-than-freehold estate

(6) Which of the following is a type of less-than-freehold estate?

(A) A mortgaged estate

(B) A leasehold estate

(C) A life estate

(D) An estate on a condition subsequent

(7) Which is the correct definition of the word 'estate' in real property?

(A)   A fee simple property ownership

(B)   All property that the deceased leaves behind

(C)   The degree and nature of interest in property

(D)   The inheritance of a particular property in the will

(8) Which of these statements gives the best assurance that one is receiving a fee simple estate ownership?

(A)   In the habendum clause, it is indicated that the ownership being conveyed is a fee estate

(B)   A warranty deed will be given by the owner

(C)   The owner may get title insurance

(D)   There is a covenant of seisin in the deed

(9) An estate administrator is selected by the _____.

(A)   Heirs

(B)   Executor

(C)   Probate court

(D)   Testator

(10) Which of these is not a characteristic of fee simple estates?

(A) Definite duration

(B) Freely transferable

(C) Freely inheritable

(D) Limitless duration

(11) If a person dies having not left a will that is valid, he has died _____.

(A) Probate

(B) Intestate

(C) Via devise

(D) Simple defeasible

(12) If a man owns a fee simple estate, what activities can he not carry out in regards to that property?

(A) Subdivide it

(B) Sell it

(C) Will it

(D) Use it in contradiction to the zoning regulations

(13) Wilson sold a piece of his land to a railway company with the condition that the land should only be used as a railway line and that the property would revert back to him or his heirs if the rail line was no longer in use. This kind of estate is _____.

(A) Tenancy at sufferance

(B) Life estate

(C) Fee simple determinable

(D) Tenancy at will

(14) Which is the highest form of ownership in the real property market?

(A) Fee simple estate

(B) Life estate

(C) Estate at sufferance

(D) Estate at will

(15) Which holder of one of the following estates is a 'non-freeholder'?

(A) Unrecorded vendor's deed

(B) Life estate

(C) Estate for years

(D) Defeasible fee

(16) Which of the following is not an activity that life estate grantors can carry out?

(A) Receive title when a life tenant dies

(B) Grant title under an unused identification

(C) Create a life estate using several people as the measure of life

(D) Take back the fee title whenever they want

(17) A certain licensee has concerns regarding some construction that is going on near the property that he is selling. He should express his concerns to the _____.

(A) Planning department

(B) Licensed surveyor

(C) Tax office records

(D) City attorney

(18) Charles sold a piece of his real estate with the condition that Moses, who was the buyer, would not sell alcohol on the premises. A few years later, Moses sold the premises to Adrian, who turned the premises into a liquor store. If Charles decided to claim the right of reentry, the lawsuit would be as a result of _____.

(A) Violating the condition subsequent

(B) Violating a covenant

(C) Violating the statute of frauds

(D) Violating the condition precedent

(19) Which one of these is personal property?

(A) Carpeting that extends from one wall to the other

(B) Household furnishings

(C) Garbage disposal

(D) A built-in dishwasher

(20) Which of the following is considered personal property?

(A) Water rights

(B) Mineral and gas rights

(C) Trees on a farm

(D) The rights of a beneficiary under a trust

(21) One of the statements below accurately describes real property. Which is it?

(A) The land, the buildings on the land and anything that is permanently affixed on the land or building

(B) The land and the air above it

(C) The land and the area that is above and below the surface as well as all improvements that are on the land

(D) The land and its mineral rights

(22) What do we call objects or things that are temporal or that can be moved easily?

(A) Devices

(B) Personalty

(C) Appurtenances

(D) Realty

(23) In a case where the contract of sale for real property includes some removable items like furniture or painting, the seller should bring a _____ when delivering the deed.

(A) Chattel mortgage

(B) Bill of sale

(C) Satisfaction piece

(D) Estoppel certificate

(24) Each of the following items is an appurtenance except _____.

(A) A fence

(B) A barn

(C) Trade fixtures

(D) An orchard

(25) Which factor should you consider most in order to determine whether certain items are fixtures?

(A) Their size

(B) Their weight

(C) The method used to attach the item

(D) The party's intention when attaching the item

(26) Which of the following is not necessary for a bill of sale to be valid?

(A) The name of the buyer

(B) The transaction date

(C) The seller's signature

(D) The item's description

(27) Personal property is best described as _____.

(A) Fixtures

(B) Chattel

(C) Appurtenances

(D) Improvements

(28) Where is littoral property located?

(A) On the seashore

(B) On a hillside

(C) Near a stream

(D) On a boundary line

(29)   Which of the following gives the closest definition of improvements in the real estate market?

(A)   Wells, fences, roadways and drains

(B)   Additions done to the initial structure

(C)   Upgrades done to the property's interior

(D)   Everything apart from the land which is constructed or artificial

(30)   What do we call the rights that a property owner enjoys exclusively that include the right of possession, enjoyment and disposal?

(A)   Bundle of rights

(B)   Corporeal ownership

(C)   Survivorship

(D)   Incorporeal ownership

(31)   Public housing encompasses _____.

(A)   A housing unit that the federal government sells below cost

(B)   A development unit with tax exemptions that is not veterans' exempt

(C)   An apartment of several units whose development is financed through a loan insured by the government

(D)   Owning a housing unit within a structure comprising several units

(32) Who owns the non-navigable part at the bottom of the river, known as the riverbed?

(A) The state

(B) No one

(C) The local community

(D) The property owner

(33) A debt can be liquidated by making payments in installments over time. This process is known as _____.

(A) Reversion

(B) Capitalization

(C) Amortization

(D) Liquidity

(34) 5½ yards as a measurement is equivalent to _____.

(A) 15 ft

(B) One rod

(C) One quad

(D) One-third of a chain

(35) Jordan, a broker, has left the city after receiving a $10,000 check as earnest money for the sale of a house. Which of the following statements is true regarding this situation?

(A) The amount received by Jordan will be considered to have been received by the seller as the principal

(B) That contract is now deemed void

(C) That contract is now indeterminate until the principal collects the amount paid

(D) The property buyer must write a different check

(36) In cases where land contracts have not been recorded, trying to ascertain if the title is actually clear sometimes causes problems. Such problems are likely to affect _____.

(A) The buyer

(B) The buyer and the trustee

(C) The buyer and the seller

(D) None of the above

(37) Appraisers sometimes use the cost method, and they can apply unit cost per square foot or cubic foot when doing computations. In terms of unit cost, _____.

(A) Two houses, one big, the other small, cost the same

(B) Between two houses of different sizes, the small one costs less

(C) Between two houses of different sizes, the small one costs more

(D) Between two houses of different sizes, the big one costs more

(38) A residential property's functional utility depends on _____.

(A) The will of the resident

(B) The floor plan and the equipment available

(C) The zoning within the region

(D) The condition of the heating system

(39) Which of the following terms means 'appreciation' in real estate?

(A) A decline in the property value

(B) A rise in the property value

(C) Something valuable that a person owns

(D) A compliment for buying property

(40) Bridge loans do not attract a lot of attention these days, and the major reason is that _____.

(A) Lenders of second mortgages have a ratio that is high in terms of loan : value

(B) Sellers are not at all interested in buyers with more than one mortgage

(C) Lenders of first mortgages already charge higher interest rates than those of second mortgages

(D) People are no longer buying residential houses

(41) When a title does not have any liens and there is no question regarding the property ownership, the title is said to be _____.

(A) A free title

(B) A good title

(C) A clear title

(D) A cloudy title

(42) The term 'collateral' is used when trying to get a home loan. It denotes _____.

(A) The home being purchased

(B) The automobile the person currently drives

(C) The borrower's respectable name

(D) The savings the borrower has in his/her bank account

(43) With a mortgage whose rate is adjustable, the date of adjustment is _____.

(A) The date when the interest rate is effectively altered

(B) One month after the day the mortgage loan was issued

(C) The date when the price index in the stock market rises

(D) The date when the mortgage is applied for

(44) A person who wants to buy real estate property can make a deposit to show seriousness in the transaction. Such a deposit is referred to as _____.

(A) A down payment

(B) Earnest money

(C) Serious money

(D) Nil ventured, nil gained

(45) The term 'subdivision' can best be described as _____.

(A) A substandard development

(B) A residential property created when a massive piece of land is divided into lots

(C) Residential units of the same size in one neighborhood are built in the same style

(D) None of the above

(46) Sometimes people make a contribution in constructing or rehabilitating a given property through other means such as rendering professional services or labor, but not by paying cash. This form of contribution is referred to as _____.

(A) Toil and labor

(B) Sweat equity

(C) A special contribution

(D) Contractor's aid

(47)   Which of the following describes a two-step mortgage?

(A)   A rate of mortgage that is adjustable; one for the initial five or seven years, and the other to cover the remaining part of the loan term.

(B)   A mortgage whose name is derived from a popular dance style

(C)   A mortgage that the lender can adjust although issued as fixed

(D)   None of the above

(48)   A/An_____ is the document legally recognized as proof that someone owns a real estate property.

(A)   Correct appraisal

(B)   Title

(C)   Quitclaim deed

(D)   Annual lease

(49)   PITI is an acronym for _____.

(A)   Principle, Interest, Taxes, Insurance

(B)   Principal, Interest, Taxes, Insurance

(C)   Prepay, Interest, Tariff, Insurance

(D)   None of the above

(50) A prepayment is best described as _____.

(A) An amount of cash paid towards reducing the interest accrued on a loan before the expected date of payment

(B) An amount of cash paid towards reducing the loan principal before the expected date of payment

(C) Cash that the borrower receives after subletting part of the home

(D) None of the above

Salesperson Test 4: Answers & Explanations

(1) The correct answer is: (C) Life estate.

For as long as she lives, the widow has life estate ownership while her child has remainder interest. Even though she has ownership rights on the property, the widow cannot tamper with the property by making changes such as bringing down the structures or converting the home into a rental facility.

(2) The correct answer is: (A) It can be created either by deed or will.

A life estate is oftentimes created through a will. A husband often leaves the property to the wife, who becomes the owner for life, after which the property is passed on to the children.

(3) The correct answer is: (B) Estate.

The quantity or degree of interest that a person has in a real property is referred to as estate. There are various types of estates ranging from absolute estate to possession.

(4) The correct answer is: (D) Reversion.

A reversion is said to take place when land is returned to a grantor or to the grantor's heirs.

(5) The correct answer is: (C) Defeasible fee estate.

In a case where ownership of land is terminated when a certain event occurs, the ownership is referred to as a defeasible fee, qualified fee or determinable fee estate.

(6) The correct answer is: (B) Leasehold estate.

Based on the ancient feudal classification, a leasehold is less than a freehold. In this classification, 'freemen' were the only ones who had court protection and the slaves had mere possessions and no interest in property.

(7) The correct answer is: (C) The degree and nature of interest in property.

In simple terms, estate can be described as the degree and nature of interest in real property. As for choices B and D, personal property is also included.

(8) The correct answer is: (C) The owner may get title insurance.

You are more assured of recovering your money from a title company than you are from the grantor. The title insurance company is, however, only responsible for insuring the title according to the stated exceptions and not for correcting actual defects which may be caused by unrecorded risks.

(9) The correct answer is: (C) Probate court.

A probate court is responsible for assigning an administrator who is supposed to manage the estates of those that pass away intestate.

(10)   The correct answer is: (A) Definite duration.

In a fee simple estate, time is indefinite unless the estate is conveyed to someone else. The only time that the estate ends is when the estate holder dies without leaving a will or heirs and in such a case the estate reverts to the government.

(11)   The correct answer is: (B) Intestate.

If the deceased did not leave a will then it is said that he/she passed away intestate.

(12)   The correct answer is: (D) Use it in contradiction to the zoning regulations.

According to the 'bundle of rights which a fee simple estate holder is granted, the holder is allowed to subdivide, sell or will the estate but is not allowed to violate government limitations.

(13)   The correct answer is: (C) Fee simple determinable.

This is a fee simple determinable estate since Wilson sold a piece of his land with a condition that it should be used for a specific purpose. When this purpose was not followed, the airport had to return the land to Wilson.

(14) The correct answer is: (A) Fee simple estate.

A fee simple estate holder enjoys the most rights and has the least restrictions to his/her estate.

(15) The correct answer is: (C) Estate for years.

A life estate and a defeasible estate are considered freehold estates while an estate for years is a non-freehold estate.

(16) The correct answer is: (D) Take back the fee title whenever he wants.

The grantor is required to surrender all control of the estate to his grantee which means that the grantor cannot take back the fee title whenever he wants.

(17) The correct answer is: (B) Licensed surveyor.

Although public records contain maps that denote accurate boundaries, they do not reveal any property encroachments so a licensee is required to hire a licensed surveyor who can verify the property boundaries and inform the licensee of any possible encroachments.

(18) The correct answer is: (A) Violating the condition subsequent.

A condition that was given to the first buyer was violated and so the owner and his heirs have a right of reentry on the grounds of violation of the condition subsequent.

(19) The correct answer is: (B) Household furnishings.

Wall-to-wall carpeting, garbage disposals and a built-in dishwasher are all considered fixtures or chattel since they are sold together with the property upon its sale. On the other hand, personal property such as household furnishings remains the seller's property.

(20) The correct answer is: (D) The rights of a beneficiary under a trust.

A beneficiary owns interest in a trust but does not become the owner of the property. The trustee is responsible for executing all contracts that involve the transfer or sale of the property.

(21) The correct answer is: (C) The land and the area that is above and below the surface, as well as all improvements that are on the land.

Improvements, land rights, air rights and subsurface rights are all included as real property.

(22) The correct answer is: (B) Personalty.

Personalty, which is a term used to also mean personal property or chattel, refers to objects or things that are temporary or that can easily be moved. Meanwhile devices, realty and appurtenances all involve real property.

(23) The correct answer is: (B) Bill of sale.

Investors mostly use bills of sale to allocate value to personal property, which tends to depreciate faster compared to real property.

(24) The correct answer is: (C) Trade fixtures.

Trade fixtures can be removed by a tenant at the end of a lease because they are not part of a landlord's property.

(25) The correct answer is: (D) The party's intention when attaching it.

The size, weight and method of attachment are all factors that can be considered in order to determine if an item is a fixture but the courts mostly emphasize the intention the party had when attaching the item.

(26) The correct answer is: (B) The transaction date.

Even though it is frequently included in a bill of sale, the transaction date is not as important as the name of the buyer, the seller's signature and the description of the item.

(27) The correct answer is: (B) Chattel.

Other terms used to mean chattel are personal property and personalty.

(28) The correct answer is: (A) On the seashore.

Littoral property is property that borders the sea or ocean while riparian property refers to property that is on a non-navigable stream or watercourse.

(29) The correct answer is: (D) Everything apart from the land which is constructed or artificial.

Improvements include everything from the land that is artificial or constructed.

(30) The correct answer is: (A) Bundle of rights.

The collective rights that one gets from the ownership of real property are known as the bundle of rights and this includes the rights of possession, enjoyment and disposal.

(31) The correct answer is: (C) An apartment of several units whose development is financed through a loan insured by the government.

Public housing is often developed with the support of government-backed loans. This ensures that affordable housing units are created for the public, especially for those who cannot afford the market rate for rental properties.

(32) The correct answer is: (D) The property owner.

Generally, for non-navigable waters, the owner of the land adjacent to the river/stream owns the riverbed up to the center of the waterway unless stated otherwise.

(33) The correct answer is: (C) Amortization.

Amortization is the process of gradually reducing a debt through installment payments over time. Each payment addresses a portion of the principal amount and the interest on the debt.

(34) The correct answer is: (A) 15 ft.

There are 3 feet in a yard. Therefore, 5½ yards equals 16½ feet. However, given the choices, 15 feet is the closest approximation.

(35) The correct answer is: (A) The amount received by Jordan will be considered to have been received by the seller as the principal.

When a broker receives earnest money, they are essentially holding it in trust for the seller. Even if the broker leaves, the earnest money is considered to be in the hands of the seller's principal.

(36) The correct answer is: (A) The buyer.

If a land contract isn't recorded, the buyer might face issues regarding the clarity of the title since the buyer is obtaining an interest in the property through the contract. Unrecorded contracts might not be known to third parties, which might lead to potential disputes over ownership.

(37) The correct answer is: (C) Between two houses of different sizes, the small one costs more.

On a per-unit basis, smaller houses often have a higher cost per square foot or cubic foot because certain fixed costs are spread over a smaller area. However, the total cost of a larger home will typically be more than a smaller home.

(38) The correct answer is: (B) The floor plan and the equipment available.

Functional utility in residential properties is typically determined by the layout (floor plan) and the amenities/equipment available in the house. While other factors like zoning and heating systems are essential, they don't directly relate to the functional utility of a residential property in the same way as a floor plan or available equipment does.

(39) The correct answer is: (B) A rise in the property value.

In real estate, the term 'appreciation' refers to an increase in the value of a property over time. This can be due to various reasons such as market demand, infrastructure developments, or other macroeconomic factors.

(40) The correct answer is: (A) Lenders of second mortgages have a ratio that is high in terms of loan : value.

Bridge loans are temporary loans taken to bridge the gap between the purchase of a new home and the sale of the current home. These loans are less common today because second mortgage lenders often lend at a high loan-to-value ratio, making bridge loans less necessary.

(41) The correct answer is: (C) A clear title.

A clear title indicates that the property is free from liens or any other encumbrances. It ensures that the owner has a rightful claim to the property without any disputes.

(42) The correct answer is: (A) The home being purchased.

When obtaining a home loan, the term 'collateral' refers to the asset that can be seized by the lender if the borrower defaults on the loan. In the context of a home loan, this asset is typically the home being purchased.

(43) The correct answer is: (A) The date when the interest rate is effectively altered.

For adjustable-rate mortgages (ARMs), the adjustment date is the day on which the interest rate changes based on a specified benchmark or index.

(44) The correct answer is: (B) Earnest money.

Earnest money is a deposit made by a potential buyer to show their genuine interest or seriousness in purchasing a property. It is a gesture of good faith.

(45) The correct answer is: (B) A residential property created when a massive piece of land is divided into lots.

A subdivision in real estate refers to dividing a larger tract of land into smaller lots that can be sold individually. Each lot can then have residential properties built on it.

(46) The correct answer is: (B) Sweat equity.

Sweat equity refers to a contribution to a project or endeavor in the form of effort and toil rather than financial investment. In the context of real estate, this means contributing to a property's construction or rehabilitation by providing services or labor instead of cash.

(47) The correct answer is: (C) An apartment of several units whose development is financed through a loan insured by the government.

A development is considered public housing if construction is financed through a government loan.

(48) The correct answer is: (D) The property owner.

Ownership of the property as marked by the lines that adjoin him/her with the neighbors extends to that part of the water that is not navigable.

(49) The correct answer is: (C) Amortization.

Once the mortgage has been fully amortized by making payments at regular intervals for a given duration, it means it has been effectively liquidated as long as the payments made are sufficient to pay the principal sum borrowed and the interest accrued.

(50) The correct answer is: (B) One rod.

If you convert 5½ yards to feet, you will have (5.5 x 3) feet; which is 16.5 ft, and one rod = 16.5 ft.

Salesperson Test 5: Questions

(1) The following statements are all true regarding 'revolving debts' apart from one. Which one is it?

(A) Revolving debt is a form of credit which is similar to credit cards

(B) The customer receives a bill for the money borrowed plus the interest due

(C) The customer borrows credit against a line of credit that is preapproved

(D) During the first six months, there is no interest incurred

(2) A survey does not show _____.

(A) Encroachments

(B) Specific legal boundaries on a property

(C) The location of furniture in the dwelling

(D) The location of easements, improvements and rights of ways

(3) Seller carry-back occurs when the seller _____.

(A) Provides financing together with an assumable mortgage

(B) Physically carries all the furnishings out of his house after closing the sale

(C) Agrees to include himself in a mortgage with his buyer

(D) Carries the loan principal without the interest

(4)Title companies are _____.

(A)   Not needed for real estate transactions to take place

(B)   Not needed until a year after close of sale

(C)   Specialized in preparing deeds

(D)   Specialized in examining and insuring titles for real estate

(5)A local or state tax that is payable upon the passing of title from one party to the other is known as a _____.

(A)   Transfer tax

(B)   Title tax

(C)   Real estate tariff

(D)   Revenue stamps

(6)Truth in lending refers to _____.

(A)   The state law that requires a lender to provide a written disclosure stating all the terms and conditions of the mortgage

(B)   The federal law that requires a lender to fully disclose the terms and conditions of the mortgage in writing

(C)   The local law that requires a lender to fully disclose the terms and conditions of the mortgage in writing

(D)   None of the above

(7) A VA mortgage is_____.

(A)   A mortgage that originated from Texas but is now found in Virginia

(B)   A mortgage that is found in Virginia

(C)   Guaranteed by the Department of VA

(D)   Available to everyone

(8) When public tax assessors assess a property, they place a valuation on the property for tax purposes. This valuation is known as _____.

(A)   Fair market value

(B)   Real value

(C)   Predicted value

(D)   Assessed value

(9) Who of the following earns the highest commission in real estate transactions?

(A)   A realtor

(B)   An attorney

(C)   A loan officer

(D)   A home warranty company

(10)   An unwritten set of laws which is based on the general customs in England and is also used in some US states is known as _____.

(A)   Casual law

(B)   Common law

(C)   Uncommon law

(D)   This is not a law since it is not documented

(11)   For real estate agents to identify the current market value of certain property, they should use recent sales made on similar property or _____.

(A)   Predicted future sales

(B)   Neighbors' estimates on the property's value

(C)   Old records from that neighborhood

(D)   Comparable sales

(12)   An individual who is owed money is referred to as the _____.

(A)   Creditor

(B)   Debtor

(C)   Lender

(D)   Mortgagee

(13) The Equal Credit Opportunity Act cannot discriminate against _____.

(A) National origin and capacity to pay

(B) Color, religion, race and income level

(C) Age, marital status and sex

(D)   National origin, color, religion, race, age, marital status or sex

(14) What do we call the mortgage which is given first priority in all recorded loans against property?

(A) First-in-line mortgage

(B) Primary mortgage

(C) The first mortgage

(D) None of the above

(15) A borrower who is in default over a mortgage payment is not entitled to interest on any of the mortgaged items. This legal process is known as a _____.

(A) Public auction

(B) Proceeds sale

(C) Takeover

(D) Foreclosure

(16) A loan against a 401(k) plan is_____.

(A) A great risk and most people would not take it

(B) Not an allowed down payment source

(C) Only allowed in cases where one has accumulated at least $50,000 in the 401(k) plan

(D) An acceptable down payment source for many loans

(17) An individual's financial responsibilities are referred to as his/her _____.

(A) Liabilities

(B) Payments

(C) Credit risks

(D) Assets

(18) Which of the following statements regarding annual percentage rates is false?

(A) It is a loan's note rate

(B) This is a value that is expressed in percentage form and is created based on a government's formula with the intention of reflecting the real borrowing cost

(C) APR is not a loan's note rate

(D) This value is always greater than a loan's note rate

(19) An independent worker who is qualified by training, education and experience in the field to estimate a property's value is known as _____.

(A) An appraiser

(B) A value estimator

(C) An underwriter

(D) An on-site inspector

(20) When a loan borrower services his mortgage using a greater amount of money than what he/she is required to pay with the intention of taking out some money for his/her personal use, the borrower performs an act called _____.

(A) Home equity refinance

(B) Refinance extra

(C) Adjustable lump sum refinance

(D) A cash-out refinance

(21) What is a certificate of deposit?

(A) A deposit that is held in the bank that pays interest over time to the account holder

(B) A down payment

(C) A deposit that is held in the bank that pays twice the normal interest rate over time

(D) A liquidated asset

(22)   What do we call short-term interim loans given to finance construction costs?

(A)   Convertible loans

(B)   Flexible loans

(C)   Promissory notes

(D)   Construction loans

(23)   What is debt?

(A)   Credit that is extended to another person

(B)   The amount that is owed to someone

(C)   A repayable amount

(D)   An amount that is owed to someone with interest

(24)   Which of the following cannot be funded by escrow disbursement?

(A)   Mortgage insurance

(B)   Real estate tax

(C)   Personal property tax

(D)   Hazard insurance

(25) When an occupant is lawfully expelled from property, we say that he/she has been _____.

(A) Convicted

(B) Evicted

(C) Divorced from board

(D) Unlawfully removed from property

(26) An agreement in writing that is made between a tenant and property owner which stipulates the conditions that a tenant may live under during the time he/she will possess that property, as well as the amount of payment due and the length of stay, is known as _____.

(A) A lease

(B) A contract

(C) Lease option

(D) An option

(27) What is the definition of a margin?

(A) A line that should not be written on in loan documents

(B) Measurements of error

(C) The difference you get when you subtract the interest rate from an adjustable rate mortgage index

(D) None

(28) Which of the following statements best describes mortgage brokers?

(A) Individuals who originate loans and sell them on a secondary market

(B) Mortgage companies which originate loans which they then place with several lending institutions

(C) A broker who receives commissions on loans

(D) Mortgage companies which originate loans which they then store in-house

(29) When you fail to make a mortgage payment, what kind of notice should you expect?

(A) A notice of default

(B) A nonpayment notice

(C) A letter written by an attorney

(D) An eviction notice

(30) When you make an insufficient payment toward your scheduled monthly payments on a mortgage loan, what kind of payment are you making?

(A) A drop-in-the-bucket payment

(B) A late payment

(C) A little payment

(D) A partial payment

(31) The meaning of 'private mortgage insurance' is _____.

(A) Mortgage insurance that the property buyer's relatives arrange for him/her

(B) Mortgage insurance whose provider is a private mortgage insurance firm

(C) Mortgage insurance that is provided by an insurance company where the buyer knows senior executives.

(D) None of the above

(32) What does 'recorder' mean in real estate?

(A) A public officer who maintains real estate records of transactions at the county level

(B) A person hired privately to write the transaction records of a purchase

(C) Registrar of births at the county level

(D) None of the above

(33) With regard to a mortgage, the amount considered the 'principal balance' is ___.

(A)   The biggest installment the borrower has ever paid

(B)   The amount of money still owed on the principal or loan borrowed

(C)   The mortgage payment paid so far on the principal

(D)   None of the above

(34) Which of the following options is false regarding qualifying ratios?

(A)   The only two kinds of ratios in real estate are 'top/front' and 'back/bottom'

(B)   'Top' ratio applies when calculating the cost to the borrower on a monthly basis based upon his/her monthly income's percentage

(C)   'Back' ratio incorporates every cost to the borrower in a month and covers any 'back' taxes

(D)   'Top' ratio and 'bottom' ratios apply in establishing how qualified a borrower is to receive a loan or mortgage

(35) A person who dies when in a joint tenancy leaves the person surviving to inherit the entire property. This situation is described as _____.

(A)   The wish of the departed

(B)   The direction of the will

(C)   Tenancy in common

(D)   Right of survivorship

(36) A loan is considered 'secured' if _____.

(A) There is collateral to back it

(B) The person borrowing makes a promise to the lending party to hand over something valuable

(C) The lending bank is not facing imminent risk

(D) The lending bank has received a bailout

(37) The law of contract demands that earnest money be submitted alongside a sales contract at _____.

(A) 6% of the offer

(B) 10% of what the asking price is

(C) A minimum of $1,000

(D) Zero

(38) Suresh is a developer of a subdivision and he decides to engage Christine as his salesperson. Hussein, who is a licensed broker, offers to purchase Lot B-2 for $25,000, and the sales contract is created. Nevertheless, there was a typographical error in the contract that nobody noticed, which said that Hussein bought Lot D-2, whose price in the listing was $30,000. What is the status of the sales contract?

(A) It is invalid

(B) It is enforceable

(C) It is void

(D) It is voidable

(39) When the property buyer and the property seller both have appended their signatures to the sale agreement, and the check of earnest money has been deposited, the money in that distinct account belongs to _____.

(A) The salesperson as his prepayment commission

(B) The property seller's initial and final payment

(C) The property buyer, to be refunded after two weeks

(D) No one until the sales transaction is finalized one way or another; through completion, rescission or a breach

(40) Abdul submitted an offer wishing to buy a home. There is a chandelier in the living room that the property owner wishes to keep for sentimental reasons, and so he signs the contract, but adds the words 'living room chandelier not part of it.' Can this contract be considered binding?

(A) No, it cannot. It is a counteroffer that the prospective buyer has to accept before the contract can be binding

(B) Yes, it actually is binding because the alteration the property seller made is minimal

(C) No, it cannot be binding and if the prospective buyer wants to accept the counteroffer, he/she must not make big modifications

(D) No. There is no way this transaction can go through now

(41) The legal position is that emblements belong to a _____.

(A) Lessor

(B) Broker

(C) Tenant

(D) Land owner

(42) The statements in escrow at the closing of a sale both for the buyer and seller are _____.

(A) Always similar

(B) Never similar

(C) Sometimes similar

(D) Prepared as escrow is opened

(43) There are some advantages FHA loans offer to borrowers that conventional loans do not. All of the following are advantages except:

(A) Monthly installments budgeted in a manner that suits each borrower's capacity

(B) Eliminating financing on a short-term basis

(C) Lower rates of insurance on mortgages

(D) Housing standards being improved

(44) A broker can apply 'use due diligence' as a counter-promise in a kind of agreement known as _____.

(A) A bilateral contract

(B) An express contract

(C) A unilateral contract

(D) A license agency agreement

(45) If a seller refuses an offer that has been presented to him/her, the seller's broker will attempt to secure _____.

(A) An alternative listing

(B) The receipt for the deposit

(C) A counteroffer

(D) A good attorney

(46) Suppose a prospective buyer directs the broker to hold his check for earnest money until the offer he/she has made gets accepted. It is the broker's responsibility to notify the property seller that there is such a check in custody _____.

(A) As the transaction nears closing

(B) At the time of presenting the offer

(C) At any stage the broker prefers

(D) None of the above. The buyer should totally refrain from making such a disclosure

(47) When there is a property takeover, you can minimize anxiety about the situation by _____.

(A) Replacing all your vendors

(B) Informing everyone concerned about what is going on

(C) Avoiding communicating with anyone

(D) Finding a replacement for your local manager

(48) Which of the following is true of rent control?

(A) The US is among the last countries to enact it

(B) It is only applied in the United States

(C) It was practiced even in ancient Greece

(D) Europe has practiced it for many years

(49) A building code requires that a building have an opening, either interior or exterior, which provides access beneath. This opening is referred to as _____.

(A) A crawl hole

(B) A catacomb

(C) A cellar

(D) A vault

(50) A board running in a diagonal manner across studs is referred to as _____.

(A) A brace

(B) A laterally running support beam

(C) A stud support

(D) A bridge

Salesperson Test 5: Answers & Explanations

(1) The correct answer is: (D) During the first six months, there is no interest incurred.
Revolving debt refers to a credit plan that works just like a credit card. It allows customers buying goods or services to borrow cash against a line of credit which is preapproved and the borrower receives a bill for the borrowed amount plus the interest due.

(2) The correct answer is: (C) Location of furniture in the dwelling.
A survey refers to a map or drawing that shows the exact legal boundaries, location of easements, improvements, encroachments and many different physical features on a property.

(3) The correct answer is: (A) Provides financing together with assumable mortgage.
In seller carry-back agreements, the property owner provides financing together with assumable mortgage.

(4) The correct answer is: (D) Specialized in examining as well as insuring titles for real estate.
Title companies specialize in examining as well as insuring titles for real estate.

(5) The correct answer is: (A) Transfer tax.
Local or state tax that is payable upon the passing of title from one party to the other is known as transfer tax.

(6) The correct answer is: (B) The federal law that requires a lender to fully disclose the terms and conditions of the mortgage in writing.
Truth-in-lending refers to the federal law that requires a lender to disclose fully and in writing the terms and the conditions of the mortgage.

(7) The correct answer is: (C) Guaranteed by the Department of VA.
A Veterans Affairs mortgage can be guaranteed by the Department of VA.

(8) The correct answer is: (D) Assessed value.
The valuation that is placed on a property by public tax assessors for tax purposes is referred to as the assessed value.

(9) The correct answer is: (A) A realtor.
A realtor generally earns the highest commission, followed by the lenders.

(10) The correct answer is: (B) Common law.
An unwritten set of laws which is based on the general customs in England and is also used in several US states is known as common law.

(11) The correct answer is: (D) Comparable sales.
Recent sales of similar property in the neighborhood can be used to determine the most accurate market value.

(12) The correct answer is: (A) Creditor.
An individual who is owed money is known as a creditor.

(13) The correct answer is: (D) National origin, color, religion, race, age, marital status or sex.
The Equal Credit Opportunity Act requires all creditors to provide credit to all individuals without discriminating based upon race, religion, color, national origin, sex, age or marital status.

(14) The correct answer is: (C) The first mortgage.
The mortgage that is given first in all recorded loans is known as a first mortgage.

(15) The correct answer is: (D) Foreclosure.
Foreclosure is a legal process that bars a defaulter from enjoying any interest that comes from the property that is being mortgaged.

(16) The correct answer is: (D) An acceptable down payment source for many loans.
A loan against the 401(k) plan is an acceptable down payment source. Some of the 401(k) and 403B plans permit loans against a person's accumulated money.

(17) The correct answer is: (A) Liabilities.
An individual's financial responsibilities are referred to as his/her liabilities. They also include short-term and long-term debt as well as any cash that is owed to other people.

(18) The correct answer is: (A) It's a loan's note rate.
APR is a percentage value created in accordance with a government's formula with the intention of reflecting the real borrowing cost. It is always greater than a loan's note rate.

(19) The correct answer is: (A) An appraiser.
Appraisers are individuals who are qualified by training, education and experience in the field to estimate a property's value. In most cases, appraisers are independent workers but some of them are employed by lenders.

(20) The correct answer is: (D) A cash-out refinance.
A cash-out refinance occurs when a loan borrower services his mortgage using a greater amount of money than what he/she is required to pay with the intention of taking out some money for personal use.

(21) The correct answer is: (A) A deposit that is held in the bank and pays a certain interest over time to the account holder.
The depositor earns interest from the deposit over a period of time.

(22) The correct answer is: (D) Construction loan.
Short-term interim loans used to finance construction costs are referred to as construction loans. The lender pays the constructor at intervals as construction work progresses.

(23) The correct answer is: (B) The amount that is owed to someone.
Debt is the amount of money that is owed to someone else.

(24) The correct answer is: (C) Personal property tax.

You cannot pay personal property tax by using escrow disbursements. However, hazard insurance, mortgage insurance and real estate taxes are typical escrow disbursements.

(25) The correct answer is: (B) Evicted.

Eviction is the process of lawfully expelling a tenant from a property.

(26) The correct answer is: (A) A lease.

A lease is an agreement in writing that is made between a tenant and property owner which stipulates the conditions that a tenant may live under during the time he/she possesses the property.

(27) The correct answer is: (C) The difference you get when you subtract the interest rate from an adjustable rate mortgage index.

The difference you get when you subtract the interest rate from an adjustable rate mortgage index is called a margin.

(28) The correct answer is: (B) Mortgage companies which originate loans which they then place with several lending institutions.

Mortgage brokers originate loans which they place with lending institutions that share a preestablished relationship with them.

(29) The correct answer is: (A) A notice of default.

When you fail to make a mortgage payment, you receive a notice informing you that you have defaulted and the lender may take legal action.

(30) The correct answer is: (D) Partial payment.

A payment that is not enough to facilitate the month's scheduled mortgage payment is known as a partial payment.

(31) The correct answer is: (B) Mortgage insurance whose provider is a private mortgage insurance firm.

Often, private mortgage insurance is required for borrowers of conventional loans. This form of insurance is meant for the protection of the party lending the money in case the borrower defaults on repayment.

(32) The correct answer is: (A) A public officer who maintains real estate records of transactions at the county level.

This public officer who maintains real estate transaction records at the county level is known as the 'county clerk' and is also referred to as the 'registrar of deeds.'

(33) The correct answer is: (B) The amount of money still owed on the principal or loan borrowed.

When the principal balance is being considered, the amount of interest paid or yet to be paid on the mortgage is not taken into account. Any additional levies related to the mortgage also are not included.

(34)   The correct answer is: (C) 'Back' ratio incorporates every cost to the borrower in a month and covers any 'back' taxes.
The 'back' ratio, also referred to as 'bottom' ratio, encompasses the cost of housing and any additional debts incurred by the borrower in a month.

(35)   The correct answer is: (D) Right of survivorship.
As long as two parties are in joint tenancy, it is obvious the surviving partner has the right to inherit the entire property owned in the joint tenancy. That is referred to as 'right of survivorship.'

(36)   The correct answer is: (A) There is collateral to back it.
A loan is termed 'secured' if there is collateral given to back it, and this collateral is the one alternatively referred to as the loan 'security.'

(37)   The correct answer is: (D) Zero.
Earnest money is not required for a sales contract to be formed or to be valid. However, the buyer can voluntarily decide to pay it or the seller can request it, but the actual amount to be paid is up for negotiation.

(38)   The correct answer is: (D) It is voidable.
Everyone involved in a contract, especially the agents, need to be careful in reading any document that is binding. In this case, the sales contract provides primary evidence of the sales agreement, and so it is imperative that it be accurate. Since this error is unintentional, the contract is voidable.

(39)   The correct answer is: (D) No one, until the sales transaction is finalized one way or another; through completion, rescission or a breach
Earnest money is held in trust by the broker and is not the property of anyone at that time. If the sales transaction is successful, the seller is entitled to the money, but there is room for the parties involved to agree on how to deal with the money.

(40)   The correct answer is: (A) No, it cannot. It is a counteroffer that the prospective buyer has to accept before the contract can be binding
Once the seller has made changes in the contract, what results is a rejection of the initial offer and a counteroffer, which is basically a fresh offer. The onus then goes to the prospective buyer to either accept that counteroffer or reject it.

(41)   The correct answer is: (C) Tenant.
'Emblements' include corn and other crops grown on an annual basis; not on a spontaneous basis. They legally belong to the tenant unless he/she plants them at a time they are not expected to mature within his/her tenancy. However, if tenancy is abruptly terminated, he/she can return to the property to harvest the crops.

(42)   The correct answer is: (B) Never similar.
One major cause of the difference is that the buyer's account is in debt while the seller's account is in credit. This is according to the Real Estate Settlement Procedures Act that stipulates that the buyer be debited with the property price and the seller be credited with the amount.

(43)   The correct answer is: (C) Lower rates of insurance on mortgages.
You do not need mortgage insurance when borrowing under conventional means, but you need it when borrowing under the FHA. As such, option (C) is an untrue statement.

(44)   The correct answer is: (A) A bilateral contract.
Each of the two parties must make a form of promise to the other and it serves as consideration, whether the promise is absolute or comes with some conditions.

(45)   The correct answer is: (C) A counteroffer.
It is normal for the broker to try and find a figure that is agreeable to both the property seller and the prospective buyer and to see the sale through. This is possible when the broker gives the seller a counteroffer that he/she thinks the buyer will agree to.

(46)   The correct answer is: (B) At the time of presenting the offer.
It is important that at the time of presenting the prospective buyer's offer, the broker inform his/her principal, the property seller, that a check has already been received.

(47)   The correct answer is: (B) Inform everyone concerned about what is going on.
In property management, effective communication is very important if you are to succeed.

(48)   The correct answer is: (D) Europe has practiced it for many years.
Even if rent control was not discussed in formal economic terms back in the day, Europe has still applied it for a long time.

(49)   The correct answer is: (A) A crawl hole.
This opening, called a 'crawl hole,' is also termed a 'crawl space.'

(50)   The correct answer is: (A) A brace.
This diagonal board that is called a brace is also referred to as a 'wind.' Another term it is given is a 'corner brace.'

Access the Bonus Flash Cards!

Scan the QR code below with your phone and you will be given a link to google drive, where you can download the flash cards.

If the QR code does not work for you, please contact us at info@newstonetestprep.com

Made in the USA
Middletown, DE
16 May 2024

54431672R00168